Sites of Slavery

SITES OF SLAVERY

Citizenship and
Racial Democracy in
the Post–Civil Rights
Imagination

Salamishah Tillet

DUKE UNIVERSITY PRESS
Durham & London 2012

Printed in the United States of America
on acid-free paper ∞
Designed by Jennifer Hill.
Typeset in Dante by
Tseng Information Systems, Inc.

*Library of Congress
Cataloging-in-Publication Data appear on
the last printed page of this book.*

Duke University Press gratefully acknowledges the University
Research Foundation at the University of Pennsylvania, which
provided funds toward the publication of this book.

For my parents,

Volora Bridget Howell

and Lennox Ignatius Tillet,

who thoughtfully

nurtured my imagination,

and for my partner,

Solomon Steplight IV,

who patiently watched the

words unfold

The paradox is American, and
it behooves Americans to understand it
if they would understand themselves.

EDMUND MORGAN,
American Slavery, American Freedom

CONTENTS

ACKNOWLEDGMENTS

LIKE ANY PROJECT that predicates itself on the delicate balance of self-doubt and utmost confidence, of writer's block and bursts of creativity, this book owes its existence to many people and institutions. Beginning as a dissertation many years ago, the scholarship, mentorship, and critical feedback of my quartet of advisors inform my analysis throughout. Henry Louis Gates Jr. was a wonderful reader and unparalleled "title man" who always provided me with an unwavering faith in the relevance of this project. I owe scarcely less to Professor Werner Sollors, whose turnaround and gentle criticism constantly forced me to rethink, reformulate, and rewrite. The project bears his stamp as much as it does mine. Farah Griffin served as both a source of inspiration and a model against which I measure my own output. Her scholarship and spirit are never simply about making it in academia, but always about keeping the faith beyond. I am also indebted to Evelyn Higginbotham, who in the early stages of this project nudged me to reconsider my topic, methodology, and theoretical framework, and thereby strengthen my intellectual foundation.

Whereas Harvard University functioned as the intellectual birthplace for the book, the University of Pennsylvania is where it grew up. I have had the rare fortune of having some of the most brilliant minds and generous hearts in academia, my colleagues Thadious Davis, John Jackson, and Heather Love, pore over every word of this manuscript. Taken together, their insights and suggestions have made this project livelier, weightier, and ultimately more ambitious. I would also like to thank my colleagues from the English Department and the Center for Africana Studies who kindly gave me feedback on some part of this manuscript: Herman Beavers, Tsitsi Jaji, Ken Shropshire, Deborah Thomas, and Tukufu Zuberi; and those who simply provided words of much needed support: Camille Charles, David Eng, Amy Kaplan, David Kazanjian, Suvir Kaul, Zachary Lesser, Josephine Park, Gutherie Ramsey, Melissa Sanchez, and Barbara Savage. While my students at Penn continue to inspire me to read more rigorously and write more creatively, their love of art and politics kept me going in the twilight hours. Special thanks to those students whose comments in class helped sharpen the thesis of this book: Joshua Bennett, Marina Bilbija, Julius Fleming, John Howard, Ryan Jobson, Samuel Mondry-Cohen, Kaneesha Parsard, Petal Samuels, Riley Snorton, Mecca Sullivan, Chloe Wayne, and Rhaisa Williams.

I am honored to have received community, funding, and mentorship from other institutions. After graduate school, I was awarded the Du Bois–Mandela-Rodney Postdoctoral Fellowship at the Center for Afro-American and African Studies at the University of Michigan. I would like to express my appreciation to Kevin Gaines and Michael Awkward for their consistent hospitality and for helping me transform the dissertation into a more mature manuscript. Funding from the Lindback Foundation in 2008 and the Woodrow Wilson Foundation in 2010–11 awarded me the valuable time and space for me to finish this project. During my fellowship year, Valerie Smith was an especially generous mentor, while Princeton University's Center for African American Studies became my intellectual home away from home. I would like to single out Daphne Brooks for her friendship, meticulous reading of an early draft of this book, and creative and book-changing suggestions. I deeply thank Eddie Glaude, Josh Guild, Tera Hunter, Imani Perry, Noliwe Rooks, and my fellow fellows—Lyndon Gill, Sarah Haley, Van Jones, and Carina Ray—for being patient sounding boards and powerful supporters. Imani is truly a person whose gentleness and generosity will never be forgotten. And special nods to Kameron Austin Collins and Brittany Edmonds, graduate students who gave me crucial support during the final stages of this book.

In addition, I would like to thank Michael Eric Dyson, Charles Rowell, and Gloria Steinem for taking me under their wings. Michael has given me an incredible amount of emotional and professional support, while always reminding me of the "bigger" picture. Charles Rowell has shared the gift of Callaloo with me since 2008. His black cosmopolitanism and his editorial vision have made be a better reader and more creative critic. Gloria is a new mentor who models the everyday politics of feminism for me, while also reminding me that I can use the pen (or the keyboard) to make a difference in the world.

The nuts and bolts of this book, however, are due to some very special people. I would like to thank Duke University Press's editorial associate Leigh Barnwell and development coordinator Bonnie Perkel for their advice throughout this process. To the four anonymous readers whom the press engaged, thank you for helping make this an intellectually richer book. The truest debt is owed to my editor, Ken Wissoker, whose friendship, insights, and encyclopedic musical taste are reasons alone to write an academic book. Many thanks for indulging my anxieties and my ambition. This book is a testament to your kind counsel.

A smile, a lunch, and a phone call are gifts to a writer that cannot be quantified. But I would like to thank my friends from graduate school and outside academia for their pep talks and distractions. Matthew Briones, Barrington Edwards, Hua Hsu, Regine Jean-Charles, Bikila Ochoa, Suleiman Osman, Brandon Terry, and Dagmawi Woubshet were all members of my Cambridge crew. By that, I simply mean those who traveled with me on that ever so difficult intellectual journey that we lightly call graduate school. I could always count on Bikila and Barrington to engage me in fertile discussions on race, sports, music, popular culture, and politics. As a scholar who always wanted to be relevant, those conversations were invaluable sites of knowledge, verbal banter, and humor. Brandon was a witty undergrad/MC whom I had the good fortune to meet during my final years of graduate school; I am deeply appreciative of his loyal friendship. Matt welcomed me to both Cambridge and Ann Arbor with open arms. His uncanny ability to build connections across race, genre, and discipline is truly inspiring. His kindness is astonishing. In our first year of graduate school, Suleiman noticed the rose-colored glasses that I adorn from time to time. Since then, he has become one of my favorite academic strategists and a loyal and committed friend. I could not ask for a better cohort member. Hua has been an undeniably wonderful colleague and friend. I am genuinely grateful for the days we spent on Magazine Street (which made Cambridge far more bearable) and our endless late night conversations about hip-hop, race, literature, love, sports, and academia. Mon autre soeur, Régine has been a fountain of love and support. Furthermore, she is one of my main models of political activism, feminism, and social change. *L'union fait la force!* My twin-soul, Dagmawi: well, words really cannot express my heartfelt appreciation to him for everything he has given me during this experience. He has bestowed me with timely feedback, thoughtful criticism, and endless encouragement. I am truly lucky to have him as my academic partner in crime. *Ameseginalehu.*

Dara Cook, Marc Hill, L'Heureux "Dumi" Lewis, Sarah Lewis, Elizabeth Mendez Berry, Joan Morgan, Lola Oguunaike, Hassan Smith, and John Stephens make up my beloved New York crew. I am especially grateful for Joan's consciousness-raising conversations and for Elizabeth's feminist wisdom and friendship over the last year. Though I fell in love with Lola's prose before our meeting, she has become one of my favorite editors, sounding boards, strategists, and dearest friends. Dumi's everyday feminism inspires me daily, and I thank Marc for his generosity and model of scholar-activism. Sarah's presence in my life has constantly pushed me to believe in more than the limits of my circumstances; her compassion and counsel have been true blessings. Thanks to Hassan for being one of my biggest fans, a kind ear, and a thoughtful friend. As my dearest confidante, Dara Cook continually keeps my life grounded with her zany brain and filled with deep and unabiding laughter. John forces everyone around him always to bring his or her A-game. I owe him for the gift of his intellectual curiosity, emotional honesty, and unrelenting loyalty. I would like to send love to my California gurls, Ty Stiklorius and Erica Edwards. Ty, you constantly give me a model of "doing it all" with style and wit, and Erica, I look forward to spending many more years of sharing our black feminist vision with the world. And I send a special thank you to my black feminist collective, to Aliyyah Abdur-Rahman, Soyica Diggs Colbert, and Koritha Mitchell, for making the academic trenches so much more manageable.

My past and present Philadelphia crew featured GerShun Avilez, Brennan Maier, Deborah Thomas, Paul Farber, the Jacksons, James Peterson, the Ritchies, Aishah Simmons, and Adenike Walker. Paul always keeps me on my toes with titles and technology; I am happy to have taken you under my wing. Brennan has been an exceptional and endearing friend since those late nights talking Ellison in the Du Bois College House multipurpose room. Thanks to JP for his humor, big heart, and affection. A shout-out to Deborah, Oliver, Marleigh, and John again for continually opening up their homes and hearts to me. GerShun has been an absolute treasure as a friend and a colleague. He read my chapters, provided kind words, and expressed continued belief in my professional success. Without him, writing both the dissertation and the book would have been far more arduous and lonely.

Isaiah and Kane supplied me with countless distractions and endless indulgences during the dissertation writing process. They constantly reminded me to enjoy each moment and forgive each seeming mistake. Isaiah has always embodied a sensitivity and compassion that we as adults so desperately need, and Kane has always personified the perseverance and curiosity without which we could not exist. Watching them grow up has been a true gift. Joe's kindness and his friendship are indispensable. It was nice to swap houses for that crazy year. Nike was my neighbor and social partner in crime (so to speak) for the three years that I lived in Philadelphia. Her ongoing thoughtfulness, laughter, and insights are pots of gold at the end of the rainbow. Aishah has been an amazing sister-friend to me. Like me, she is a fellow survivor who uses her art to help others heal; however, I am forever grateful to her for providing endless emotional and political support to me throughout my entire graduate school career and beyond.

Words cannot describe my gratitude to the people who make up A Long Walk Home, Inc. I would like to shout out our board members, soars cast, and all our Girl/Friends staff and students. In their own unique way, these men and women have taught me the miracle of compassion and political commitment. They all are Oshun's Children . . .

Special thanks to Veronica Ryback and Jane Abrams for their kindness and insight and Tia Gist for her patience. I could not have endured graduate school in Massachusetts without the support and love of my extended family. Specifically, I am indebted to Uncle Terry, Auntie Andrea, Tariq, Rafiq, Nadja, Aaliyah, Auntie Yvette, Uncle Everett, Nigel, Chris, Giselle, Crystal, Rhonda, and of course Nicole, Auntie Annie, Auntie Suzie, Uncle Keith, Keisen, Keisha, and Uncle Trevor. I also would like to express my gratitude to Marilyn "Mert" Strickland, who has opened her home to me and my family far too many times to count; she is the definition of generosity. Additionally, I would like to big up Darryle Steplight because he has always welcomed me as another member of his family. I cannot forget my grandmothers Hilda "Dolly" Tillet and Luretha Griffin, whose independent spirits and love for their grandchildren and for their respective cultural identities of Trinidad and the American South have forever shaped my understanding and my appreciation of the connections that constitute the African diaspora.

Unbeknownst to him, my brother Shaka Davis inspired me to become a teacher. Shaka's kindness, charm, and intellect are both fascinating to witness and thrilling to encourage. He always keeps me honest and relevant—and for that he acts as my informal muse. Much love to Jasmine Reynolds and the joy of all our lives, Jaliah. My sister Scheherazade Tillet is not only my best friend but my soul mate. Her vision has transformed the world for the better, but her creative thoughtfulness and her unconditional love defy language and narrative. She is simply the *best* person I know. Thank you. My father, Lennox Tillet, is such a kind, gentle soul whose compassion for others and commitment for social justice, especially for those who live in the "Third World," have completely influenced how I interact with and define the world in which we live. Never shy of thinking beyond national borders, my father taught me to love and to identify with vulnerable people throughout the world and continually fight for their/our freedom. If my father influenced my political outlook, my mother, Volora Bridget Howell, the most courageous and ambitious person I know, shaped my love of the culture. She taught all her children to love art and encouraged me to think past disciplinary boundaries and locate the conversations that artists have with each other. As such, the interdisciplinary focus of this entire book stems from growing up with a mother who is an artist ahead of her own time. Her sacrifices are not forgotten or taken for granted. I thank both my parents for their love and encouragement.

Finally, I could not ask for a better reader than my life partner, Solomon Steplight, who has survived the cluttered rooms, tense deadlines, and sleepless nights that this book produced. He has read every word, quieted almost every panic attack, encouraged me to push past my intellectual threshold, and pulled me in when I got lost in my mental wonderland. You are the love of my life.

Sites of Slavery

Yet, despite being an antique, the old black American narrative of pervasive victimization persists, denying the overwhelming evidence of change since the time of my parents and grandparents, refusing to die. . . . It has become ahistorical. For a time it served us well and powerfully, yes, reminding each generation of black Americans of the historical obligations and duties and dangers they inherited and faced, but the problem with any story or idea or interpretation is that it can soon fail to fit the facts and becomes ideology, even kitsch.

CHARLES JOHNSON, "The End of the Black American Narrative"

Slavery can never be exhausted as a narrative. Nor can the Holocaust; nor can the potato famine; nor can war. To say slavery is over is to be ridiculous. There is nothing in those catastrophic events of human life that is exhaustible at all.

TONI MORRISON, in Kevin Nance, "The Spirit and the Strength"

INTRODUCTION

Peculiar Citizenships

ON THE EVE of Barack Obama's historic presidential election in 2008, Charles Johnson appealed to African American writers to lay slavery and its long arm of segregation—what he calls the "group victimization" narrative—to rest. "I think writers should be free to go wherever their imagination takes them," Johnson writes, "but I do think clearly that slavery-era and segregation-era stories are stories about the past."[1] Even though Johnson set his most famous novels, *Oxherding Tale* (1982) and *Middle Passage* (1990), in the antebellum South, he argues that the unprecedented political success of Obama, the emergence of a "true" black middle class, and the influx of African and Caribbean immigrants over the last forty years redefine the terms of the black narrative. In Johnson's view, the quintessential black narrative is one of protracted interracial conflict—a narrative, moreover, that long ago climaxed and achieved resolution during the civil rights movement. Despite the codified political gains of the Civil Rights Act of 1964 and Voting Rights Act of 1965, African American academics and writers continue to peddle a "pre-21st-century black American narrative" of disenfranchisement and racial injustice. Urging writers to move beyond slavery's constitutive role in African American arts and letters, Johnson calls for "new and better stories, new concepts, and new vocabularies and grammar based not on the past but on the dangerous, exciting, and unexplored present."[2] This twenty-first-century black aesthetic should eschew the retrospective for the absolutely presentist and should attend to slavery not as a useable past but as a thoroughly ahistorical thematic. In effect, to best reflect the political present, Johnson believes that contemporary African American artists must abolish slavery as the master trope for African American identity.

In her novel *A Mercy* (2008), Toni Morrison nevertheless returns to slavery as a central theme. Published the same year as Johnson's manifesto (and, notably, after Obama's election to office), *A Mercy* is set in late-seventeenth-century Virginia on the cusp of the American experiment and American racial slavery. Unlike *Beloved* (1987), Morrison's Pulitzer Prize–winning novel on slavery and its immediate afterlife, *A Mercy* is a pastoral narrative that moves "beyond the Puritan, Plymouth Rock stuff" and is set in a period before blackness and slavery became "constructed, planted, institutionalized, and legalized" in American society.[3] So while Johnson would cast *A Mercy* as a literary throwback, as fiction grounded in the concerns of the pre–civil rights era, Morrison's novel is quite emblematic of, rather than an exception to, a dominant trope in late-twentieth-century African American poetics and politics. Since the 1970s — the period commonly referred to as post–civil rights — African American artists, writers, and intellectuals have produced a large corpus of works that take American chattel slavery as their central theme. Contrary to Johnson's claims, these post–civil rights representations of slavery are neither antediluvian nor anticlimactic; instead, they reveal an African American preoccupation with returning to the site of slavery as a means of overcoming racial conflicts that continue to flourish after the height of the civil rights movement in order to reimagine the possibilities of American democracy in the future.

In this book I contend that contemporary representations of slavery in African American literature, film, theater, visual culture, and lawsuits do not simply envisage or presage the debate about new black narratives between Johnson and Morrison. Instead, such engagements reconcile what has been one of the fundamental paradoxes of post–civil rights American politics: African Americans' formal possession of full legal citizenship and their inherited burden of "civic estrangement." Here, my use of the phrase "civic estrangement" recalls and extends Rogers Smith's influential *Civic Ideals*, in which the author shows that race, gender, ethnicity, class, and religion historically determined the "ascriptive" aspects of U.S. citizenship.[4] While legal citizenship includes suffrage and the right to participate in government, civic membership predicates itself on abstract signs and symbols or the civic myths of the nation. In the case of African Americans, civic estrangement occurs because they have been marginalized or underrepresented in the civic myths, monuments, narratives, icons, creeds, and images of the past that constitute, reproduce, and promote an American national identity. Civic estrangement is both ascriptive and affective. As a form of an ongoing racial inequality, civic estrangement describes the paradox post–civil rights African Americans experience as simultaneous citizens and "non-citizens," who experience the feelings of disillusionment and melancholia of non-belonging and a yearning for civic membership.

This book theorizes how many post–civil rights African American writers, artists, and intellectuals respond to this crisis of citizenship by revisiting the antebellum past and foregrounding what I call a "democratic aesthetic" in their representations of slavery. Michael Bennett's *Democratic Discourses* is particularly instructive here. Bennett emphasizes the "realness" of radical abolitionists' depictions of slavery, arguing that they enabled the production of a democratic aesthetic that created emancipatory space for African Americans while making room for the uniquely American genre of the slave narrative.[5] My formulation of a "democratic aesthetic," while indebted to Bennett, departs significantly in order to consider the demands of a post–civil rights political project and its influence on African American cultural production. Unlike their antebellum counterparts, whose primary goal was to render the horrors of that peculiar institution in the service of abolition, contemporary African American artists and intellectuals have neither the political nor the aesthetic imperative to depict realistic representations of slavery. The recent surge of late-twentieth-century African American cultural production that centers on American chattel slavery becomes even more striking. Producing in the age of what the cultural critic Greg Tate refers to as the "post-liberated black aesthetic," contemporary African Americans are the beneficiaries of putative juridical and legislative equality born of civil rights agitation.[6] In contrast to their antebellum predecessors who shaped their rhetoric around the demand for legal freedom, this democratic aesthetic, while revealing a lingering DuBoisean "twoness" at the dawn of yet another century, distinguishes itself by shuttling between the pessimism of civic estrangement and the privilege of African American legal citizenship.

The critical distance between the antebellum period and the contemporary moment affords contemporary artists and writers the opportunity to reshape, deviate from, and experiment with the form and content of the slave autobiography. Because of the centrality of the nineteenth-century slave narratives, most contemporary critics have attended to the newly emerging "neo-slave narratives" through only that lens, paying less attention to slavery as a central leitmotif within broader contemporary African American art and rhetoric.[7] Here I aim to broaden and complicate the ways in which scholars define and critically interrogate contemporary representations of slavery, so as to expose the ways that, beyond the novel, multiple cultural forms — from drama, dance, cinema, and visual art to heritage tourism, reparations legal cases, and critical race historiographies — engage in rituals of collective remembering, recuperative forms of recognition, and revisionist forms of historical representation.

As a way of providing a comprehensive analysis of how historical circumstance, nationality, gender, and genre influence these varied post–civil rights African American representations of slavery, I study the following four sites of slavery: the allegations of a sexual relationship between Thomas Jefferson and Sally Hemings; the representations of enslaved African Americans in Harriet Beecher Stowe's *Uncle Tom's Cabin*; African American "Back to Africa" travel and tourism; and the ongoing legal challenges of reparations movements. Inspired by both Pierre Nora's seminal work "Les Lieux de Mémoire" and Toni Morrison's essay "The Site of Memory," I employ the term *sites of slavery* to refer to historical figures, objects, texts, and places that commemorate enslaved African Americans, formally remember American slavery, and thereby democratize U.S. memory. For Nora, sites of memory preserve those aspects of the past that uphold national identity and then legitimate and transmit those histories to present and future generations. Objects, texts, and places become sites of memory when they lose their original functionality and become commemorative and tangible links between the national past and contemporary citizens.[8] Sites of memory, then, gain their national import precisely because they celebrate selective objects (Plymouth Rock and the Statue of Liberty), places (Gettysburg National Park and Jamestown), and events (the annual fireworks displays on the Fourth of July) from the American past that continue to uphold and promote national identity in the present.

Departing from Nora's more nationalistic definition of sites of memory, Toni Morrison in her essay "The Site of Memory" defines the African American slave narrative as the quintessential site of memory. She observes that the authors of the slave autobiographies, such as Frederick Douglass in the *Narrative of the Life of Frederick Douglass: An American Slave* (1845), shaped their "experience to make it palatable to those who were in the position to alleviate it; they were silent about many things; and they 'forgot' many other things."[9] In response to these literary omissions, Morrison understands her role as a late-twentieth-century African American writer as one that "extends" and "fills-in the autobiographical slave narrative" and thereby provides enslaved African Americans with an interiority and subjectivity denied to them in American history.[10] Developed from Nora's and Morrison's "sites of memory," I posit "sites of slavery" as the objects, texts, figures, places, and narratives from the American past that provide tangible links between present-day Americans and American chattel slavery. Like Nora's sites of memory, the sites of slavery on which I focus produce discourses about how best to remember American democracy and to construct national identity. Following Morrison's sites of memory, I argue that post–civil rights African American writers and artists claim and reconstruct pivotal figures, events, memories, locations, and experiences from American slavery in order to provide interiority and agency for enslaved African Americans and write them into the national narrative. Historically, the four sites of slavery on which I focus all consistently generate debates about how best to memorialize slavery and assume a metaphoric or synecdochic relationship to African American political identity: they are loci at which definitions of "Americaness" and "African diaspora" hinge, always simultaneously establishing, questioning, and reconstituting those very identities. As a result, they produce narratives of contestation and potential resolution as well as sites of rich textual inquiry.

THE RITES OF AMERICAN CITIZENSHIP

In the case of the United States, we should not think of citizenship solely in terms of political rights; rather, following T. H. Marshall, we can understand it to have evolved into three dimensions in order to accommodate the changing demographics, industries, and histories of liberal democratic societies.[11] Building on Marshall, my analysis suggests that African Americans shape their post–civil rights representations of slavery to gain access to this multidimensional American citizenship, particularly the extralegal markers of citizenship such as the economic (the right to earn) and civic (the right to recognition). For Americans, civic myths directly influence the parameters of civic citizenship by playing off the American creed or what Gunnar Myrdal defined in *The American Dilemma* as "liberty, equality, justice, and an opportunity for everybody."[12] On the one hand, civic myths sustain the durability of the American creed and have the ability, as Seymour Martin Lipset notes, to display "more continuity than change with respect to the main elements of the national system."[13] Civic myths, as a form of collective memory, must continually adapt to changing social and political conditions in order to successfully promote the American creed in successive generations and different groups. But, on the other hand, civic myths not only transmit the ideology of the American creed to present and future American citizens, but also elide, discard, or co-opt historic events and experiences that contradict their supremacy. By omitting such historical realities, American civic myths not only bear partiality toward certain interpretations of the past but also privilege those members of society who find themselves represented in these versions of history. Even though countless events have challenged the reality of an unfettered American democracy, most specifically slavery and Jim Crow segregation, civic myths marginalize these contradictions and dismiss them as aberrations in American history. The end result is a civic culture that either forgets or casts itself in contradistinction to the lives and contributions of enslaved African Americans.

Initially, the civic estrangement of antebellum African Americans was yet another tragic byproduct of their political disenfranchisement and purported ontological difference. During slavery, the law relegated African Americans to "a subordinate and inferior class of beings" or "a people of the law."[14] Consequently, the status of African Americans as the categorical non-citizen was not simply a legal matter, but extended into a civic sphere in which both caricatured blackness and the coffled black body became the criteria against which to define and uphold the nation. For example, the Supreme Court's landmark decision in *Dred Scott v. Sandford* (1857), which explicitly ruled African Americans ineligible for citizenship, implicitly reinforced the racial ridicule commonly found on the minstrel stage and in the broader visual culture. In a similar vein, as Jim Crow legislation replaced slavery as the definitive site of African American political oppression, late-nineteenth-century and early-twentieth-century African Americans were forced to endure both civic and legal segregation. In *Race and Reunion*, David Blight explains that the post–Civil War reconciliation achieved by the North and the South occurred by excising slavery from the memory of the war and by omitting African Americans from the myths of reunification.[15] The results were so devastating for African Americans that by 1915 W. E. B. Du Bois wrote, "We have in fifty years, by libel, innuendo, and silence so completely misstated and obliterated the history of the Negro in America . . . that today it is almost unknown." "History had been effectively used," he maintained, to teach Americans to "embrace and worship the color bar as social salvation."[16] According to Du Bois, the national forgetting of African American experiences in slavery helped sustain the legal segregation—the "color bar"—that characterized the United States for most of the twentieth century.

Du Bois argues that similar to slavery, segregation not only limited African American citizenship but also denied African Americans access to the historical myths that constituted national identity. This combination of legal and civic alienation further relegated African Americans to a social existence "outside the mainstream of retrospective consciousness" that constituted the reunified nation.[17] Primarily responding to *de jure* practices of racial discrimination, pre–civil rights African American artists and writers were veritably preoccupied with the law; much of their artistic dissent—from slave narratives to poetry to the "protest" writings of Richard Wright—took legality as its central theme.[18] Understandably, the law held the ultimate significance for antebellum and pre-civil rights African Americans because it was the site of their political exclusion. However, through the Civil Rights Act of 1964 and the Voting Rights Act of 1965, African Americans gained legal enfranchisement, first-class citizenship, access to the polity, and protection by the law. Ostensibly, legal citizenship also ensured that they had attained all the benefits that came with lawfully belonging to the nation. Nonetheless, post–civil rights African Americans, according to Mark Weiner, emerged as legal but not necessarily as civic citizens of the United States: "For a group to enjoy full citizenship in the cultural sense, the civic majority must recognize that the group 'belongs,' that it shares certain basic characteristics with the community." Weiner goes on, "This is a subtle phenomenon—it is usually less tangible than, say, a statute denying women the right to vote—but it is partly the intangibility of this aspect of citizenship that makes it so important."[19] Therefore, while successfully gaining legal citizenship within the nation to which they, by birthright, should have access, post–civil rights African Americans became simultaneously part of and tangential to the citizenry.

This political ambiguity tied to ongoing racial discrimination and socioeconomic inequality made it even clearer that the legal extension of citizenship to African Americans would not singularly solve the racial problem.[20] Civic estrangement, then, not only highlights the non-legal or ascriptive marks of American citizenship, such as civic membership, but also unveils the formative role of affect as well. In *The Melancholy of Race*, Anne Cheng argues that the founding paradox of American freedom and slavery, fictionalized by Morrison in *A Mercy*, created a "melancholic bind between incorporation and rejection" for people of color since the nation's beginning.[21] Following Sigmund Freud's "Mourning and Melancholia," Cheng theorizes that the democratic rhetoric of belonging and equality ("incorporation") and the practice of racial exclusion ("rejection") produce melancholia, an affective state of inevitable and interminable loss. By pointing out how melancholia results from the fissures between civic myths and "constitutional practices," Cheng's readings underscore a theory of a multidimensional American citizenship. In the case of African Americans, the institutions of slavery and segregation are stark examples of the failure of the United States to apply its principles of democracy and equality to all its citizens. African Americans have not only had the unfortunate fate of existing outside of the founding narratives and selective visions of the American

past that made up the "we" in the American people, but are also subject to the continual repression of their economic and material contributions, "busily disavowed" in and by civic myths.[22] The very rhetoric
of American citizenship—an eighteenth-century discourse of individuality, equality, and freedom—became formed and fortified through the
affect of black loss and yearning.

African Americans (and other people of color) continue to experience what David Eng and Shinhee Han describe as "racial melancholia" in the post–civil rights era. They remain in a state of "suspended assimilation" in which they "are continually estranged" from the ultimate
object of American citizenship: the ideal of whiteness.[23] Because racial
exclusion had become part and parcel of African American political
identity since slavery, it cannot simply be willed or wished away. This
protracted experience of disillusionment, mourning, and yearning is
in fact the basis of African American civic estrangement.[24] Its lingering
is not just a haunting of the past but is also a reminder of the present-
day racial inequities that keep African American citizens in an indeter-
minate, unassimilable state as a racialized "Other." While the affect of
racial melancholia was bred in the dyad of slavery and democracy, it
persists because of the paradox of legal citizenship and civic estrangement. However, Eng, Han, and I, unlike Freud, do not see this form of
melancholia as destructive or damaging, but recognize it as a potentially
productive state. Quoting José Esteban Muñoz's *Dis-Identifications*, Eng
and Han offer a corrective to Freud's pathology, for Munoz proposes
that melancholia "is a mechanism that helps us (re) construct identity
and take our dead with us to the various battles we must wage in their
names—and in our names."[25] In turn, by reconstructing these sites of
slavery, post–civil rights African American artists and intellectuals are
able to speak out against their racial plight (the living) and on behalf of
their enslaved ancestors (the dead).

By doing so, African Americans not only call the legitimacy of
American civic myths into question, but also reconfigure these civic
markers in order to accommodate the constitutive sites of American
history that the national memory has forgotten or excised. To combat this erasure and elision, contemporary black cultural producers engage in what Charles Taylor aptly terms "the politics of recognition,"
the formal battle for equality that requires a revision of symbols and
images.[26] Whereas the debates for legal citizenship largely took place in

the juridical and political realms, civic membership is symbolic in form. The demands for civic membership, therefore, have mostly taken place in the aesthetic and cultural realms. As Ralph Ellison put it, "The society is not likely to become free of racism, thus it is necessary for Negroes to free themselves by becoming their idea of what a free people should be."[27] In order to gain this Ellisonian freedom, post–civil rights African Americans have attached themselves to the myths, monuments, narratives, icons, creeds, and images that render them eligible for civic membership; they do so precisely by revising the very same elements of national identity from which they have been rejected. Those most likely to engage the abstract signs and symbols that make up the national identity have been contemporary African American artists, writers, and legislators whose projects contest the hegemony and racial homogeneity of American civic myths while simultaneously creating more historically faithful and more democratic national narratives.

TOWARD A CRITICAL PATRIOTISM

In the quest to expose and consequently undermine the racial contradictions of American civic culture, contemporary black activists and artists have not always replaced civic myths with rival myths but with what Rogers Smith defines as "complex truths."[28] While Smith concedes that civic myths "may contain factual elements," he simultaneously warns that "stories buttressing civic loyalties virtually always contain elements that are not literally true." Thus, in order for citizens to actualize democracy, they "must strive to be skeptical of flattering civic myths. . . . They must try to look unblinkingly at the realities of their history and their present, with all their deficiencies as well as their great achievements on view."[29] Presumably, the role of the citizen in a liberal democratic society does not always mirror the task of the artist or intellectual. Not all late-twentieth-century African American writers and activists challenge civic myths. Nevertheless, the texts that I focus on self-consciously return to antebellum chattel slavery as a way of remembering a forgotten past and gaining equal recognition in the present. By foregrounding American slavery, these artists and writers, to quote Brook Thomas's Civic Myths, "form a discourse capable of working on myth, drawing on its narrative power to generate compelling stories."[30] These representations of slavery contest the singularity of American civic myths to reconfigure a democratic aesthetic and praxis, and by extension write themselves into the ultimate ur-narrative of the United States.

Unlike the civic myths, this democratic aesthetic neither encourages idolatry of the nation's past nor champions a blind loyalty to the state. Staunch allegiance and an inflexible attachment to the country are the normative terms of patriotism, but dissidence and dissent, what I call "critical patriotism," form essential components of this democratic aesthetic's discourse. In no way do I mean to suggest that civic skepticism and criticality is novel, for we have only to return to the nineteenth-century abolitionist movement to locate such rhetoric. For example, Frederick Douglass's speech of July 5, 1852, allows us to trace a genealogy of this critical patriotism. In "The Meaning of July Fourth for the Negro?" Douglass asked his northern white audience if they meant to mock him when they invited a former slave and non-citizen to speak in honor of the anniversary of the signing of the Declaration of Independence. To Douglass, the occasion was theirs, not his; a day of melancholia, not a day to "rejoice." The biggest irony, however, was America's refusal to live up to the democratic ideals of the founding fathers, those "statesmen, patriots and heroes" and "the principles they contended."[31] Instead of rebuking the founding narrative of the nation that did not guarantee him legal rights or liberties, Douglass appropriates its legacy in order to launch his critique of its slaveholding present. By exhorting his "fellow citizens" to understand that "America is false to the past, false to the present, and solemnly binds herself false to the future," Douglass's critical patriotism enables him to become the model citizen, one who does not repudiate but reifies, does not dismantle but re-engages the meta-discourse of American democracy. Similar to Douglass, post–civil rights African American cultural producers depict the coupling of slavery and freedom as ironic and constitutive. However, unlike Douglass, contemporary black writers and artists do not disaggregate slavery from the narrative of American democracy. Instead of representing slavery as the foil to American democracy, contemporary African Americans foreground slavery as the mnemonic property of the entire nation, and not, as Charles Johnson posits, the exclusive intellectual property of blacks. As Edmund Morgan articulates in *American Slavery, American Freedom*, the United States was born of a marriage between democracy and slavery.[32] Similarly, in *Blackface, White*

Noise, Michael Rogin notes that the Declaration of Independence "bequeathed a Janus-faced legacy to the new nation—the logic on the one hand that the equality to which white men were naturally born could be extended to women and slaves, and the foundation on the other white freedom on black servitude."[33]

In turn, contemporary narratives on slavery transform this founding moment of slavery as the primary trope through which to articulate a post–civil rights African American belief in the restorative and curative possibilities of American democracy. Neither born into nor burdened by the need to end slavery, contemporary African Americans have invoked what Saidiya Hartman calls slavery's "scenes of subjection" as a useable past.[34] Their new narratives on slavery are radical mnemonic strategies that privilege the idea and ideal of democracy, yet all the while remaining skeptical of its materialization. Described by Ralph Ellison as "antagonistic cooperation," their democratic discourse not only works as a corrective against monolithic, cult-like narratives of an uncritical (white) patriotism, but also serves as a discourse of patriotism based on dissent, criticality, and inclusion.[35] As a result, this democratic aesthetic is backward-looking (in its return to slavery) and forward-thinking (a way of rendering the African American patriot, estranged, second-class, or disenfranchised, as the ultimate model of American citizenship).

As I identify the democratic aesthetic as the dominating mode of poetics and politics of contemporary narratives of slavery, I do not neatly separate it from the concurring postmodernist epistemologies. Many of these texts I study, from Barbara Chase-Riboud's novel *Sally Hemings* to Carrie Mae Weems's photograph "Elmina Cape Coast Ile de Goree," easily fall into what Linda Hutcheon thoughtfully calls "historiographic metafiction" of postmodernism. According to Hutcheon, "its theoretical self-awareness of history and fiction as human constructs (historiographic metafiction) made the grounds for its rethinking and reworking of the forms and contents of the past."[36] Here, the past is neither stable nor fixed but a malleable subject that present-day writers and artists can reappropriate, reconstruct, and reclaim. In many ways, the post–civil rights depictions of slavery are examples of a postmodernist practice, for they employ the formal techniques of fragmentation, intertextuality, and discontinuity, while also engaging in deconstructionist critiques of the totalizing narratives embedded in American law and civic culture.

However, instead of arguing that these post–civil rights narratives on slavery begin and end in the postmodern tradition as many critical works on the neo-slave narrative have posited, I contend that this subgenre incorporates formal and thematic aspects of postmodernism in its larger yearning to enact democracy.[37] When contemporary African American artists and activists display a fidelity to the cohesive metanarratives of freedom and American democracy, they are not necessarily contradicting their postmodernist intentions; rather, they reveal the limits of postmodernism as the primary philosophy through which to theorize post–civil rights African American subjectivity and cultural production. Similar to bell hooks's argument that postmodernism provides "new strategies of resistance," these contemporary narratives on slavery appropriate certain forms and features of postmodernism to challenge the racial hegemony of American civic culture.[38] Instead, much like the fugitive slave writer Douglass, and the African American modernist Ellison, post–civil rights writers and intellectuals appropriated and contoured their period-specific aesthetic, in this case postmodern irony, to articulate the need for a deep and justifiable skepticism about past and present practices of racial democracy: a need that paradoxically has maintained itself by the durability of an American civic myth whose promise of equality continually disputes the reality of African American life. In some ways, it is the stability of these contradictions, the longevity of American racial injustice itself, that has sustained the determinate and unequivocal African American allegiance to this grandest of all American myths.

This loyalty to democracy in the midst of the postmodern influence, however, has not produced a homogenizing notion of blackness, upheld one particular political critique against racism, or assumed that racial progress is static. In fact, it incorporates many of the aesthetic and philosophical concerns of what is routinely called "Post-Soul" studies.[39] Inspired by the founding Post-Soul critics of Trey Ellis, Nelson George, Thelma Golden, and Greg Tate, Mark Anthony Neal in Soul Babies says that Post-Soul rhetoric is preoccupied with "continuously collapsing on modern concepts of blackness and reanimating 'premodern' (African?) concepts of blackness," ultimately rendering many "traditional 'tropes' of blackness dated and even meaningless."[40] While the post–civil rights contemporary narratives on slavery build on the Post-Soul emphasis of refusing thin tropes and redefining complex notions of blackness, they are distinguished by their preoccupation with the ante-bellum past to work through discourses of citizenship, democracy, and African American political identity in the present. Further differentiat-ing the contemporary representations of slavery in my study are their varied deployments of the democratic aesthetic: historical (How do these texts supplement and subvert the national forgetting of slavery?); generic (Why do these narratives formally privilege satire over melo-drama to launch their civic critiques?); geographic (Where does one locate counter-narratives to American civic myths?); and ethical (What do these narratives imagine a fair and just materialization of equality and racial justice to be?).

The chapters of this book each take into account how representa-tions of slavery change over time and how artists and writers revise the democratic aesthetic itself to suit the political moment and cultural period. The first two chapters examine how contemporary African American artists reconstitute icons—be it the historical figures of Sally Hemings or Thomas Jefferson or the fictional characters of Uncle Tom and Topsy—as metaphors for post–civil rights racial melancholia and yearning. The last two chapters focus on collective and public forms of memory such as commercial tourism to West African slave forts and formal demands for reparations for slavery. In an attempt to interro-gate the limitations of this democratic aesthetic in post–civil rights nar-ratives, the epilogue puts forth a sustained reading of the implications of representations of slavery in the most recent period of the post–civil rights era: the Age of Obama. Specifically, I discuss the conflicts and collaborations that generated the national exhibition "The President's House: Freedom and Slavery in the Making of a New Nation." Sitting directly in front of the Liberty Bell and Independence Hall in Phila-delphia, the President's House commemorates the nation's first execu-tive mansion in which Presidents George Washington and John Adams lived, while primarily memorializing the lives of the nine enslaved Afri-can Americans who served Washington, thereby making it the first American commemorative site to formally recognize the founding paradox of slavery and democracy.

Chapter 1 focuses on how Barbara Chase-Riboud's novel *Sally Hemings* (1979), the playwright Robbie McCauley's *Sally's Rape* (1994), and the historian Annette Gordon-Reed's *Thomas Jefferson and Sally Hemings: An American Controversy* (1998) and *The Hemingses of Monticello*

(2008) reconstruct the narrative of Hemings and Jefferson in order to provide Hemings with an agency and subjectivity denied her in her own life and in American historiography. By doing so, these works not only posit the black female body as the central focus for engaging with Jefferson's slave past, but also as a uniquely constitutive and generative element of post–civil rights memory/remembering of slavery. The emphasis on black female corporeality within these texts importantly disrupts the limiting categories of "man" and "slave" as famously opined by Frederick Douglass.[41] Their depictions also signal the emergence of "woman" and "slave" as an essential and repeated trope within contemporary African American representations of slavery. In this sense, the chapter and this entire book are influenced by Hartman's provocative question in *Scenes of Subjection*: "What happens if we assume that the female subject serves as a general case for explicating social death, property relations, and the pained and putative construction of Blackness? . . . What possibilities of resignification would then be possible?"[42]

To answer this question, this book theorizes the ways national fictions of whiteness, blackness, and femininity have overdetermined black women, like Hemings, as spectacles that, to quote Hortense Spillers, are "vestibular to culture" and subsequently in direct opposition to the rights and rites of U.S. citizens.[43] In this sense, enslaved black women are not simply denied access to feminized civic myths — such as the "mother of the nation" — that are crucial to the national identity, but are also relegated as the permanent others of the United States. My intervention, however, is to understand how post–civil rights African American writers and artists reimagine enslaved black women as a source of critical patriotism and model citizenship. These new narratives heed Frederick Douglass's warning that through slavery the United States "binds *herself* false to the future," while offering the enslaved black woman as the embodiment of a democratic future and the ultimate liberator of a nation bound by the dyads of slavery and freedom and civic estrangement and legal citizenship.

Chapter 2 marks a generic shift. I contend that the post–civil rights narratives of Ishmael Reed's novel *Flight to Canada* (1976), Bill T. Jones's dance *Last Supper at Uncle Tom's Cabin / The Promised Land* (1990), Robert Alexander's play *I Ain't Yo' Uncle: The New Jack Revisionist of "Uncle Tom's Cabin"* (1991), and Kara Walker's large-scale silhouette *The End of Uncle Tom and the Grand Allegorical Tableau of Eva in Heaven* (1995) all reclaim

Stowe's most racially problematic characters, Uncle Tom or Topsy, by using satire and signification to destabilize the narrative control of Harriet Beecher Stowe's classic *Uncle Tom's Cabin* (1852). These artists do not simply substitute Stowe's sentimentality for satirical derision. Their democratic aesthetic encourages different forms of attachments to the nation, engendering more complex affective relationships to the nation that extend beyond either blind loyalty or uncritical love of national achievements. In these narratives, critical and reflexive emotions like shame, disillusionment, and yearning become the basis of civic membership as well.

Chapter 3 looks at the possibilities and limits of a supranational democratic discourse. It argues that the late-twentieth-century "Back to Africa" discourse departs from the nineteenth-century emigrationist and mid-twentieth-century expatriate "Back to Africa" movements; the contemporary discourse predicates itself more on a commemoration of slavery's past than on the creation of a programmatic solution for the future by way of the establishment of an alternative homeland in an emancipated African postcolonial present. While most studies on diaspora and black tourism have been anthropological, my analysis of the photographs from Carrie Mae Weems's *Slave Coast* (1993) and Chester Higgins's *Middle Passage* (1994) series, along with Haile Gerima's film *Sankofa* (1993), marks a turn to the aesthetic. The advent of African American heritage tourism, I argue, enables post–civil rights African Americans to replace (and thus temporarily reconcile) their sense of exclusion from America's canonized national self-narrative. These representations produce an alternative diasporic site of origin while also reproducing an almost exclusively American narrative of return and redemption.

Unlike the cultural texts that engage the past with an eye toward revision, early-twenty-first-century calls for reparations invoke the past as a way of imagining and constructing a model of democracy for the future. As such, the past is a signifier for the yet-to-be-seen possibilities and potential of American democracy. Chapter 4 analyzes how contemporary African American reparations discourse exemplifies an ethical commitment to democracy through its legal arguments that redistribution of economic resources to the descendants of enslaved African Americans is a precondition for a democratic state. I examine the reparations discourse of Randall Robinson's *The Debt* (2000) and

Mary Frances Berry's *My Face Is Black Is True* (2005), and also the legal cases of *Cato v. United States* (1995) and *African American Slave Descendants Litigation* (2003), which put forth different claims of both material and mnemonic restitution in order to challenge the purposeful and polite national amnesia around slavery. Here, democracy distributes itself ... ...tergenerational monetary compensation and the restruc-
ican civic memory.

'oject is heavily indebted to Ashraf Rushdy's *Neo-Slave*
ent works by Madhu Dubey, Arlene Keizer, A. Timothy
isa Woolfork, I also depart from these studies in my
disciplinarity, tropological revision, and transnation-
rpio's *Laughing Fit to Kill: Black Humor in the Fictions*
articularly important. Her interdisciplinary analysis
and fiction on slavery investigates "the relationship
d humor and complicate[s] distinctions between
resentations of slavery in the past forty years."[45]
ılar attention to the constructive possibilities
...erican humor in the post–civil rights era, I am trying
to think through the ways that contemporary African American rep-
resentations of slavery examine the relationship between democratic ideals and civic entitlements, on one hand, and the ways that slavery continues to be bound up with American national narratives, on the other. In this way, the title of this introduction, "Peculiar Citizenships," becomes more than a simple allusion to slavery. Clearly, it recalls the southern euphemism of "our peculiar institution" to describe the systemic exploitation of enslaved African Americans during the eighteenth and nineteenth centuries. But the reference to peculiar citizenships also resonates with the radical tradition of postbellum black writers, such as Pauline Hopkins, author of the musical *Peculiar Sam, or The Underground Railroad* (1879), in which the title character's rebellious escape from slavery renders the trope of "the peculiar" as a form of dissidence and resistance. Like Hopkins's reclamation of "peculiarity" from southern slaveholders and her inversion of Sam, the avuncular icon of the American nation-state, the notion of peculiar citizenships moves between invocations of the "peculiar" as private property and as political oddity, between slavery and subversion. It stretches the black radical tradition into the present, while modeling challenges to ongoing forms of racial retrenchment and imagining an unfinished revolution of

black freedom. A move, this book argues, that enables post–civil rights African Americans to stage the ultimate rhetorical coup, one in which they wrestle with and eventually recuperate the primordial site of black racial inequality — slavery — as the basis for a more racially democratic future.

All in all, Sally's story and the Jefferson it asks us to believe in, if credited as true, would require us not merely to change some shadings in his portrait but literally to reverse the picture of him, as an honorable man, painted by contemporaries who knew him well and by the multitudes of later scholars. . . . The personality of the man who figures in Sally Hemings's pathetic story simply cannot be assimilated to the known character of Thomas Jefferson.

DOUGLASS ADAIR, "The Jefferson Scandals"

I said, "Thomas Jefferson was my great-great-great-great-great-great-grand-father." The teacher told me to sit down and stop telling lies.

SHANNON LANIER, quoted in Anita Hamilton, "A Family Divided"

ONE

Freedom in a Bondsmaid's Arms

Sally Hemings, Thomas Jefferson, and the Persistence of African American Memory

AT THE DAWN of the French Revolution, a teenaged Sally Hemings, coiffed with lovely brown curls and adorned in the finest Parisian silks, begins an exchange with Thomas Paine and Thomas Jefferson during a garden party at the Palace of Versailles. Awed by Paine's presence yet confident in her powers of persuasion, Hemings approaches both men by quoting excerpts from Paine's provocative pamphlet *Common Sense* (1776): "Weak men cannot see and prejudiced men will not see" and "We have it in our power to begin the world again."[1] Transfixed by her wit and beauty, Paine first bows and then, turning to Jefferson, whispers, "Well, if ever there were reason to accept Washington's appointment and push an anti-slavery bill through Congress, dear boy, she is the best." In this brief scene from

African American screenwriter Tina Andrews's four-hour television miniseries *Sally Hemings: An American Scandal* (CBS, 2000),[2] Hemings, played by the British actress Carmen Ejigo, is the ultimate cosmopolitan and patriot. Andrews depicts Hemings as a bilingual aesthete who exudes a worldly self-assurance that matches the charisma of the statesman Jefferson. Once back in Virginia, Hemings not only ensures that her children will be manumitted, but she illegally teaches enslaved children how to read and write, privately opposes Jefferson's purchase of the slaveholding territory of Louisiana, and challenges Jefferson's scientific racism by confronting him with his own copy of *Notes on the State of Virginia*. Through this fictionalized Hemings, Andrews not only reminds viewers of the presence of African American women during the formation of the American nation-state, but also casts the slave-born Hemings as the ultimate heir to Paine's revolutionary rhetoric, more faithful to the democratic ideals of the nation than one of its most esteemed founding fathers, Thomas Jefferson.

In contrast to Jefferson's extensive legacy, the only remaining historical records of Sally Hemings are a bill from a boarding house on the Rue Seine, her passport, the ledgers from Jefferson's household detailing how much he spent on her clothes, the memoirs by her son Madison, newspaper accounts of her relationship with Jefferson in 1802, and the slave inventory at Monticello in which, at age fifty-seven, she was valued at fifty dollars.[3] As a result of these material and discursive silences, there is no simple method to access her past, no way, as Hortense Spillers remarks, "to easily form in the inner ear an aural image of the sound and grain of Sally Hemings's voice, the shape and meaning of her words, or how she might have felt."[4] In the absence of written and visual records, Andrews turns to speculation and imagination in order to reconstruct "Sally Hemings's perspective, the disregarded perspective, the slave perspective" at Monticello.[5] Although Andrews's re-creation of Hemings is unique, her teleplay is part of a larger critical intervention by post–civil rights African American women writers such as Barbara Chase-Riboud, Robbie McCauley, and Annette Gordon-Reed, whose texts also reclaim Hemings as the symbol of a multiracial American democracy. Moreover, as these contemporary representations put forth novel and radical readings of Hemings, they continue to incorporate African American oral histories that, as Clarence Walker notes, actually kept the story of Hemings and Jefferson in circulation for some two hundred years.[6] Until recently, when DNA validated that Eston Hemings was in fact Hemings's and Jefferson's biological son, the official history of the Hemings–Jefferson relationship included only Jefferson's correspondences, the oral testimonies of his white grandchildren, and Dumas Malone's and Merrill Peterson's estimable biographies. Through omission, redirection, or outright rejection, all these accounts disputed the legitimacy of a sexual relationship, be it romantic or coerced, between Jefferson and Hemings.[7]

Nonetheless, the Hemings–Jefferson relationship was so significant to African American abolitionist culture that the first African American novel, William Wells Brown's *Clotel: or, the President's Daughter: A Narrative of Slave Life in the United States* (1852), used the rumor that Jefferson had fathered slave children and that one of his daughters had been sold on the auction block for a thousand dollars as its central plot device. Brown chose Jefferson because he unambiguously embodied the contradictions that hovered around the nation's founding, for Jefferson "had written magnificently about human freedom" while "buying, working and selling slaves."[8] Even though Jefferson is not among the main characters in *Clotel*, by depicting him as both the father of Clotel and a founding father of the United States, Brown depicted the incongruity between the democratic rhetoric of American civic myths and the reality of chattel slavery. Brown also cast Hemings and her children within the national allegory as tragic symbols of black non-citizenship and enslavement in the antebellum period. According to Werner Sollors, the fictional Clotel was emblematic of the lamentable legal status of nineteenth-century African Americans who had "white America as the father figure, black America as the mother," but as offspring were "the problematic, truly American heir who is denied his/her birthright and inheritance by his/her father."[9]

Over a century later, in 1954, when *Ebony* published "Thomas Jefferson's Negro Grandchildren," readers learned about "a handful of elderly Negroes who traced their ancestry back to Jefferson."[10] Similar to Brown's retelling, *Ebony* reframed Jefferson's real and metaphorical racial contradictions as the perfect foil against which to protest second-class black citizenship. By legitimating Jefferson's paternity of Hemings's children, these written accounts used African American oral histories to democratize perspectives of the past while simultaneously framing their interpretations of the Jefferson–Hemings relationship to directly protest black disenfranchisement in slavery and Jim Crow segregation. As Ann Du Cille writes, the "rumor" of their relationship was never simply "the idle gossip of maiden aunts, distant cousins, and community busybodies." But "the carefully guarded family records of a people denied access to their own heritage, except by word of mouth," thereby providing what Michel Foucault defined as a "counter-memory" to the official absence of Hemings from Jefferson's historiography.[11] Rather than embrace the power of historical narratives and the authority of totalizing national myths, Foucault argued that counter-memory looks to the past for the hidden histories excluded from dominant narratives.[12] George Lipsitz notes that for African American writers, counter-memory not only excavates buried histories, but simultaneously contests and revises hegemonic images, traditional icons, heroes, rituals, and narratives.[13] Protesting against slavery and segregation, these earlier African American counter-memories fought for racial equality by appealing to rights and rituals of legal citizenship. In such representations of slavery, it was Jefferson, not Hemings, who emerged as the more accurate symbol for America's racial paradox and who thereby compromised democracy.

Because contemporary African American artists and intellectuals do not have to contest legal slavery or segregation, their representations of slavery in general and of Hemings in particular do not have to be realistic and are decidedly more experimental, multidimensional, and focused. The critical distance between the antebellum period and our contemporary moment gives modern-day texts, such as Barbara Chase-Riboud's novel *Sally Hemings* (1979), Robbie McCauley's play *Sally's Rape* (1994), and the historian Annette Gordon-Reed's *Thomas Jefferson and Sally Hemings: An American Controversy* (1997) and *The Hemingses of Monticello: An American Family* (2008), the privilege of depicting Hemings with a measure of authority unknown to her in her real life.[14] So while these texts do not have the same political burden to render slavery "palatable," as Toni Morrison writes, to those who were in the position to alleviate it, these contemporary writers render her a national allegory for a vexed post–civil rights citizenship. The past in this sense serves the present. Hemings did not benefit from the rights and privileges of nineteenth-century U.S. citizenship. However, rather than use Hemings as an empty signifier of the slave past, a historical womb that both mourns and mirrors black disenfranchisement, Chase-

Riboud, Gordon-Reed, and McCauley interrogate the past of slavery by reimagining her as a radical black female subject. By casting Hemings as America's prodigal daughter, their texts remind us of the importance of black female corporeality to slavery's scenes of subjection and the genealogy of that subjection. This use of Hemings, in many ways, recalls what Spillers meant when she wrote that in the American practice of slavery the "quintessential 'slave' is *not* male, but a female."[15] Yet for these writers, Hemings not only represents the forms of black resistance that flourished in spite of slavery. They also characterize her as America's founding mother, a crucial symbol of the constitutive relationship between slavery and the formation of the American nation-state in which black women, not the founding statesmen, emerge as the true progenitors and guardians of democracy. Through African American (postmodern) memory, Chase-Riboud, Gordon-Reed, and McCauley help write African Americans back into the nation's founding and justify black birthright claims, thereby invoking a democratic aesthetic that substitutes sanitized, racially homogeneous civic myths with the complex truths of interracial ties of intimacy. By shifting the focus from Jefferson to enslaved African Americans such as Hemings, these contemporary representations of slavery provide a radical insight into American history in which Hemings, not Jefferson, becomes the racial metonym of the nation on the one hand and a model for post–civil rights civic membership on the other.

DUSKY SALLY AND SOOTY CHARMS: GENDER, RACE, AND AMERICAN CITIZENSHIP

> The patriot, fresh from Freedom's councils come,
> Now pleased retires to lash his slaves at home;
> Or woo, perhaps some black Aspasia's charms,
> And dream of freedom in his bondsmaid's arms.
>
> THOMAS MOORE, *Epistle VII*

If, as Merrill Peterson argued, Thomas Jefferson is America's "mirror of the race dilemma," then Sally Hemings darkly stood on the other side of the looking glass.[16] This dialectic between belonging and non-belonging, recognition and invisibility, not only defines the civic segregation that Hemings experienced in the antebellum culture, but was simply the logical extension of the legal and economic disenfranchisement of millions of free and enslaved African Americans. Unfortunately, stereotypes of racial alterity not only justified black non-citizenship, but the rhetoric of early American citizenship was gendered male, racialized as white, and defined against the black body.[17] In this vortex of defining what and who belong to the nation, enslaved African American women were in a particularly estranged and subordinate position. As Patricia Hill Collins thoughtfully notes, "As the 'Others' of society who can never really belong, strangers threaten the moral and social order. But they are simultaneously essential for its survival because those individuals who stand at the margins of society clarify its boundaries." Regrettably, "African American women, by not belonging, emphasize[d] the significance of belonging."[18]

Caught in this gendered racial discourse from 1802 to 1808, Sally Hemings was not simply denied access to feminized civic myths, such as the "mother of the nation," that were crucial to the national identity. She became a spectacle that, to quote Hortense Spillers, was "vestibular to culture" and mirrored for the society around her what a citizen was not.[19] In both Federalist verse and prose, the image of "Dusky Sally" was the subject of more newspaper stanzas than any contemporary American female, black or white.[20] Most famously, Hemings first appeared on the national scene when James T. Callender published the article "Reading Improves the Mind" in the *Richmond Recorder* on September 1, 1802, in which he described the Jefferson–Hemings relationship as follows:

THE PRESIDENT, *AGAIN*

It is well known that the man, *whom it delighteth the people* to honor, keeps, and for many years past has kept, as his concubine, one of his own slaves. Her name is SALLY. The name of her eldest son is TOM. His features are said to bear a striking resemblance to those of the president himself. The boy is ten or twelve years of age. His mother went to France in the same vessel with Mr. Jefferson and his two daughters. . . . By this wench Sally, our president has had several children. . . . THE AFRICAN VENUS is said to officiate, as housekeeper at Monticello.[21]

Callender goes on in subsequent articles to describe Hemings as a "wench," "a slut as common as the pavement," as having "had fifteen or thirty" different lovers "of all colours," and referred to her children as a "yellow litter."[22] Drawing on eighteenth-century European scientific and travel discourse that stereotyped African women as sexual and moral deviants, Callender's article initiated the public discourse that purported Sally Hemings to be innately lewd and lascivious and therefore not simply a threat to Jefferson, but to the national racial order itself.[23]

While Callender's publicizing of this local rumor did not directly damage Jefferson's reelection campaign, it provided fodder for the president's political adversaries. Because many contemporary newspapers continued to adapt Callender's claims, the popular press kept the Jefferson–Hemings story alive. Like Callender's story, these writings depicted Hemings as seductive and promiscuous, contrasting Hemings's womanhood to the idealized femininity of Jefferson's white wife and daughters in ways that further demonized her. In October 1802, Joseph Denzie, the editor of the genteel and popular Philadelphia magazine *Port Folio*, composed "A Song Supposed to Have Been Written by the Sage of Monticello":

> Of all the damsels on the green
> On mountain or in valley,
> A lass so luscious ne'er was seen
> As Monticellian Sally.
> *Chorus*: Yankee Doodle, who's the noodle?
> What wife were half so handy?
> To breed a flock of slaves to stock,
> A blackamoor's the dandy.[24]

In this song Denzie satirized the optimistic nationalism of the popular *Yankee Doodle Dandee* with Jefferson's love for the "blackamoor" Hemings who he insinuated was more valuable to Jefferson than a white wife because her children, as slaves, added to the value of his property. Because prevailing stereotypes defined African American women as loose and amoral, these women were more likely to experience public ridicule of their procreative capacities. Moreover, once slave women's reproduction became a topic of public conversation, so did their sexual activities. People accustomed to reading and writing about the nature of bondswomen's reproductive abilities could hardly help associating Sally Hemings's children with licentious behavior.

Under the anonym of Thomas Jefferson, the *Boston Gazette* published another poem:

Thou, Sally, thou, my house shalt keep,
My widow'd tears shall dry!
My virgin daughters—see! they weep—
Their mother's place supply.
Oh! Sally! Hearken to my vows!
Yield up thy swarthy charms—
My best beloved! my more than spouse,
Oh! take me to thy arms.[25]

In this song Jefferson ignores his grieving daughters' tears and exalts Hemings, a slave woman, to the position of "more than spouse," a position that rightfully belonged to a white woman. Looking at the roles that white women and black women played in antebellum America, Hazel Carby concluded, "Black womanhood was polarized against white womanhood in the metaphoric system of female sexuality, particularly through the association of black women with overt sexuality and taboo sexual practices."[26] Unlike Jefferson's wife and his white daughters, Hemings as a slave could clean Jefferson's home, but she should not be able to "keep" his home. In the *Gazette* poem, the white women weep because Jefferson has given their precarious domain of power—the home—to Hemings largely because of sexual prowess and her "sooty charms."

For many white Americans, Hemings's relationship with Jefferson insulted the integrity of his family while simultaneously agitating the deep anxiety they felt toward miscegenation and African American equality. Hemings did not simply "keep his home" but symbolized the potential integration of African Americans into the national identity—a nation over which she suddenly loomed as a sort of founding mother. However, because stereotypes of black alterity were central to the production of ideologies of white citizenship, her sexual intimacy with Jefferson was not only seen as in the public domain but also perilous to the racial structure of the republic. While Jefferson initially warded off these allegations through reticence, Jeffersonian historians in collusion with his white grandchildren emphasized Jefferson's abstinence. The idea of Jefferson's sexual virtue and racial purity not only misrepresented his actual historical legacy but also perpetuated stereotypes of Heming's immorality and sexual aberrance that linked her and her children to Jefferson's nephews, the Carrs, or brother, Randolph. Therefore, even though Hemings received substantially more attention than her African American female contemporaries, her exceptionality in early-nineteenth-century discourse originated in and perpetuated a racist anxiety about miscegenation and African Americans as morally unfit for citizenship. As Jefferson's civic iconography, based upon his standing as a founding father and author of the Declaration of Independence, became a restatement of America's greatness, the growth of Jefferson's prestige was enabled by the deliberate and continual excising of Hemings, her children, and all black kin from his personal record. Ironically, this erasure did not lead to Hemings's disappearance from Jefferson's historiography, but to a rearticulation of her illegitimacy and immorality into a negative symbol that helped justify African American political inferiority and second-class citizenship well into the mid-twentieth century. To paraphrase Spillers, Sally's country needed her, and if she had not been there, she would have had to have been invented.[27]

THE AMERICAN HOUSE OF ATREUS: BARBARA CHASE-RIBOUD'S *SALLY HEMINGS*

[Barbara] Chase-Riboud is faced with a dilemma: Hemings, the main character, is encased in myth; yet she lingers in the margins of historical records. Because Chase-Riboud must rescue her heroine from myth, she cannot completely free herself from the conventional trappings of the historical novel.

BARBARA CHRISTIAN, "Somebody Forgot
to Tell Somebody Something"

In 1979, when Barbara Chase-Riboud decided to write the novel *Sally Hemings*, she wanted to use the intimacy between the fictional Jefferson and Hemings to counter the hypocrisy of an American national identity that "perceives itself as a white man's country," even though this perception "has nothing to do with reality." After reading Fawn Brodie's *Thomas Jefferson: An Intimate History* (1974), Chase-Riboud fictionalized Hemings as a slave woman with whom Jefferson had a thirty-eight-year monogamous relationship.[28] Before Brodie and Chase-Riboud, historians had primarily used James Callender's slanderous articles and the oral testimonies of Jefferson's white grandchildren to describe Hemings.[29] Rejecting these derivative and reductive representations, Chase-Riboud constructs Hemings as a figure of America's multiraciality and as proof that the United States has always been a "mulatto country."[30] By writing these multiracial origins back into Jefferson's iconography, Chase-Riboud tells an American founding narrative that rightfully includes its African American members. Furthermore, Chase-Riboud recognizes that the absence of formal signs and symbols of an African American past creates a larger crisis of recognition and African American civic estrangement. As she stated in an interview, "There comes a time in the life of a nation when certain facts have to be faced and included in the national identity," and that remembering slavery, and even more specifically resurrecting Hemings, is "not only . . . a matter of record, but . . . a matter of survival."[31]

While the novel is nominally set in post-Revolutionary America, Chase-Riboud transforms Jefferson's Monticello into a site of slavery that personifies what Stephanie Camp describes as "the crime and seduction of miscegenation; the ambiguities of black and white racial identities and meaning; the coexistence of prejudice and power with family, intimacy, and sex."[32] In *Sally Hemings*, we learn that Sally is also the offspring of the interracial sexual relationship between Jefferson's white father-in-law, John Wayles, and his slave mistress, Elizabeth Hemings. Consequently, Sally Hemings was not only the half-sister of Jefferson's white wife, Martha Wayles Jefferson, who died in childbirth four years before the Jefferson–Hemings relationship began, but also the biological aunt of Jefferson's two surviving daughters. Through the complicated entanglements of the Jefferson–Hemings family, Chase-Riboud emphasizes that America's incestuous ties and multiracial origins not only literally bind blacks and whites together, but also subvert the founding mythopoeia upon which the United States built itself. In place of civic myths that deny America's mixed-race beginnings, Chase-Riboud turns to the Hemings family to unveil the historical presence of antebellum interracial relationships and the possibilities of a post–civil rights multiracial community. In the scene in which Jefferson's "white" family and Hemings's "black" family dance in a circle, Sally cannot help but notice that she was "only one in the web of ties that weaved itself in and across and around the two parts of the circle, binding one half to the other in arabesques as twisted and complicated as the hanging strands of silver cord on the tree above us."[33] Here, Chase-Riboud uses the trope of interracial intimacy to undermine the rigid racial lines of Monticello, for Hemings is not exceptional but "only one" of many who compose this circle of overlapping relationships: parent-child, master-slave children, mistress-owner, sister-brother, black-white. The circle and the silver umbilical-like cords hanging above them represent the potential of racial harmony, one in which blacks and whites can acknowledge their intimacy and their shared origins.

However, at the end of the dance, when the families return to their stations as slave and master and black and white, Chase-Riboud does not offer interracial romance as a simple solution to American racism. She presents Jefferson as a man who consistently struggles with his simultaneous sexual desire for and enslavement of African American women. This fictional Jefferson philosophizes that slavery inevitably corrupts the moral integrity of the nation, and yet he spends the bulk of the novel owning and exploiting the labor of his African American slaves. Hemings is literally at the heart of Jefferson's inner conflict in which loving and owning her co-exist. In public, Jefferson does not formally acknowledge his relationship with her, while in private their "love story" defies the slave-master relationship based completely on exploitation and subjugation. Although Hemings is fifteen years old at the time of their first sexual encounter, Chase-Riboud does not entertain the possibility that Jefferson sexually exploited Hemings. Instead, she depicts Hemings as a woman with whom Jefferson would inevitably fall in love.[34] As in Tina Andrews's miniseries, Chase-Riboud not only portrays Sally as cosmopolitan and erudite, but also describes her as extraordinarily striking:

> [Her eyes were] of a deep amber yellow, mark of a quadroon, which gave her whole face an illusion of transparency. Eyes that were liquid gold in an ivory mask; windows onto banked and mysterious fires that burned day and night, absorbing everything and returning nothing the surface. The skin was drawn, smooth. There was no way to tell age; neither in the lines of her face nor the contours of her body — which was small and low, compact and strong, with that wiry vivacity of congenital thinness. (4)

Anticipating Spillers's claim that we have no access to Hemings's interiority ("how she might have felt") or exteriority ("the sound and grain of her voice"), Chase-Riboud supplements Hemings with a wonderful description of her appearance. Her Sally is so beautiful that she transcends Jefferson's idealized perception of white female beauty.

In *Notes on the State of Virginia*, Jefferson argues that the physical differences between blacks and whites are so strong that in "their own judgment" black men chose "in favour of the whites . . . as uniformly as is the preference of the Oran-ootan for the black women over his own species."[35] In order to mitigate Jefferson's own racist rhetoric and therefore dismiss claims that he could not have been attracted to her, Chase-Riboud's Sally is so "physically appealing and sexually alluring," in the words of Andrew Burstein, that no "white man could resist her," thus elevating her from her status as a slave to that of an incomparable romantic partner, a bilingual woman with elegant instincts, enduring beauty, and a fine eye for decor.[36] And while Hemings is legally Jefferson's slave, she also remembers that "on my left hand, I wore a wide yellow band of gold. Wife" (278). The romantic narrative encourages the possibility that this thirty-eight-year relationship was based mostly on respect and mutuality and involved minimal coercion. While the emphasis on romance was inconceivable to earlier African American reconstructions of their relationship, it is integral to Chase-Riboud's vision of Hemings as the prodigal founding mother of a multiracial America. Cast as Jefferson's partner, lover, and slave, Chase-Riboud imbues Hemings with what Kimberly Brown describes as a gift of "uncomplicated agency" that works against the "aggressive nature of corporeal imperialism" upon which slavery was built.[37]

Yet despite the fact that Chase-Riboud recuperates Hemings from the annals of American history, her narrative of freedom within the text is decidedly ambivalent. Much like the misrecognition of African Americans in the civic sphere, the character Sally Hemings cannot escape permanently being "defined by others, particularly by men" throughout the novel.[38] In the pivotal scene in which the pregnant Hemings promises to stay with Jefferson on the condition that their children will be manumitted:,

"Promise me you will not abandon me again."

"I promise, Master."

"I swear to cherish you and never desert you."

"Yes, Master."

"I promise solemnly that your children will be freed," he said.

"As God is your witness?"

"As God is my witness." (143)

Instead of empathizing with Hemings's desire for freedom, Jefferson coerces a promise to her "master," rather to a "lover" or "husband," that she will never forsake him. Then a teenager, Sally sacrifices her freedom for Jefferson because as a slave girl, she thinks perpetual bondage is her destiny. Hemings remembers that during their first sexual encounter, "I was seized with a terrible yearning. I thought of my mother and her mother before her. Nothing would ever be the same again. Nothing would ever free me of him. Nothing would erase those strange words of love which I had to believe in my weakness" (103). Even though Hemings is initially presented as a character enraptured by Jefferson's desires, she eventually develops a deep ambivalence for the man who forces her into the contradictory role of maternal concubine.[39]

In the beginning of their relationship, Hemings convinces herself that she is more than property because she believed that "in the hierarchy of slavehood I stood at the pinnacle, even before [her mother] Elizabeth Hemings, for I was the 'favorite,' the untouchable. I was far above the station of the other slaves" (181). But as the novel progresses, Hemings's recognizes what Saidiya Hartman describes as "the confusion between consent and coercion, feeling and submission, intimacy and domination, and violence and reciprocity" that defined slave law.[40] Ultimately, Chase-Riboud uses the ambiguity of a relationship founded on both interracial violence and interracial romance to represent the novel's constant negotiation between the official history of Thomas Jefferson and the oral testimonies of African American slaves. Because nineteenth-century slaves were unable to tap into what Barbara Christian calls the "deeper labyrinths of dream and memory," Hemings has to use her private memory based on her diaries, newspaper accounts, letters, conversations, burial grounds, and portraits to re-create the life she has lived.[41] Recalling the entirety of their thirty-eight-year relationship from the point of view of its title character, *Sally Hemings* constructs a counter-narrative in which interracial intimacy works to democratize the past and dispute the racial hegemony upon which Jefferson's stature and American civic myths rest.

Through the character of Nathan Langdon, a census taker who lists the whites and free blacks of Albermarle County, Chase-Riboud further literalizes the tension between civic myths and black civic estrangement. The novel begins and ends with the meetings between Langdon and Hemings, who, as a former slave, is "a person with an unrecorded history and unofficial past."[42] Like Jefferson, Langdon becomes a representative of the state whose function is to uphold and repeatedly institutionalize antebellum racial norms. However, because he is unable to reconcile the reality of Hemings's life with her conspicuous absence in Jefferson's narratives, Langdon deliberately writes her out of the historical record. Instead of listing Hemings as an ex-slave and thus black, he counts her and her two sons, Madison and Eston, as white in the Albermarle County census. Langdon believes that the racial designation of black would formally recognize that Jefferson had a sexual relationship with an African American woman. He deliberately rewrites the past, for "if Sally Hemings was who and what people said she was, then Thomas Jefferson had broken the law of Virginia" (16). Although Hemings never forgets that she is black, Langdon imposes "whiteness" on her because he is "determined that Thomas Jefferson would not be guilty of" and not be formally remembered for "the crime of miscegenation" (16). Through Langdon's intentional exclusion of Hemings's blackness, Chase-Riboud reenacts an originary moment of black civic estrangement. Even after Hemings shares "drawers and drawers of memories" (39) with him, Langdon upholds the official, anesthetized Jefferson within American civic myths. Instead of respecting the right that African Americans have "to define their own reality, establish their own identities, name their history,"[43] Langdon, as the agent of official history, believes that he can and should define, create the identity of, and name African American history in a way that defends Jefferson's status in the national memory.

When Hemings learns that Langdon has listed her sons as white, she recognizes "that she owned nothing, except the past. And now, even that had been taken away from her. She had been raped of the only thing a slave possessed: her mind, her thoughts, her feelings, her history" (53). By intentionally misrecording her identity, Langdon endeavors to deny her right of self-definition; similar to Jefferson, he effaces her history, knowing she cannot formally contest his account. She realizes that because she is a black, her entire life has been overdetermined by "white men playing god with my flesh and my spirit and my children and my life" (51). These gods, however, have not only played with her life, but, as custodians of official history, have also shaped her legacy within American civic culture. Denied access to what Daphne Brooks has termed the "patriarchal fantasy of writing herself into being,"[44]

Hemings then turns to her "unending stream" (53) of memories as a counterpoint. Unlike the public act of writing, her memories fully maintain her interiority for she can now choose to keep them silent or to share them. Hemings, in an effort to reconstruct herself and to challenge white male authorial control of American history, destroys all the printed records of her life with Jefferson, beginning by burning John Trumbull's "pencil drawing, a portrait of her as a girl in Paris" (53). Even though the portrait is the only physical image of Hemings that is described in the novel, she now perceives it as proof that she has conspired with white men to record and to define her past.[45] In addition to burning the picture, she also burns both her diaries and her letters from Jefferson. Afterward she concludes that her "blood sacrifice" was an "act of her very own . . . neither black nor white, neither slave nor free, neither loved or loving" (54). Setting out to remember her past in order to control it, she is no longer confined by Jefferson's or Langdon's approach to history, and she begins to see herself as "beyond love, beyond passion, beyond History" (343). By doing so, she begins to assert a subjectivity that culminates the democraticizing project of the entire novel.

In the end, Chase-Riboud gives Hemings authority over her story and the ability to control her own voice. Unfortunately, this agency is short-lived and nontransferable. Because Hemings denies her sons, the next generation of Hemings, access to her past, the sanitized Jefferson continues to dominate the historical record. She has never told her sons her "history" or theirs because "they are safe without it" (44). Their social safety, however, comes at the cost of historical obscurity.[46] As Chase-Riboud says of her son Madison, "His mother had never told him anything of his origins. He knew that slave women never told their offspring anything. So slave children learned what they could when they could, in bits and pieces from older slaves, mammies, white people's conversation, and the bitterness of what they learned was all the more wounding. It intensifies the shame without alleviating the burden" (23). Instead of depicting African American oral memories as full a counterweight to the founding mythology, Chase-Riboud reveals that segregated interpretations of the past maintain African American inferiority. Hemings's refusal to share her past with her children is not simply familial silence, but also a symbol of the national amnesia about slavery and America's multiracial origins. Even though Langdon never solves the mystery of Sally Hemings, he solidifies his version of the past by writing it into the official record. And as she remembers her past as both slave and lover, Hemings's narrative does revise Jefferson's—as well as American—history, by means of Chase-Riboud's deliberate inclusion of black and white social intimacy. Through Hemings's "mulatto country," Chase-Riboud writes them back into being by redefining the national narrative of American democracy as a multiracial narrative. However, because Hemings remains on the margins of American history here, Chase-Riboud tempers the optimistic notion that interracial romance or the simple acknowledgment of African American oral histories alongside racially exclusive civic myths is enough. To do so would only ensure that African Americans continue to experience civic estrangement, and, like Hemings, have their founding pasts willed out of history.

"ONLY THE MOST CONVENTIONAL AND PROPER RELATIONSHIP": ANNETTE GORDON-REED AND THE PROPAGANDA OF HISTORY

> Even today the Jefferson scholars wary of the impulse to sanctify are nevertheless its victim; they glorify and protect by nuance, by omission, by subtle repudiation, without being the least aware of the strength of their internal commitment to canonization. This we see particularly in their treatment of the story of Sally Hemings. This liaison, above all others in Jefferson's life, is unutterably taboo.
>
> FAWN BRODIE, *Thomas Jefferson: An Intimate History*

While the novel *Sally Hemings* incorporates African American oral histories of Hemings and Jefferson within its fictional framework, Annette Gordon-Reed posits historical writing itself as a contested ground of African American non-belonging. Though written almost a decade apart, Annette Gordon-Reed's *Thomas Jefferson and Sally Hemings: An American Controversy* (1997) and *The Hemingses of Monticello: An American Family* (2008) complement each other. In the earlier book, Gordon-Reed employs oral histories to examine the biases of traditional interpretation, thus questioning the ways in which these official narratives shape our ways of seeing and remembering the past. She is not overly concerned with proving Jefferson's paternity of Hemings's children, but with exploring the racism that has plagued the representations of the Jefferson–Hemings liaison in American historiography. The latter book, buttressed by the DNA proof of Jefferson's paternity of Eston Hemings, fills in those former historical silences by literally retracing the lived experiences of Sally Hemings and her family at Monticello. Her first book analyzes the history of Jefferson scholarship to undermine the construction of American civic myths that deride black subjectivity and thereby exposes the constitutive and enduring moments of black civic estrangement. This book reconciles African American oral memories and the written historical record, thus racially integrating both Jefferson's legacy and American history as well.

Gordon-Reed's main argument in *Thomas Jefferson and Sally Hemings* is that prominent Jefferson historians, such as Dumas Malone, Merrill Peterson, and Douglass Adair, systematically privileged the historical accounts put forth by Jefferson's white descendants at the expense of his African American slaves and his black descendants. Gordon-Reed employs two main devices to challenge these Jefferson scholars' assessments of African American sources: first, she examines the Jefferson biographies produced by an earlier generation of Jefferson scholars as individual case studies, thereby portraying Jeffersonian history as a field of active contestation. Second, by juxtaposing the biases of Jefferson scholars to the credibility of Madison Hemings's memoir, the only account given by a child of Hemings and Jefferson, she writes African American oral accounts of slavery into the historical record. By examining history based on a respect for African American counter-memories, her book successfully provides agency to her African American historical actors, Sally and Madison Hemings, while simultaneously entering their voices into the official national narrative.

Gordon-Reed structures *Thomas Jefferson and Sally Hemings* around the five characters most relevant to the investigation of the relationship: Madison Hemings, alleged to be one of Jefferson's slave sons; James Callender, who first reported the story; the Randolphs and the Carrs, two white families with blood ties to Jefferson; and Jefferson and Hemings themselves. Sifting through Jefferson's historiography with a lawyerly precision, the author investigates why and how Jefferson scholars have repeatedly allowed their own partiality and preconceptions about the statesman to infect their historical writings. Despite the historiographical revolutions in the study of slavery over the last thirty years, Gordon-Reed notes, "The consideration of the Sally Hemings story remained in a curious time warp. When confronting this issue, scholars fall back upon notions and make arguments that seem to reverse the steady progress away from the too romantic or 'through-eyes-of-white-southerners' view of slavery" (xiv).[47] Almost complete deference had been given to the interpretations of the more established Jefferson studies, such as Peterson's *The Jefferson Image in the American Mind*, Malone's five-volume Jefferson biography, and Adair's posthumous essay "The Jefferson Scandals." All these works unequivocally reject rumors of the liaison, despite the fact that other reputable historians, such as Winthrop Jordan, author of *White over Black: American Attitudes towards the Negro, 1550–1812* (1968), as well as Fawn Brodie, validated these same rumors. And despite the fact that most Jefferson scholars have never made a "serious and objective attempt to get at the truth of the matter" (224), they were, as professional historians, vested with the authority to authenticate or disprove the historical veracity of the Hemings–Jefferson relationship. Gordon-Reed asserts that well into the 1980s and 1990s, Jefferson biographies such as Andrew Burstein's *The Inner Jefferson: Portrait of a Grieving Optimist* (1995) and Joseph Ellis's *The American Sphinx: The Character of Thomas Jefferson* (1996), continued to "dismiss the allegation out of hand with no evidence of having attempted to investigate the facts themselves" (5).

Even though Gordon-Reed reassesses the Jefferson–Hemings controversy, she dismisses neither the integrity of the historical profession nor the authority of written historical records. Influenced by Brodie's research, Gordon-Reed uses Madison Hemings's oral testimony in the 1873 *Pike County Republican* newspaper article entitled "Life among the Lowly No. 1" to corroborate the Hemings–Jefferson liaison. In this article, Madison Hemings told the editor S. F. Wetmore that their relationship began when Sally Hemings traveled to France as the personal servant of Jefferson's younger daughter, Maria. Once there, Jefferson impregnated Hemings and she initially refused to return with him to the United States. Much like the scene in Chase-Riboud's novel, Madison recounted that Jefferson "promised her extraordinary privileges, and made a solemn pledge that her children should be freed at the age of twenty-one years. In consequence of his promise, on which she implicitly relied, she returned with him to Virginia. Soon after their arrival, she gave birth to a child."[48] Once again, Gordon-Reed does not try to prove if Madison was telling the truth, but instead investigates why scholars have either ignored it or "dismissed it out of hand" (viii). Even though Madison's published testimony is "the only known recitation of the details of this controversial story by any of the parties involved" (135), according to Gordon-Reed, most Jefferson scholars (when they have bothered to address the existence of Madison's testimony at all) have attacked it on a number of fronts.

For example, Dumas Malone and co-author Stephen A. Hochman critically examined Madison's statement in their essay "A Note on Evidence: The Personal History of Madison Hemings" (1975). Gordon-Reed argues that these historians attacked Madison's statement primarily to discredit the motivations of S. F. Wetmore. Since Wetmore's newspaper was affiliated with the Republican Party, Malone and Hochman insinuated that Wetmore had been "rewarded with federal patronage by the Republican administration" to collect and write down a series of short biographies of the African American residents of Pike County.[49] His motive, they suggested, was "judging from its title, 'Life among the Lowly, Number One,' to create sympathy for the freedmen just as *Uncle Tom's Cabin* did for the slaves. That the freedmen needed sympathy and that the Republican Party needed support in Ohio becomes abundantly clear on examination of the local situation. Pike County was a Democratic bastion, and anti-Negro sentiment was very strong there."[50] Rather than scrutinize the historical accuracy of Madison's testimony, most Jefferson scholars, Gordon-Reed contends, simply distrusted his version because it painted an alternative and sometimes oppositional view of Jefferson. Unfortunately, many Jefferson scholars could easily dismiss Madison's statement because his former slave status and his accompanying blackness rendered him untrustworthy. According to Gordon-Reed, to deny his story, to deem it useless, continues to deny African Americans access to Jefferson's legacy. More egregiously, by erasing the Hemingses from Jefferson's civic iconography, these Jefferson historians re-created a past in which enslaved African Americans had no import and contemporary African Americans could lay no claim.

According to Jacques Le Goff, "Impartiality requires no more than honesty on the part of the historian, while objectivity requires more than that. . . . The historian engages in abuses of history only when he himself becomes partisan. A politician, or a lackey of political power."[51]

Following suit, Gordon-Reed's analysis reveals the high political stakes of Jefferson biographies, for those scholars who refused to question the (white) sources that dismissed the relationship compromised the craft of history itself. Instead, they privileged the narratives of the masters like Thomas Jefferson and his grandchildren over the narratives of former slaves like Madison Hemings, who "said something that historians do not want to believe" (86). Gordon-Reed's scrutiny of written histories of the Hemings–Jefferson relationship shows that most Jefferson historians have been overly concerned with protecting Jefferson's legacy from interpretations that they believed would tarnish or compromise his cultural value. Like Chase-Riboud's Nathan Langdon, these conservative Jefferson scholars recorded the past the way Jefferson wanted rather than the way he actually lived it. Unfortunately, through overlooking and misrepresenting the historical and genetic evidence that supports the existence of the Hemings–Jefferson relationship, these scholars have neglected large portions of American history that Jefferson's African American slaves both embodied and articulated. The net impact of such purged histories has been the denial of one of the constitutive markers of American citizenship, the right to recognition. While this civic exclusion ultimately compromises African American civic membership, for Gordon-Reed such partiality jeopardizes democracy and "our possible destiny as Americans" (5).

While *Thomas Jefferson and Sally Hemings* methodically lays out the case of black civic estrangement through Jefferson's legacy, Gordon-Reed reconciles this paradox in *The Hemingses of Monticello* by reclaiming and democraticizing the historical record itself. Trying to reconstitute this "elusive historical actor from a myriad of creative angles,"[52] the author uses "the memories of those enslaved, the records of white owners who in taking care of business kept track of their human property, and information about the larger historical contexts in which all these individuals operated" to contextualize the legacy of the Hemingses.[53] For Gordon-Reed, getting to this last source and reconstructing historical context is "to a great degree an imaginative enterprise" in which historians "call upon what we know in general about mothers, fathers, male-female relationships, power relationships" (32) in order to better understand the complex truths that make up American history. Consequently, not only does her depiction of Sally Hemings differ greatly from the negative racist images of Hemings that dominated nineteenth-century and twentieth-century historiography, but also, like Chase-Riboud, Gordon-Reed theorizes that Hemings's relationship with Jefferson likely originated in reciprocal love and consent rather than sexual coercion and gendered racial violence.

Using the evidence that Hemings had children with only one partner and that Jefferson had no other lovers for thirty-eight years, Gordon-Reed argues against retrospective readings that assume that their relationship had to contain a certain degree of force. She writes that such interpretations deny the singularity of Hemings and Jefferson and treat them "as symbols of the institution—the violation of an entire people by the system of slavery, the violation of countless black women—reenacted in the lives of these two human beings, who because of their fame are easy to use as stand-ins for those larger phenomena" (365). Refusing to frame their intimacy as interracial violence like McCauley's *Sally's Rape*, or as a conflicted symbol of America's multiracial origins as Chase-Riboud does, Gordon-Reed situates the Hemings–Jefferson encounters almost exclusively within the narrative of romance. Instead of viewing interracial intimacy between master and slave mistress with caution or suspicion, she uses it as a trope to undermine simplistic notions of American slave life and illuminate Hemings's individuality: "Hemings, lived in her own skin, and cannot simply be defined through the enumerated experiences of the group—enslaved black females" (290).

As a historian committed to recuperating Hemings's singularity, Gordon-Reed uses conjecture, imagination, and oral and written histories to fill in "the uncertainty about the precise origins" (364) of the Jefferson–Hemings relationship. However, in her alternative genealogy of their encounters, love and sex emerge as great social equalizers. Gordon-Reed deduces that if affection existed between Jefferson and Hemings, "Hemings would necessarily have had gained some measure of power over Jefferson."[54] In an attempt to treat Hemings as a historical actor and not a "statistic, the difference between being forced, physically or psychologically, by a man and being charmed by him would have made all the difference in the world to her inner life, a thing that was and is, indeed, always a great moment" (320). Assuming Jefferson's sincerity and Hemings's humanity, Gordon-Reed subverts the social and racial hierarchies purported by traditional Jefferson scholars. Here, the exceptional Jefferson is an ordinary slaveholder who fell in love with one slave but owned many more. While he bore traits that were worth defending, he also lived a life that was worth reviewing thoroughly. Hemings, however, emerges as neither a temptress nor a victim, but as a model of black republican motherhood who desperately upheld the ideals of the nation by successfully negotiating the manumission of her four slave children. Whether it was by loving her master or protecting her children from slavery, Gordon-Reed reconstructs a Sally Hemings that defies "the stereotypes that historians seem to have wanted the public to assume" (226).

Ironically, Gordon-Reed's historical romance not only challenges those Jefferson scholars who have vigorously denied the possibility that Jefferson might have coerced Hemings, but it is also a radical departure from canonical black feminist scholarship on enslaved women, consent, and rape.[55] Arguing against what she calls the "no-possible-consent rule" (315) that suggests that enslaved African American women could not willingly engage in sexual encounters with white men without coercion, Gordon-Reed's romance imagines a scenario in which Jefferson and Hemings's love provided them an extralegal space of mutuality and respect. For Gordon-Reed, the "no-possible-consent rule" as put forth by Hemings's supporters "suggests that individual personalities, life stories, and dignity of enslaved women are meaningless or, in the case of 'dignity,' even nonexistent" (315). Analyzing in detail the two different scenarios of master-slave sexual relationships, Gordon-Reed uses the famous rape case of an enslaved woman, Celia, and the lesser known interracial romantic relationship between Hemings's sister Mary and her master, Thomas Bell, to make a poignant distinction between coercion and romantic love. While Gordon-Reed acknowledges the "confusion between consent and coercion" that Hartman notes undergirded slave law, her more pointed message is that antebellum interracial intimacy also included scenarios in which enslaved women could renegotiate their status with their masters. Essentially, despite the rigid racial and social structures, some blacks and whites could and did express affection and love for each other. To oppose such a possibility, Gordon-Reed concludes, not only grants slaveholders like Jefferson absolute sexual power over enslaved black women, but simultaneously suggests that the actual biographical details of individuals like Hemings are "meaningless" (161). By providing an alternative "origin" for Hemings and Jefferson from those that excise her from his legacy or retroactive readings of Hemings's sexual victimhood, Gordon-Reed offers a third interpretation, not a founding violence but a founding love, which simultaneously rescues Hemings from marginality while claiming her exemplarity.

The critical acclaim of *The Hemingses of Monticello* suggests that lives and contributions of enslaved African Americans are now fully included in American historiography. As the recipient of the 2009 Triple Crown—the National Book Award, the Pulitzer Prize, and George Washington Book Prize—Gordon-Reed indicates by her success that civic stories are becoming more heterogeneous and racially complex, and thereby that African American oral histories are essential to understanding early America. Gordon-Reed wrote about Sally Hemings as a way of reminding Americans of the contributions of those slaves whose stories have been told by others, scholars who denigrated (intentionally or not) the humanity of African Americans. In 2008 she painted an image of Jefferson and Hemings that rejects reading them only as national allegories. However, when she restores Hemings's exceptionality in order to privilege black agency, she seems unable to do so without a romantic rhetoric of interracial intimacy. Thus, while Gordon-Reed casts Hemings as a person, the textual narrative itself frames the Jefferson–Hemings interracial relationship as a romantic rewriting of the nation's founding and, as her first book attests to, American history itself. Desegregating their sexual histories, social standing, and, yes, mnemonic meaning, Gordon-Reed supplements American historiography and appears to reconcile the two parallel narratives of civic myths on one hand and African American counter-memories on the other. Instead of replacing one civic myth with a rival one, Gordon-Reed's books use multiple histories to democratize American civic culture.

"AIN'T NO RAPE CRISIS CENTER ON THE PLANTATION": ROBBIE MCCAULEY'S *SALLY'S RAPE*

> I wanted to keep myself pure; and, under the most adverse circumstances I tried hard to preserve my self-respect; but I was struggling alone in the powerful grasp of the demon Slavery; and the monster proved too strong for me.
>
> HARRIET JACOBS, *Incidents in the Life of a Slave Girl*

Similar to the works of Andrews, Chase-Riboud, and Gordon-Reed, Robbie McCauley's Obie Award–winning play *Sally's Rape* (1992) privileges interracial intimacy as a useful metaphor through which to explore the history of black non-citizenship and the contradictions of civic estrangement in post–civil rights America. Set in the early 1990s, *Sally's Rape* is the third installment of the trilogy entitled *Confessions of a Working Class Black Woman*. In the mid-1980s McCauley wanted this series to be staged as works in progress, all of which focused on oral stories from her familial history. The first, *My Father and the Wars*, explored McCauley's relationship with her father and his life in military service. The second was *Indian Blood*, a meditation on her Native American grandfather's participation in the genocide of his own people. In *Sally's Rape*, McCauley shifts her focal point to the experiences of women in her family. Each play is about ancestral survival and about how the past shapes and collides with present racial conflicts. As a two-woman performance, *Sally's Rape* elides the heternormative romance narrative that has typically framed black women's interpretations of Hemings's relationship with the founding father, choosing instead to incorporate the voices of female slaves like Sally Hemings and her own great-great-grandmother Sally to focus on the exploitive sexual relationships between slave masters and slave women. Examining the specific trauma of rape, *Sally's Rape* engages in a double revision of the hitherto iconic Jefferson: first McCauley challenges versions of the American past that exclude the myriad of slave women's voices and bodies; and second she calls into question the sentimental representations of Jefferson with American civic culture. In *Sally's Rape*, antebellum interracial relationships are not metaphors for racial reconciliation but the historical foundation for racial inequities, such as civic estrangement, in the present. McCauley's narrative reminds the audience that racism continues "to shape the bodies and memories and attitudes that she brings into the performance and that these events have contributed not only to the constitution of her own subjectivities but also of theirs."[56]

Because traditional American history has generally ignored the voices of Jefferson's African American slaves, McCauley invokes memory—as personal, familial, and collective—to reclaim the power to speak and to generate dialogue with her audience. By personalizing collective memory, McCauley challenges the disconnection between civic myths and its recipients, the individual citizens. Here, McCauley radically insinuates that individual Americans (and, even more unconventionally, individual African American women) better serve as symbols of American democracy than traditional icons and heroes, such as Thomas Jefferson, because they reflect the real rather than the ideal experiences of the nation. Instead of simply replacing one dominant narrative with another, McCauley uses the local and personal aspects of African American oral histories to redefine the meaning of the citizenry. Instead of linking "the people" by perpetuating civic myths that are divorced from the individual memories and perpetuate monolithic, uncomplicated narratives of the past, McCauley provides a post–civil rights discourse of civic membership based on dissent, criticality, and inclusion.

By retelling the story of Sally Hemings alongside the stories of other black women, *Sally's Rape* attempts to augment American history, thus reworking the master narrative. For example, when the performers re-enact a scene from 1964 between McCauley and a white Smith College graduate, the playwright juxtaposes the national memory of Jefferson with the "real" history lived by her ancestors. The Smith graduate, a U.S. history major, tells McCauley, "I never knew white men did anything with colored women on the plantations"; in response, McCauley writes, "I said, 'It was rape.' Her eyes turned red. She choked on her sandwich and quit her job."[57] Like the white census taker in Chase-Riboud's novel, the Smith graduate eventually resigns from her library job with McCauley because of her inability to reconcile the differences between the oral testimonies of African Americans slaves and the official written record. McCauley suggests that historical narratives that deny the lived experiences of African Americans are incomplete and only give white Americans the ability and the permission to forget their past by being "ignorant, mean, or idealistic" (229). Playing themselves, McCauley explains to her white co-performer, Jeannie Hutchins, that she has learned more history from "sitting around her grandmother's kitchen table" (225) than the Smith graduate who "studied U.S. history and comes out sounding dumb about what went on during slavery time" (226). As McCauley celebrates complex truths like her grandmother's that "chronicled history amongst black people," she also underscores that such African American oral histories, like those of Hemings's descendants, are devalued in the larger society.[58] Instead of simply dismissing stories passed down from generations of African American families, McCauley suggests that African American memory can be authoritative and trustworthy. Further, she insists that history should not only be a "catalogue of dates and events significant" to historians, but should include "the concrete experiences of the powerless who survive it."[59]

McCauley's use of African American oral histories writes "against the myth of the romance of the slave master and the overseers with the slave women, even Thomas Jefferson" (215). Using African American counter-memories to legitimize her depiction of Sally Hemings, McCauley positions the story of her great-great-grandmother Sally and that of Sally Hemings as almost indistinguishable. As enslaved women, both Sallys were subject to slave law and vulnerable to sexual abuse, and they bore their masters many children: "They say Sally had dem chillun by the massa like it was supposed to mean something. Shit, Thomas' Sally was just as much a slave as our grandma and it was just as much a rape. One Sally's rape by the massa no gooder n'an n'other" (232). Contrary to Gordon-Reed's message of Hemings's exemplarity, McCauley's Hemings does not have an exceptional life but is the quintessential slave woman who "worked in the house, but she stayed down in the quarters . . . He took Sally out on the ground" (232). Disagreeing with the romance discourse of Chase-Riboud and Gordon-Reed, McCauley's story is also an intergenerational narrative that attributes the contemporary violence inflicted against black women to Jefferson's founding interracial violence. Despite being the master's mistress, Hemings was like the majority of Jefferson's slaves—a woman without choice.

Even though McCauley invokes the rape of black women as the central symbol of African American racial oppression, she does not completely deny agency to rape victims. Instead, she examines the negative impact rape and slavery have had on the psyche of African Americans while simultaneously celebrating African American survival strategies. Despite the abuse that her forebear Sally suffered during and after slavery, McCauley remembers in the voice of her Aunt Jessie:

that they say sally was tough. bought a house after slavery time. taught her daughters to be ladies. asked the white man, how much was the house on 23rd street. he told her and laughed. living in one of the red houses, paying by the month, took in washing, cleaned up their houses for money. took $750 to the bank, which is where the colored had to go to get the paper for property. said she did all that and none of us ever had to be whores. (231)

For McCauley, the everyday acts of rape on the plantation changed the identities of African Americans: "That kind of rape changed who we were as a people and that was not our choice. We didn't choose to make ourselves as a result of rape, we had to improvise ourselves."[60] In order to prevent the sexual and social subjugation of her African American descendants, Sally, like many freedmen and women who sought reparations after slavery, defines her freedom through the ultimate symbol of American citizenship, property. For those who had previously been "propertied" themselves, land ownership alone should have given them access to economic rights that slavery had denied them. In the end, such improvisations were limited in how successful they could be because as Sally was subverted into the racial exclusivity of American economic culture, she and her daughters remained victims of its legal and civic segregation.

McCauley reconstructs Hemings as a figure of both submission and survival and recasts her as a metaphor for post–civil rights African American identity. By universalizing Hemings, McCauley does not use her beauty, charm, or intelligence to differentiate Hemings from other enslaved women. In fact, unlike Andrews, Chase-Riboud, and Gordon-Reed, McCauley refutes those narratives of exceptionality because being Jefferson's mistress "was supposed to have meant something" (232). Rather than rewrite Jefferson and Hemings as a romance and imbue their love as a symbol of interracial optimism, McCauley treats antebellum interracial sexuality with great suspicion. In turn, she uses her skepticism to deconstruct historical writing itself. When McCauley strips naked on stage and stands on a bench that serves as an auction block, Jeannie Hutchins invites the audience to participate in the scene and chant, "Bid 'em in, bid 'em in, bid 'em in." For her American audience members, this blurring of histories forces them to come to terms with the unacknowledged and the unheroic American history of black subjugation and white supremacy.

Sally's Rape challenges the audience to accept and to identify with the visceral image of the enslaved black female body. Although McCauley's message that the inequality of the master-slave relationship continues to be the present-day paradigm for black civic inequality, she asserts that Americans can begin the process of racial healing and reconciliation only by remembering our murky history. Therefore, unlike Chase-Riboud, who puts forth Hemings and Jefferson as figures of racial reconciliation, McCauley invokes interracial feminist solidarity as the site of reconciliation and integration. McCauley's destabilization of the romance narrative in which Jefferson and Hemings's fractured relationship function as a stand-in for modern racial inequality is an essential feature to her critical reimagining. If McCauley rejects using Jefferson and Hemings as figures of interracial redemption, she does not abandon the possibilities contained in interracial intimacy altogether. Onstage she and Hutchins wrestle with and resolve their own interracial tension about history and authority. Throughout the play, Jeannie undergoes several racial transformations that include embodying the slave auctioneer, learning to speak in African American vernacular, and arguing with McCauley about "playing the stupid white girl."[61] Through this slippage of historical figures and space, Hutchins stands in for white privilege, liberal guilt, and interracial alliance. Her metamorphosis both echoes and subverts the racist power dynamic that founded Hemings and Jefferson, slave and master. As McCauley and Hutchins banter, the audience actually witnesses a barter of histories, in which black women's histories are not tangential to the conversation but are central to their understanding of American history.

It is, however, through McCauley's experimental, interactive, and improvisational narrative structure, one in which the plot travels back and forth from earlier moments to the present to retell the story of Sally Hemings, that she disciplines and democratizes historical narrative. The postmodern nonlinearity of *Sally's Rape* allows for McCauley to travel throughout time between slavery, the civil rights movement, and the present day.[62] Instead of privileging one version of history, *Sally's Rape* collapses narrative authority into the multiplicity of African American women's voices, a heterogeneity further emphasized when McCauley and Hutchins invite members of the audience to participate in the onstage conversation. As McCauley and Hutchins discuss subjects ranging from charm school to Marxism, *Sally's Rape* breaks the fourth wall of theater and engages the audience in dialogue—sometimes directed, sometimes leaving space open for impulse.[63] At various points in the play, the actors turn to the audience and ask their opinions. By sharing the stage with her audience, McCauley models an interracial democracy in which the majority-white audience must acknowledge and perhaps identify with the particular identities, subjectivities, and motivations of her African American ancestral characters. According to

William Sonnega, "In these dialogues, white spectators are encouraged to publicly perform—for one another—their real, imagined, or desired affiliation with both the represented and actual histories of the rape of an African American slave woman, which occurred more than one hundred years ago."[64] Once the fourth wall that segregates actor and audience collapses, McCauley, Hutchins, and the audience must now find new intimacies and identifications through which to bond. In order for the audience members to understand their own histories, McCauley states that they first must recognize that "my personal history is all of our story" (214). By encouraging the spectators to share their experiences watching the performance, *Sally's Rape* also compels the audience to reclaim history, and even the histories of slavery, as their mnemonic property. As such, McCauley distinguishes the live performance of theater to be a living, open-ended model for a new imagined community. The interracial exchange both onstage and offstage, between the actors and the audience, models the sort of democratic citizenry to which McCauley's aspires, in which African Americans in general and African American women in particular become the basis of a new American people.

EMBODYING HISTORY: DNA AND
AFRICAN AMERICAN LEGITIMACY

When the late historian Nathan Huggins remarked that the story of Sally Hemings persisted among African Americans because it directly reflected African American desires of integration into the larger national identity, he highlighted the paradox between American history and African American memory. Until the 1998 DNA test that demonstrated a genetic connection between the Jeffersons and the Hemingses, the official historiography of Thomas Jefferson and Sally Hemings was filled with what Huggins describes as "gaps and problems with evidence." But because of the persistence of an African American countermemory, "most black people *know* the rumors are essentially true."[65] Whether or not the story "was actually true," and regardless of the DNA results, Huggins concludes that the story of Sally Hemings has always held a symbolic significance for African Americans. More than anything else, the story of Sally Hemings and Thomas Jefferson spoke to the durability of myths. The rumor of their relationship always represented the contested racial terrain of the United States. For those like James Callender who publicized the rumor to insult Jefferson, the relationship signified the corruption of American civic ideals and white superiority. For those like Jefferson's white grandchildren and his canonical biographers who denied the relationship, Jefferson's legacy meant preserving the myth of a seamless American democracy. For others from William Wells Brown to Annette Gordon-Reed, who believed in the probability of their affair, Jefferson and Hemings embodied both the possibilities and failures of the American creed. Because of the collision and collusion of perspectives, the DNA test legitimized and incorporated the once-marginalized memory of Hemings's African American descendants into the national memory, while maintaining the metonymic value of the Hemings–Jefferson union.

Like other legitimizing myths that became part of our culture as historical memory, the Sally Hemings story ties black people to the founding of the nation, reinforces birthright claims, and gives them access to a "kind of epic American identity" previously unavailable to them.[66] Nevertheless, the investment in a Jefferson–Hemings romance, as opposed to what Suzette Spencer describes as "coersubmission" or the sexual violence experienced by black women in slavery, is not without risks.[67] For example, in both the Merchant-Ivory film *Jefferson in Paris* (1995) and the kitschy "Tommy Heart Sally" flyer (figure 1) distributed by a now-defunct University of Virginia student group, the Committee for Jeffersonian Tradition, the image of Hemings and Jefferson produces the illusion of civic integration while actually proffering the rhetoric of an ahistorical interracial optimism. In *Jefferson in Paris*, the setting for the relationship between the young Hemings, played by Thandie Newton, and the aging Jefferson, played by Nick Nolte, is Paris. Unlike Virginia, France has abolished slavery in its metropolis, and Hemings and Jefferson begin their liaison outside the limits of slave law. Unfortunately, the plot of their passionate romance is a throwback to early-nineteenth-century depictions of Hemings, and all enslaved black women, as lascivious and unfit for freedom.

In *Jefferson in Paris*, the teenage Hemings is neither an aesthete nor cosmopolitan, but she is highly skilled in the art of seduction. The discourse of seduction here, as Saidiya Hartman suggests, not only "obfuscates the primacy and extremity of violence in master-slave relations," but ultimately becomes proof of his racial liberalism and enlightenment

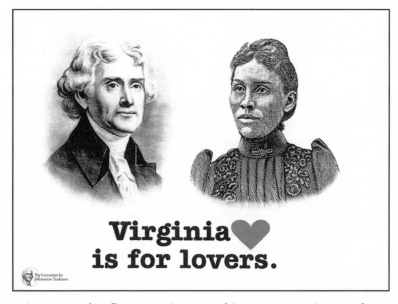

Virginia♥ is for lovers.

The Committee for Jeffersonian Traditions

1. The Committee for Jeffersonian Tradition's use of the state's tourism slogan to reflect on the relationship between Thomas Jefferson and Sally Hemings in this flyer is also a comment on the enduring malleability of her iconography among conservatives.

ideals rather than his contradictions and complicity in slavery.[68] Similarly, by absorbing the familiar image of Jefferson and a random image of an anonymous nineteenth-century black woman for Hemings into the slogan "Virginia is for lovers," the Committee for Jeffersonian Tradition tries to absolve Jefferson's own complicity in maintaining slavery. In addition, in their attempt to project love as a uniting force, the flyers obscure the fact that Virginia, until the 1967 landmark civil rights case *Loving v. Virginia*, vigorously upheld anti-miscegenation laws. Ironically, for this visual reenactment of the lovers to do its symbolic work, the image must exaggerate phenotypical racial differences between Hemings and Jefferson while deracinating their romance in the conservative framework of racial neutralism or color-blindness. By completely extricating their relationship from its historical context, rather than imagining its interiority and contradictions, these narratives of racial reconciliation flatten Sally Hemings in the civic landscape. In contrast to Chase-Riboud's vivid description of Hemings's exceptional countenance, the image assumes that black women's exteriority is at once generic and interchangeable. By reconstructing Hemings's life, Chase-Riboud and Gordon-Reed challenge the hegemony of the blind interracial optimism and frame an American history that integrates those counter-memories of African Americans who helped to found the nation. By connecting Hemings's individual story to those of generations of African American women, McCauley reconstructs a lineage of critical patriotism that centers black women's dissent. While civic myths will most likely continue to uphold Jefferson as the unadulterated father of American democracy, for a brief moment, thanks to the imagination and speculation of contemporary African American women writers, we remember those forgotten, ignored, or silenced. In the end, we are left remembering a woman of whom so little is known, but whose image has resisted the confines of historical obscurity and lingers in the American cultural imagination as the complicated symbol of America's — vis-à-vis Jefferson's — peculiar memory of slavery.

Yet three of the enduring archetypal characters in her novel are Negroes, as seems only fair in light of the fact that, for better or worse, it was Mrs. Stowe who invented American Blacks for the imagination of the whole world.

LESLIE A. FIEDLER, *The Inadvertent Epic*

For all its undeniable, even seductive, narrative powers, *Uncle Tom's Cabin*—both in itself and in the "fallout" it induced—might be regarded as a lethal weapon, or *because* such powers, and for at least once in the history of literary production, we can say that we have found in this work a "poem" than *can* "kill."

HORTENSE SPILLERS, "Changing the Letter"

TWO

The Milder and More Amusing Phases of Slavery

Uncle Tom's Cabin and Black Satire

ACCORDING TO LEGEND, on the dawn of Emancipation Abraham Lincoln remarked upon meeting Harriet Beecher Stowe, "So this is the little lady who made this big war." Lincoln's comment on the novel's profound effect in provoking anti-slavery sentiments reflected its popular success, for *Uncle Tom's Cabin* was the first novel anywhere in the world to sell over a million copies. In its first year alone it sold 300,000 copies in the United States and a million in England. When *Uncle Tom's Cabin* appeared in 1852, many of Stowe's African American contemporaries welcomed the novel because of its unique ability to popularize abolitionism. For more than any other abolitionist text, including Frederick Douglass's *Narrative* (1845), Stowe's novel appeared to capture both the imagination and hearts of northern whites. Nineteenth-century African American responses to *Uncle Tom's Cabin* varied from highly favorable to severely critical.[1] After the Civil War, as Stowe's novel became popularized and distorted in hundreds of American minstrel shows and films, two of her most memorable characters, Uncle Tom and Topsy, had become full-blown racial caricatures. Recalling the pro-slavery use of Sally Hemings as a symbol of black inhumanity in the early nineteenth century, the images of a servile Uncle Tom and an unruly Topsy helped promote anti-black discourse and legislation throughout much of the Jim Crow era. And it was this docile Uncle Tom and bastardly Topsy, born on the pages of Stowe's novel, that James Baldwin lambasted in his essay "Everybody's Protest Novel" (1949), the most trenchant racial critique of Stowe's sentimental novel to date.

In his essay Baldwin observes, "Apart from her lively procession of field hands, house-niggers, Chloe, Topsy, etc. — who are the stock, lovable figures presenting no problem — she has only three other Negroes in her book. These are the important ones and two of them may be dismissed immediately, since we have only the author's word that they are Negro and they are, in all other respects, as white as she can make them."[2] Well into the twentieth century, then, Stowe's problematic representations of black slave characters continued to impact the American cultural landscape and haunt the African American aesthetic imagination. Nevertheless, African American artists have always shaped their responses to the novel (and later theatrical and cinematic adaptations of it) as aesthetic interventions and in accordance with their present social and political needs. As such, it should not be especially surprising that the post–civil rights narratives have maintained this discursive tradition. It is, however, striking that texts such as Ishmael Reed's novel *Flight to Canada* (1976), Bill T. Jones's dance *Last Supper at Uncle Tom's Cabin / The Promised Land* (1990), Robert Alexander's play *I Ain't Yo' Uncle: The New Jack Revisionist of "Uncle Tom's Cabin"* (1991), and Kara Walker's large-scale silhouette *The End of Uncle Tom and the Grand Allegorical Tableau of Eva in Heaven* (1995) reclaim rather than reject Stowe's most racially problematic characters, Uncle Tom or Topsy, as post–civil rights symbols of racial resistance or reconciliation.

While Baldwin's rebuke might be the most canonized African American literary critique of Stowe's novel, his scathing assessment of her portrayals of enslaved African Americans was part of a long genealogy of African American objections that began with Martin Delany's debate with Frederick Douglass in 1852 about the merits of Stowe accurately depicting black slave life.[3] Almost seventy-five years after the Delany–Douglass debate, Harlem Renaissance writer William Stanley Braithwaite continued this line of black criticism when he described the novel's negative impact in Alain Locke's *The New Negro*: "The moral gain and historical effects of Uncle Tom have been an artistic loss and setback. The treatment of Negro life and character, overlaid with these forceful stereotypes, could not develop into artistically satisfactory portraiture."[4] Using even more forceful language, Richard Wright's short story collection *Uncle Tom's Children* (1945) underscored the fact that by the mid-twentieth century many African American artists developed an adversarial relationship to Stowe's characters. Wright's epigraph declared: "The post Civil War household word among Negroes—'He's an Uncle Tom!'—which denoted reluctant toleration for the cringing type who knew his place before the world of white folk, had been supplanted by a new word from another generation which says—'Uncle Tom is dead!'"[5]

As Thomas Gossett points out in *Uncle Tom's Cabin and American Culture*, "Stowe would be intensely surprised, were she alive now, to discover the opinion that she had denied Tom humanity by making him excessively meek."[6] In fact, what Baldwin regarded as a stereotype of an Uncle Tom "robbed of his humanity and divested of his sex" (578) Stowe most likely understood to be signs of his moral virtue and proof of humanity. As such, "it is ironic," observes Wilson J. Moses, "that the humble heroism of old Uncle Tom has been transmuted into racial treason by the subtle alchemy of social amnesia."[7] While "social amnesia" partly explains why many African Americans still hold Stowe responsible for the caricature of Uncle Tom, Stowe is not entirely blameless for the critiques against her because her novel calls for the end of slavery while also putting forth an ambivalent depiction of African American citizenship. For despite her best anti-slavery intentions, according to Richard Yarborough, Stowe's racial stereotypes were able to leap "with incredible speed to the status of literary paradigms and even cultural archetypes," because white readers could easily assimilate Topsy and Tom and, to a lesser extent, the exiled Eliza and George into their nineteenth-century rhetoric of black inferiority.[8] At the end of *Uncle Tom's Cabin*, as Tom presumably goes to heaven, Stowe deports her most aggressive, intelligent, black characters, George, Eliza, and Topsy, to Africa. When she concluded her novel with her black characters either dying or emigrating to Liberia, Stowe created an image of American democracy that excluded African Americans.

In this sense, Baldwin was right to point out that Stowe's racial taxonomy went hand in hand with her failure to imagine political equality for blacks (free or slave, mulatto or full-blooded). First published in *Zero* in 1949 and later that year in *Partisan Review*, Baldwin's "Everybody's Protest Novel" has a two-part critique of *Uncle Tom's Cabin*: first, he accuses Stowe of birthing an American literary tradition that sacrifices the individuality and humanity of African Americans. Second, Baldwin denounces the political efficacy of the sentimental novel as a form of radical protest. It must be noted that James Baldwin had a more complicated relationship to *Uncle Tom's Cabin* than "Everybody's Protest Novel" suggests. Well before rejecting Stowe's novel, Baldwin read the book "over and over and over again" as a child, immersed so deeply in the book that his mother confessed, "I even hid it away up in the closet. But he rambled around and found it again. And, after that, I stopped hiding it."[9] Baldwin would later write in *The Devil Finds Work* that he read the novel obsessively because he "was trying to figure out something, sensing something in the book of some immense import for me." The young Baldwin, however, through his identification with Tom, also renounced him because "Uncle Tom would not take vengeance into his own hands, he was not a hero for me."[10] Anticipating Hortense Spillers's claim that "Stowe, the writer, casts a long shadow, becomes an implacable act of precursor poetics that the latter-day black writer would both outdistance *and* forget," Baldwin's ambivalence toward *Uncle Tom's Cabin* marks it as a signal novel on slavery.

Later critics such as Philip Fisher would defend Stowe's sentimental excess by arguing "sentimentality, by its extension of humanity to prisoners, slaves, madmen, children, and animals," is inherently democratic, for it "exactly reverses the process of slavery itself which has at its core the withdrawal of human status." In sharp contrast, Baldwin believed that "*Uncle Tom's Cabin* is a very bad novel" whose "self-righteous, virtuous sentimentality" exploits, rather than invokes sympathy for, the pain and suffering of enslaved African Americans.[11] For Baldwin, Stowe's sentimentality risked making scenes of black pain and powerlessness, like Tom's fatal whipping and Topsy's beating at the hands of Miss Ophelia, pleasurable spectacles to a white American audience that was already conditioned to experience excessive violence against black bodies as humorous and normative. Drawing on Baldwin's reading, Lauren Berlant in "Poor Eliza" notes that despite its racial liberalism, Stowe's novel had its political limits. Sentimentality is an affective strategy that is "deployed mainly by the culturally privileged," Berlant writes, "to humanize those very subjects who are also, and at the same time, reduced to cliché within the reigning regimes of entitlement or value."[12] In other words, the "feeling politics" of *Uncle Tom's Cabin* are contradictory. They can be productive, when white northern audiences identified with enslaved black characters, and oppressive, when that same identification is based on a reifying whiteness, through Eliza and George, or brutalizing blackness, as in the case of Tom and Topsy. Even though Stowe's racial sentimentalism has abolition as its goal, Baldwin and Berlant call out the novel for privileging the affect of white sympathy over structural and symbolic justice for her African American characters. Rather than reject racial stereotypes and grant African Americans like Tom political as well as spiritual agency, Stowe withholds racial equality in the earthy realm while foreshadowing freedom in the heavenly one. In the end, her black characters not only stimulated a national debate about slavery, but provided the visual, performative, and literary lexicon for a denigrated "blackness" in post-slavery America.

It was the innumerable theatrical versions of the play, widely known as Tom shows, that nevertheless solidified the derogatory images of African Americans in the national culture. Thus, any reconsiderations of Stowe's novel in the contemporary moment should also include its impact on American theater and dance. For these performances "changed the landscape of American theater, increased its audience base, and spawned a long-lasting genre of their own," as Judith Williams notes; "the essence of the stereotype was present in Stowe's novel, yet the embodiment that occurred on stage added another dimension to it."[13] While Baldwin's condemnation underscores how Stowe's sentimental depictions of African Americans birthed some of the most controversial stereotypes of African Americans, his castigation of her novel excludes how the stage and film versions of *Uncle Tom's Cabin* exaggerated and more often than not reinvented Stowe's characters into full-fledged minstrel caricatures. In the case of Uncle Tom, many of the early stage versions of the novel, even those endorsing a clear anti-slavery message, chose to rewrite Tom's fate as happy, thereby further anesthetizing black suffering in slavery and flirting with the plantation myth of the happy slave.[14] For example, in 1852, in what was perhaps the most influential theatrical adaptation of *Uncle Tom's Cabin* during the antebellum period, George Aiken's script and George Howard's production of *Uncle Tom's Cabin* shifted the attention away from Tom's experiences on the Legree plantation to focusing almost exclusively on his interactions with Eva.[15]

Although Aiken and Howard intended to create an anti-slavery play, by diverting the audience's attention away from Stowe's most tragic slave character, they cushioned Stowe's abolitionist rhetoric. Worse than simply redirecting the audience's gaze from Tom to Eva, by casting white actors to play such serious African American characters in blackface, Aiken and Howard opened up space for the later minstrel adaptations of the novel. According to Eric Lott in *Love and Theft*, the use of blackface may have been inevitable, for Tom shows "could not in any case have avoided making use of blackface devices: minstrelsy was the current material condition of theatrical production in the representation of racial matters."[16] However, in the minstrel adaptations of *Uncle Tom's Cabin* the actors did not simply "blacken up" Stowe's characters, but also imbued Tom and Topsy with unflattering, racist characteristics that were not present in the novel.

While blackface performances of *Uncle Tom's Cabin* were staged in Britain during the 1850s, in the United States these minstrel versions became popularized in the United States only after the Civil War.[17] The Tom shows completely supplanted Stowe's vision of Tom by replacing his piety with their gray-haired, bumbling, self-hating, obeisant, blackface versions. Likewise, as the number of plays increased, Topsy, not Tom, emerged as the focal point. Taking cues from Stowe's Topsy, the blackface minstrel version exaggerated Topsy's "black" features, rendered her a completely comical and impish figure, and cemented her status as the most famous "pickaninny" in American culture. Unfortunately, the iconic image of Tom as servile, slow-witted, and old, and Topsy as impish, unruly, and wicked, justified both pro-slavery and pro-segregation debates about the alleged inferiority of African Americans and their inability to function as good citizens. James Dorman recognized that because the minstrel stage had already denied African Americans both performative and political agency, "the arrival of Jim

Crow was to provide the final ingredient in the total pattern of anti-black prejudice."[18] In other words, if before reading *Uncle Tom's Cabin* white Americans had suspected African Americans of being racially deficient, after witnessing its numerous theatrical adaptations Stowe's stock African American characters and stereotypes became the racial norm. As such, although the minstrel shows departed from Stowe's social vision of American democracy in which her African American characters either die or emigrate, these shows enthusiastically supported the prevailing anti-black prejudices of their time. Whether it was the 1850s or 1880s, the popularity of the minstrel Tom shows further justified the legal exclusion of African Americans from the polity. As David Roediger argues in *Wages of Whiteness*, when the minstrel stage offered a transitional democratic social space for whites, it always did so at the expense of African Americans.[19]

In response to these literary and performative racial stereotypes, several twentieth-century African American artists, including Richard Wright, Ralph Ellison, and James Baldwin, to quote Yarborough again, were determined to "distance themselves from all that *Uncle Tom's Cabin* represents."[20] If, as Lott and Roediger argue, blackface minstrelsy was a site of interracial possibility for white working-class men, it was conversely a space of racialized shame for African American audiences. Likewise, Saidiya Hartman describes, "the seeming transgressions of the color lines and the identification forged with the blackface mask through aversion and/or desire ultimately served only to reinforce relations of mastery and servitude."[21] Black suffering might have produced positive intraracial identifications and affects for white audiences, but for African Americans, Tom and Topsy were abject images worthy of an exorcism. Before Richard Wright's premature announcement of Uncle Tom's death, nineteenth-century poet Albery Whitman listed the negative effects that these characters produced for postbellum African Americans: "All 'Uncle Toms' and 'Topsies' ought to die. Goody goodness is a sort of man worship: ignorance is its inspiration, fear its ministering spirit, and beggary its inheritance."[22] Whitman, like Baldwin, sought to replace these debasing, shameful images with representations of three-dimensional African American characters. Like preceding generations of African American artists, the post–civil rights artists Ishmael Reed, Bill T. Jones, Robert Alexander, and the younger Kara Walker shape their responses to *Uncle Tom's Cabin* in accordance with their varying historical circumstances and political needs. Now, wrestling with a new paradox — the privilege of legal citizenship and pessimism of civic estrangement — these contemporary narratives on slavery nonetheless do not reproduce realism or racial sentimentality. Instead, paying little heed to Baldwin's critique, they enlist satire to reclaim Stowe's Tom or Topsy, exaggerating stereotypes and turning the negative affects of revenge, fear, or shame, into the basis of new democratic collectivities.

Most black abolitionists, like Frederick Douglass in the novella "The Heroic Slave" (1853), did not satirize *Uncle Tom's Cabin* but engaged Stowe's characters by supplanting them with realistic yet noble portrayals of enslaved and newly freed African Americans.[23] The turn to satire, then, is a peculiarly post–civil rights African American response to *Uncle Tom's Cabin*. This move can partly be explained by the aesthetic and ideological freedoms that postmodern satire offers contemporary artists. "Postmodernism," Linda Hutcheon writes, entails a deliberate "rethinking and reworking of the forms and contents of the past."[24] But unlike the recuperations of Sally Hemings by contemporary black women writers who primarily used the postmodern techniques of nonlinearity, polyvocality, and fragmentation, postmodern satire is also made up of anachronisms, pop-culture referentiality, hyperbole, and reductio ad absurdum. By applying these postmodern techniques to satire, contemporary African American writers not only have an irreverent attitude toward dominant historical narratives, but now can upset the hegemony of Stowe's sentimentality and its attendant racial and racist iconography. Black postmodern satire gives artists as disparate as Ishmael Reed, Robert Alexander, Bill T. Jones, and Kara Walker the opportunity to abuse, subvert, and challenge the past in order to examine the effects of an enduring American racism, both direct and indirect, upon the African American citizen.

These contemporary artists do not simply supplement these figures of racial subjugation with either realistic or hyper-dignified ones, but they also exaggerate the very qualities of obeisance or absurdity for which Baldwin famously castigated Stowe, turning sentimental excess into satirical excess. But like the "feeling politics" that Berlant associates with Stowe's sentimentality, satire too has its affective dimensions and limits. While sentimentality seeks to get those in the dominant group to identify with the dispossessed and disenfranchised, satire has no such lofty goals. By definition, satire is a literary subgenre in which prevailing vices, values, or follies are denaturalized and held up to ridicule. According to Guillermo Hernández, the satirist is "a subversive whose art represents an opposing incompatible, and overwhelming evaluative norm that challenges the legitimacy of cherished normative values and figures."[25] The targets of their jokes are narratives that idolize the nation's past and emphasize an uncritical loyalty to the state, the hallmarks of civic myths, so to speak. Affectively, however, satire not only thrives in irony but produces a range of emotions different than patriotism's normative affects of love, pride, or sympathy. Reveling in the excessive affects of satire rather than those of sentimentality, these versions of Toms and Topsys produce different affects, like anger, shame, or revenge that can potentially serve as the basis of democratic collectivities. In this way, it is the perfect genre for black dissent and dissidence in the face of ongoing political invisibility and civic estrangement. To combat this excising upon which civic estrangement rests, these contemporary artists use satire's intrinsic qualities of criticality and reflexivity to produce a democratic aesthetic that radically revises symbols and images and engages in a post–civil rights era battle for equality through the politics of recognition.

TRUTH STRANGER THAN FICTION: THE SATIRE OF ISHMAEL REED AND ROBERT ALEXANDER

What advantages I may have lost, by thus throwing away an opportunity of obtaining freedom I know not; but the perception of my own strength of character, the feeling on integrity, the sentiment of high honor, I have experienced.

JOSIAH HENSON, *The Life of Josiah Henson*

Ishmael Reed's novel *A Flight to Canada* (1976) and Robert Alexander's play *I Ain't Yo' Uncle: The New Jack Revisionist Uncle Tom's Cabin* (1991) both reclaim Tom as a figure of racial transgression and refashion him as a metaphor for post–civil rights African American political identities. Playing with the similarities between antebellum and Civil War America and the cultural imaginary of the 1970s, Reed's novel is anachronistic. It traces the escape of three fugitive slaves (one of whom makes it to the U.S.-Canadian border) and deliberately collapses the temporal boundaries between the antebellum period and the immediate post–civil rights period in which the novel is published. Alexander's play is set in the 1990s and uses the late-twentieth-century racial spectacle of Rodney King's beating as the backdrop for the set. Similar to Reed's anachronistic use of time, Alexander transports Stowe's characters to a more contemporary moment during which they put Stowe on trial for her novel's troubled depictions of enslaved African Americans. Much like Stowe's *Uncle Tom's Cabin*, these two texts position Tom's enslavement as proof of a failed American democracy. However, instead of depicting Tom's tragic fate as a byproduct of a slaveholding America, *Flight to Canada* and *I Ain't Yo' Uncle* recast Tom as a figure who embodies the racial self-awareness and political pessimism of the post–civil rights era. Even though Reed and Alexander published these texts more than a decade apart, their preoccupations with Uncle Tom indicate the durability of both Stowe's sentimental depiction of black suffering and the minstrel-stage adaptations of Tom in the popular imagination. In order to challenge the sense of civic estrangement that many post–civil rights African Americans endured due to their mischaracterizations or absence in American civic myths, Reed and Alexander tap into satire's fluidity and freedom. Satire becomes a genre that affords the artists the opportunity to escape the binaries of realism and sentimentalism, reclaim Tom, and destabilize the cultural hegemony of both the martyred and minstrel Toms.

Despite the fact that they posit Stowe as the butt of their satirical jokes, racial inequality is the real target of their scathing social criticism. Both the time of production and genre differences influence how Reed and Alexander uniquely reimagine Uncle Tom, at what ideologies they aim their satirical jabs, and who they cast as post–civil rights racial villains. Most critics consider Reed's reverence of the novel's Uncle Tom–like character, Uncle Robin, in *Flight to Canada* (1976) to be an intraracial indictment of the racial essentialism of the Black Power movement.[26] Although Reed's Black Power contemporaries categorized civil rights leaders as modern-day Uncle Toms because they refused to endorse strategic violence over civil disobedience, Reed defamiliarizes the Uncle Tom trope by making Uncle Robin the most successfully rebellious character in the novel. Instead of deriding Uncle Tom's pacifism as Christian martyrdom or passive submission, Reed repositioned Uncle Tomming as a subversive performance used by African Americans to outwit and eventually defeat their racial oppressors. Through Robin,

Reed not only revolutionizes the figure of Uncle Tom, but argues that post–civil rights racial equality entails a radical integration of American multiracialism, or what Reed notes as his "Neo-HooDoo Manifesto" into our nationalist myths.[27]

In an equally bold move, *Flight to Canada* enacts its democratic aesthetic by revealing cynicism with the racial politics of the post–civil rights Black Power movement and by refashioning Uncle Robin as a civil rights icon. In *I Ain't Yo' Uncle*, Robert Alexander manifests a democratic aesthetic by invoking its Uncle Tom character as a symbol and redeemer of post-industrial racial disparities and interracial urban violence. More specifically, Alexander provides a genealogy of post–civil rights African American experiences with racial brutality when the actors in *I Ain't Yo' Uncle* reenact Simon Legree's famous whipping of Tom to death in front of a videotape still of Rodney King's police beating as the stage backdrop. By paralleling these scenes of black male victimization, he not only reveals how the modern-day practices of racial violence originated in the flawed founding dyad of American democracy and American slavery, but also underscores the fact that the gains of legal citizenship alone have not ensured post–civil rights African Americans like Rodney King the benefits and protections of full citizenship and civic membership.

In order to reappropriate Tom, Reed and Alexander recognize that they first must upset Stowe's authority over her literary creations because *Uncle Tom's Cabin* functioned as the signal novel on slavery for more than a hundred years after its publication. Satirizing Stowe's sentimentality, her writerly persona, and her canonical scene of black suffering, Reed and Alexander supplant what Robert Stepto has called her "authorial control" of Tom.[28] As such, Reed's and Alexander's modern usage of satire is not arbitrary but, as Henry Louis Gates concludes, "a subtle and profound" strategy to undermine the conventions and traditions of the sentimental writer.[29] To counter Stowe's admixture of romantic liberalism and sentimentality, Reed and Alexander embrace the satirical because this genre inherently mocks institutional authority and renders ideology and history as the objects of its ridicule. Moreover, as Darryl Dickson-Carr points out, satire has enabled African American artists to employ humor and aim their barbs at American racism not so much to tear down the American body politic as to inspire a remodeling.[30] Consequently, as an artistic genre, satire not only undermines the racial conservatism of Stowe's sentimentality but induces a trickster affect, a laughter that African American abolitionists once used to signify, in the words of Glenda Carpio, "a wrested freedom, the freedom to laugh at that which was unjust and cruel in order to create distance from what would otherwise obliterate a sense of community and self."[31] Here, the laughter, steeped in a tradition of racial resistance, reveals both the limits and the possibilities of post–civil rights American race relations. While the object of their satire begins with Stowe's sentimental affect, when Reed and Alexander completely supplant her narrative control over Uncle Tom and invoke him as their respective model of post–civil rights racial democracy, their jabs must extend beyond the sentimental and aim at Stowe herself.

In the first chapter of *Flight to Canada*, "Naughty Harriet," Reed strategically begins to undermine Stowe's status as the writer who "started the big war."[32] By calling her "naughty," Reed situates himself as the conveyer and punisher of Stowe's two unpardonable of literary crimes: plagiarism and fabrication. Instead of supporting Stowe's alleged claims that "God wrote *Uncle Tom's Cabin*" (11), Reed insinuates that she "borrowed" the story from Josiah Henson because she "wanted enough money to buy a dress" (8). Here, Reed moves the argument of cultural authority from Stowe's admission that she modeled Uncle Tom's pious passivity on Josiah Henson to insinuating that Stowe lifted her plot in *Uncle Tom's Cabin* and titular character from Henson's slave narrative in *The Life of Josiah Henson, Formerly a Slave, Now an Inhabitant of Canada, as Narrated by Himself* (1849). In *Flight to Canada*, the distinction between authorship and plagiarism is especially important because Stowe, not Henson, benefitted financially and politically from the success of *Uncle Tom's Cabin*. Even though Stowe refers to Henson's autobiography in her *Key to Uncle Tom's Cabin*, she did so to ward off attacks that her northern ignorance precluded her ability to write a realistic novel about slavery. For Henson, this claim led to a sudden rise in prominence in abolitionist circles. Although they both profited from the story that Henson was the real-life Uncle Tom, *Flight* quickly reminds us that their equality was short-lived: "Harriet gave Josiah credit in her The Key to Uncle Tom's Cabin. What was the key to her Cabin? Strange woman, that Harriet. Josiah would never have thought of waging a plot-toting suit against her, Couldn't afford one anyway" (8). Reed suggests that her plagiarism coupled with economic exploitation was a cultural, bodily, and economic appropriation of African American labor that was, of course, the essence of American slavery.

In the wake of Henson's relative obscurity, the enormous success of *Uncle Tom's Cabin* becomes a metaphor for Stowe's complicity in slavery—a slavery no longer limited to the South but bred in "A Virginia plantation in New England" (8). Instead of depicting Stowe as the mother of abolitionist literature, Reed recast her as literary slave master. By doing so, Reed completely undermines Stowe's narrative control, exposes her hypocrisy, and attempts to sully her legacy. In other words, Reed, as Stowe does to Henson, completely revises the "original" text. Ultimately, by dethroning Stowe's cultural authority, Reed is able to create a democratic aesthetic, which empowers late-twentieth-century novels on slavery to produce what Ashraf Rushdy considers "fresh readings of the co-opted slave narratives."[33] In this way, we can think of Reed's project as a form of literary reparations in which contemporary African American writers seek restitution and recognition on behalf of the former African American slaves, like Josiah Henson, who died uncompensated for their manual and literary labor.

While alluding to *Uncle Tom's Cabin*, Reed's novel does not make Harriet Beecher Stowe a formidable character. Confining her to a few pages at the beginning and the end of the novel, Reed re-creates Stowe in the original Uncle Tom image, flat rather than whole, a character that simply talks rather than is a speaking subject. As such, Reed ultimately mocks and minimizes Stowe's literary presence in his book as a strategy of resistance in which the satirical novel supplants her master narrative. As Reed's fictional character, Stowe appears only when she telephones Uncle Robin to convince him that she is the best person to write his slave narrative. Unlike Josiah Henson, when Robin refuses to grant Stowe narrative control over his biography, he symbolically contests Stowe's cultural authority as the progenitor of the prototypical anti-slavery novel. Instead of having Stowe plagiarize his slave narrative, Uncle Robin gives the rights to his story to his fellow slave, Raven Quickskill. By turning down Stowe's offer, Robin and Raven not only wrestle literary dominance away from Stowe, but also provide competing narratives and heterogeneous interpretations of slavery. By writing Stowe's unwanted advances into *Flight to Canada*, Reed does not declare a Barthesian "Death of the Author"; rather, he decenters the racial hegemony of Stowe's black characters. By not removing her entirely from the novel, Reed reveals that Stowe and Uncle Robin, rather than she and Uncle Tom, are inextricably linked. Therefore, while Reed's satire renders Tom's "original" literary creator inoperative, his narrative also recognizes that Stowe remains essential to any project that attempts to reconsider Tom. Reed never seems to forget that without Stowe there would be no Tom to reclaim and without an overly sentimentalized Tom there would be no Stowe to satirize.

Like *Flight to Canada*, Robert Alexander's revisionist play *I Ain't Yo' Uncle: The New Jack Revisionist Uncle Tom's Cabin* displaces Harriet Beecher Stowe's literary authority. *I Ain't Yo' Uncle*, one of Alexander's best-known works, was originally written for the internationally renowned San Francisco Mime Troupe in 1991. In this burlesque reexamination of *Uncle Tom's Cabin*, the book's characters, costumed in the well-known cartoony mime troupe aesthetic of black hats and white hats, put Stowe on trial for perpetuating racial stereotypes and for "failing to get their story right." Whereas Reed accuses Stowe of plagiarism and quickly renders her opinion suspect, Alexander's play presents her as a well-intentioned, racially misguided, white liberal writer. The play opens as a mock trial in which Stowe is prosecuted for "writing stuff she couldn't possibly know about. A slave's experience. The black experience."[34] In this trial, the novel's main black characters, Topsy, George, Eliza, and Tom, preside as the prosecutor, judge, and jury. As a defendant, Stowe must explain her depiction of enslaved African Americans and justify why she created such "a burdensome legacy of images of black identity."[35] As each black character challenges her authority, they upset her narrative control and assert their right to "control their own representation, to re-right [sic] history by telling their own truth."[36]

As the trial ensues, Stowe appeals to the sympathy of her best and most beloved character, Uncle Tom: "There seems to be confusion as to who's on trial here. I'm glad you've come back, Uncle Tom. I know you'll defend me" (25). Understandably, Stowe assumes her writerly privilege and believes that appearing before her is the unflinchingly loyal Tom. However, instead of Tom remaining faithful to her and her text, Tom defiantly replies, "Let's get a few things straight, Ms. Stowe. First of all, I ain't yo' uncle!" (25). Completely rejecting Stowe's avuncular term for him, Tom differentiates his self-creation in this play from Stowe's paternalistic image. To declare that he is not her uncle, Tom makes a symbolic break from his literary connection to Stowe's original Tom and its subsequent iterations. As the cross-examination continues, Tom probes Stowe's authorial intent: "Yeah, your book turned some folks against slavery, but it created a big image problem. 'Uncle Tom,' that's what they call that new Supreme Court justice, ain't it? Why did you give me that cross to carry? Why did you paint me like Jesus, instead of painting me like a man . . . a whole man?" (25). Of course, the Supreme Court justice to whom Tom refers is the conservative Clarence Thomas. Establishing the appellative link between him and Clarence Thomas, Tom not only reveals the longevity of his image, but also shows an acute sense of how his image has metamorphosed.[37] Here, Tom understands that he has become a symbol of both emasculation and intraracial betrayal and blames Stowe for his mischaracterizations. Moving past Stowe's one-dimensional, Christ-like character, Tom shows a high level of self-reflexivity here. Instead of accepting his fate as a fictional character created by Stowe's racial sentimentalism, Tom wants to know why Stowe sacrificed his humanity. Through his interrogations of Stowe's intentions, Alexander's Tom does not submit to the authority of Legree, Stowe, or even a Christian God, as an alternative Tom becomes an existential figure that has moved from serving as an object of Stowe's text to becoming a speaking subject who questions the varied meanings of his own existence. By completely sidelining and silencing Stowe's character after her initial plea to Tom, Alexander ensures that Tom's existential crisis here will catalyze his later act of self-actualization. Moreover, since Stowe never directly addresses the audience, Tom engages the audience with his asides and monologues. By doing so, Tom removes Stowe as his literary intermediary, and in a Baldwinesque manner reveals his own desire to transcend Stowe's imagination and remake himself into a three-dimensional fictional character.

Once Reed and Alexander use satire to debunk Stowe's authorial control over Uncle Tom, they are able to reject the limitations of the Uncle Tom of yesteryear. These writers now can reimagine what the racial possibilities of Tom, or at least a post–civil rights version of him, can be. To do so, they recognize that they must not simply caricature Stowe, but rewrite her ultimate scene of black suffering, Tom's death, in order to configure their Toms as metaphors for post–civil rights race relations and reconciliation. In *Flight to Canada*, Reed's Uncle Robin superficially appears to embody the loyalty of Stowe's Uncle Tom and the dumb-wittedness of the minstrel Tom. Satirizing the titular character of the first pro-slavery response to Stowe's text, John H. Page's 1853 *Uncle Robin in His Cabin in Virginia and Tom without One in Boston*, Reed's Uncle Robin is engaged in a performance of tomming rather than being the historic Tom's doppelganger.[38] After visiting the Swille plantation in *Flight to Canada*, the Abraham Lincoln character realizes that he has only four of the five gold coins that Swille told Robin to give him. When asked whether "the nigger" Robin shortchanged him, Lincoln immediately responds, "I doubt it. Poor submissive creature. You should have seen him shuffle about the place. Yessiring and nosirring. Maybe he didn't intend to give me four" (50). Rather than imagining that Robin could either outwit Lincoln or steal from Swille, Lincoln misinterprets Robin's "mistake" as a function of a submissive nature. Here, Reed reveals that Lincoln's inability to recognize the possibility of black subjectivity precludes an accurate reading of Robin. However, Lincoln's misrecognition symbolizes the historiography of Tom's image in American culture. Recalling Stowe's depiction of Tom, Robin's alleged complacency enables Lincoln, like the minstrel version of Tom, to infantilize him. Moreover, Lincoln's reference to Robin's shuffling alludes to the caricaturing of Stowe's Tom in the twentieth-century Tom shows. Robin's alleged "yessiring and nosirring" reflects the pejorative response of African Americans toward the minstrelization of Tom's image. Ironically, Robin is fully aware that Lincoln's misreading grants him an agency (or at least a gold coin that can be used to help other slaves escape) that neither Stowe nor Lincoln could envision.

Through Robin's guile, Reed signifies on readings of Uncle Tom as racial spectacle by reminding his readers that the performance of subservience was a method of survival and resistance for many enslaved African Americans. Admittedly, Robin's tomming is a form of self-fashioning and black subjectivity that often defined antebellum black life but, partly due to Tom's popularity as either an emasculated martyr or blackface minstrel, was often forgotten or omitted in the civic culture. While Uncle Robin remains a fictional substitute for the lived experiences of actual slaves, unlike Stowe's and the minstrel Toms, he is not a passive spectacle of blackness. Rather, Robin's actions redress Tom's racist iconography and replace the racial script of black victimization and emasculation with a new narrative of black heroism and resistance. Moreover, Robin's subversive performance not only satirizes

Tom's racist iconography in American cultural practices such as the minstrel stage, but also parodies Tom's demonization within the Black Power movement. Because of Tom's refusal to rebel and because his forgiveness seemed to suggest compliance, many Black Power activists denounced the preceding generation of civil rights leaders such as Martin Luther King Jr. because they refused to engage in civic disobedience. In 1966 Stokely Carmichael publicly repudiated the NAACP executive director Roy Wilkins as an "Uncle Tom." In a position paper on black power, the Student Nonviolent Coordinating Committee compared Uncle Tom and the most vicious of the novel's slave owners: "Who is the real villain—Uncle Tom or Simon Legree?"[39] As such, by the 1970s, Henry Louis Gates Jr. points out, the character Tom, whose "very soul bled within him" for the wrongs he witnessed, had become "the most reviled figure in American literary history."[40]

The ideological differences between the Black Power movement and the preceding civil rights movement stemmed from the fact that the fight against desegregation and for legal citizenship alone did not produce racial equality. Thus in their quest to dismantle racist structures and provide full equality to African American citizens, many black nationalists cast and therefore discredited civil rights leaders as the ultimate race traitors, Uncle Toms, in order to reject and differentiate their tactics from the non-violence of the civil rights movement. While these black nationalist myths of racial solidarity came about to oppose American founding myths, they do so at the expense of and by forgetting those African Americans whose experiences and contributions complicate the totalizing narratives of the Black Power movement. For Ishmael Reed, such divisive politics were dangerous because they put forth a discourse of racial unity that inevitably denied the ideological complexity of those very same African Americans that the Black Power movement claimed to help. In a piece that he wrote for *Black World* in 1973, Reed critiqued those "who've tried to build a politics or culture based on the assumption that we're going to be here have been regarded as Uncle Toms. These 'judgment day' assumptions have been enervating and wasteful."[41]

Unlike his fellow protagonist Raven Quickskill, Robin never physically escapes from slavery, and his willingness to remain on Master Swille's plantation puts him at risk of being "called Uncle Tom" even by his fellow slaves. However, once Reed reveals that Robin's tomming was a subversive performance rather than his state of being, the reader simultaneously recognizes that the joke, or rather the object of Reed's satire, includes members of the black community as well as Stowe. To quote Dickson-Carr, the African American "satirist's 'eye for contradiction and pretensions' does not limit itself to targets outside the satirist's group; intra-group, even that which indict the satirist, is frequently within the bounds of fair play."[42] Here, the "target and topic" of his satire is Stowe's narrative authority and the racial essentialism of what Hortense Spillers describes as his "putative community of African American readers."[43] So, in addition to rebelling against civic estrangement and writing enslaved African Americans back into the national consciousness through this narrative, *Flight* assumes a syllogism between post–civil rights interracial inequality and the intraracial policing of the Black Power movement: "Perhaps the civil rights movement lost its steam because people notice that blacks weren't practicing civil rights among themselves."[44] Ironically, Reed responds to this post–civil rights racial pessimism by creating a new mythology, not of American founding narratives, but one in which the civil rights movement is a model for American democracy and Uncle Robin its new icon.

Flight to Canada reverses Stowe's ending by foregoing a spectacular and fatal beating of Uncle Robin at the hands of an evil slave master and concluding with the mysterious death of his master Arthur Swille. Moreover, much to the surprise of the Swille family, Swille appears to have bequeathed his entire plantation to Robin. However, because Swille had dyslexia and allowed Robin to serve as his scribe, Robin was able to doctor Swille's will so he could inherit all his property. After confessing his forgery to his wife, he states:

> Yeah, they got down on me an Tom. But who's the fool? Nat Turner or us? Nat said he was going to do this. Was going to do that. Said he had a mission. Said his destiny was a divine one. Said that fate had chosen him. That the gods were handling him and speaking through him. Now Nat's dead and gone these many years, and hereI am master of a dead man's house. Which one is the fool? One who has been for these many years or a master in a dead man's house. I'll bet they'll be trying to figure that one out for a long time. A long, long time. (178)

Uncle Robin's closing speech argues against remembering Tom as either a simpleton or a race traitor. Instead, Uncle Robin celebrates his own pragmatism in which "property join[s] forces with property" (171). Unlike the preferred icon of the Black Power movement, the more openly rebellious Nat Turner, Robin's tomming ultimately affords him the legal and financial resources to resist enslavement. Also, unlike Stowe's Tom who dies because he refuses to disclose the whereabouts of the fugitive slaves, Cassie and Emmeline, Robin's self-sacrifice is really an act of self-preservation. By tomming, he outwits his master's family, manumits himself, and frees all of Swille's slaves. As a satire of *Uncle Tom's Cabin*, *Flight to Canada* does not repudiate Robin's unselfishness, but rather transforms Tom's tragedy into Robin's last laugh. By doctoring the will, Robin funds a fugitive slave-writing colony in which Raven can write his and Robin's narratives. Once Robin establishes himself as financial and cultural agent, he gains complete authorial control of his story and invokes an agency similar to Sally Hemings's first-person narration in Chase-Riboud's novel that fills in, extends, and counters black exclusion in civic myths.

At the end of *Flight to Canada*, when Stowe telephones Robin, she demands that he sells the rights to his story. When Robin replies, "I got somebody already, Ms. Stowe" she condescendingly asks, "*You have somebody? Who could you know?*" (174). Robin responds by hanging up the phone, which fully silences Stowe's presence in the text. With the absence of both Stowe and Swille, Robin discards his masquerade and reveals that he, even more than the fictional Lincoln, is the true emancipator and fighter for racial justice. While the Swille-turned-Robin plantation is an anomaly in the slaveholding south, it becomes a site of political and artistic authority for African Americans. However, because Robin's community celebrates American multiracialism and black heterogeneity, his colony enables the former slaves to have both a literary and a literal freedom. In effect, through Robin's fate, Reed's novel puts forth a model of reparations for slavery that celebrates the cultural and racial hybridity of the United States as well integrates the complex histories of African Americans into the new narratives of the American past.

Unlike all the other black characters in *I Ain't Yo' Uncle*, the Tom character chooses to keep his original fate in *Uncle Tom's Cabin*. Alexander refashions Stowe's Topsy as a symbol of the late-twentieth-century urban blight in which she embodies economic despair and black rebellion. Whereas Stowe describes Topsy as a pickaninny who remains loyal to her white owners, Eva and Miss Ophelia, this modern Topsy murders Eva, leaves Miss Ophelia after gaining freedom, and wreaks havoc in her neighborhood. The play ends with her confessing, "Dat's right. Topsy-Turvy in effect. This ain't no mother-fucking play. I'm the governor of this bullshit story. Harriet didn't make me up" (89). George in *I Ain't Yo' Uncle* is even more rebellious in attitude and speech than he is in the original novel. Although Stowe depicts George as a man who would fight and die for his freedom, Alexander recasts George as a late-twentieth-century version of Nat Turner. Rather than emigrating to Liberia after he and his family have successfully escaped slavery as he does in *Uncle Tom's Cabin*, George leads a slave insurrection on the Legree plantation. Even though he never interacts with Tom in the novel, in the play George visits Tom at the Legree plantation to enlist him in the revolt and exclaims: "I've come to lead you to freedom. Tomorrow night, I will strike like a panther at the Fulton plantation. Then my posse shall pay your Mr. Legree a visit. Be ready. You hold your freedom in your hand, Tom. We shall fall on our oppressors with fire and sword! We're gonna see these swamps run with slaveowners' blood" (78). George, in a Nat Turner–like apocalyptic rhetoric, tries to persuade Tom to avenge his enslavement by destroying the Legree plantation and murdering Legree. Unlike Stowe's George, whose purpose is to convert and to educate Africans, Alexander's George is a self-proclaimed insurrectionist. However, George's mission fails, and Legree eventually hangs him.

Given Topsy's and George's reconstructions, Alexander's preservation of Stowe's original fate for Tom appears even more ironic and problematic. At the end of the play, George turns to him and asks, "Tom, we all changed our endings. Why didn't you change yours?" To which Tom replies, "If I live, nobody'll remember me. My dying stays in everybody's face" (89). Here, Tom recognizes that his act of self-sacrifice in and of itself is not problematic. Instead, the tragedy lies in Stowe's paternalism, for she depicts Tom's religious devotion and godliness as traits that disable him from physically defending himself from Legree's whips. By choosing to die, Tom is able to turn his victimization into agency and his ignorance into subjectivity. Tom realizes that he "lives on" more through his death than by actually remaining alive. However, Tom's statement that "dying stays in everybody's face" takes on even greater significance and relevance when Alexander set this scene against the backdrop still of George Holliday's twenty-minute video of Rodney King's police beating. By adding the still to later versions of the play, Alexander reveals the tragic continuity of interracial violence in post–civil rights African American life. Juxtaposed with one another, these scenes put forth a visual lineage of racial terror that originates modern-day police brutality in American racial slavery. As such, Alexander's reappropriation of Uncle Tom underscores the fact that the gains of the civil rights movement did not do away with racial subjugation; instead, in 1992, contemporary African Americans continued to exist in a liminal state of citizenship and a different mode of racial alterity. When Tom echoes Rodney King and when Simon Legree becomes the four white Los Angeles police officers who viciously assaulted King, Alexander reveals the consequences of forgetting American slavery and ignoring its ongoing legacy in the present. However, unlike the actual Rodney King, Alexander's Tom is not a lingering reminder of "the visual and *voiceless* slave," as Houston Baker so eloquently noted of Rodney King's silence throughout the trial, but a subject who speaks out against racial oppression, whether it is Stowe's liberal condescension or Legree's lethal blows.[45] By choosing his death, Tom forces the audience to recognize the contradictory history of American slavery, abolitionism, minstrelsy, civil rights, and state-sanctioned acts of police brutality.

Yet by keeping Uncle Tom around, Reed and Alexander risk chaining him rather than liberating him from his racial paradox. Given that Uncle Tom has had such a sordid past, these contemporary works raise the following question: "Is his image actually reversible or recoverable?" Even more important, once contemporary African American writers rescue Tom, do they successfully reappropriate him as a cultural hero? Instead of an outright rejection of Stowe's literary creation, Reed and Alexander use the satirical mode to disrupt her sentimentality. Because satire allows Reed and Alexander to engage and to confront *Uncle Tom's Cabin*, they enable themselves to remember Stowe's Tom without reproducing him. However, these new Toms also challenge the civic myths of a seamless American democracy. Like James Baldwin, Reed and Alexander contest prevailing racial stereotypes and create more radical and racially inclusive national narratives. But unlike their literary forebears, Reed and Alexander create their texts in response to a post–civil rights American culture. Free of having to construct African American characters that help abolish slavery or over-throw segregation, these contemporary writers have the opportunity to imagine and to remember the contradictions of not only the United States, but of African American political identity. For their works do not simply protest Stowe's sentimentalism or minstrelsy, but resist the demonization of Tom as the ultimate racial traitor. Instead of belaboring his suffering or his subjugation, Reed's and Alexander's Toms model a politics of recognition. This recognition is a form of literary reparations that perhaps only satire can offer, in which the very act of exaggeration contests a problematical American past while materializing racial fluidity and heterogeneity in the present.

MINE EYES HAVE SEEN THE GLORY: BILL T. JONES AND THE AMERICAN SUBLIME

> At this moment, the sudden flush of strength which the joy of meeting his young master had infused into the dying [Tom] gave way. A sudden sinking fell upon him; he closed his eyes; and that mysterious and *sublime* change passed over his face, that told the approach of other worlds.
>
> HARRIET BEECHER STOWE, *Uncle Tom's Cabin*

In 1990 Bill T. Jones launched the international tour of his three-and-a-half-hour dance opus, *Last Supper at Uncle Tom's Cabin / Promised Land*. Inspired by the AIDS-related death of his longtime lover and company partner, Arnie Zane, Jones's *Last Supper* explores the intersection of faith, death, oppression, and democracy in contemporary American culture.[46] *Last Supper* is divided into four sections; it begins with a nod to Stowe in "The Cabin," follows with a dance performance of Leonardo da Vinci's painting *The Last Supper* (1498), reenacts the Old Testament story of Job in which he dances to his mother reciting scripture, and later debates a local priest, minister, or rabbi about the usefulness of religion as solace. The performance ends in "The Promised Land." Like the Martin Luther King Jr. "I See the Promised Land" speech of 1968 to which Jones's title alludes, Jones's "Promised Land" envisions a society in which there is social equality and a genuine recognition of each other's differences.[47]

However, Jones realizes that to literalize democracy onstage means to imagine a sociopolitical reality that he has never experienced.

Furthermore, since American narratives of democracy have tradition-
ally excluded or ignored African Americans, Jones recognizes that he
has to write enslaved African Americans back into the national memory
in order to guarantee their equality in his "Promised Land." Similar to
Reed and Alexander, Jones remembers African American agency during
slavery by turning to and reconsidering the ur-text of American slavery,
Stowe's *Uncle Tom's Cabin*. With the aim of revising Stowe's stereotypi-
cal black characters, Jones satirizes and then "corrects" Stowe's ultimate scene of suffering, Tom's death. By changing Stowe's ending from
Tom's sacrificial death to his resurrection, Jones imbues this character
with a subjectivity and resistance analogous to Reed's Robin. However,
even though Jones begins by satirizing the sentimentality of *Uncle Tom's
Cabin*, he concludes with a sublime vision of American democracy in
which the entire cast and local community members dance onstage
naked as a celebration of racial, sexual, and bodily differences.

Jones engages *Uncle Tom's Cabin* in the first act, "The Cabin," in order
to grapple with racial difference, particularly what it means to have a
flexible, heterogeneous blackness in the post–civil rights period. It is
only after reconciling the racial iconography embedded in Stowe's text
with a counter-memory of African American slave resistance that he
is able to perform his own definition of American democracy in the
final act, "The Promised Land." In a darkened theater, *Last Supper* begins with curtained performers reading varied chapter titles from *Uncle
Tom's Cabin*.[48] The performers do not recite the titles in chronological
order but appear to shout out arbitrary words and phrases. Similar to
Chase-Riboud's flashback structure in *Sally Hemings*, their non-linear
reading indicates early on that *Last Supper* intends to disrupt historical
sequencing and thereby restructure Stowe's novel. As the deep blue
lights baptize the stage, the audience meets R. Justice Allen, the African American male narrator, who introduces a middle-aged Harriet
Beecher Stowe, played by Sage Cowles. While Allen remains in modern clothing and presumably plays himself, Cowles is supposed to be
Stowe, but donning an oversized black petticoat and a bulky white wig,
she appears to be an exaggerated version of her.

Through both the non-chronological invocation of her chapter titles
and sartorial hyperbole, Jones, like Reed and Alexander, uses satire to
challenge Stowe's narrative control. Next to the bored, articulate, and
thoroughly modern Allen, Stowe's nineteenth-century exhortations

and burlesque dress humorously cast her as an unreliable narrator. Although Jones does not accuse Stowe of plagiarism, his caricature of her suggests that we should not take her reputation and her literary creations at face value. After appearing before the audience as the author of *Uncle Tom's Cabin*, Cowles-as-Stowe begins reading from an oversized edition of *Uncle Tom's Cabin*. Suddenly, Allen yawns, interrupts her sermon, and initiates "The Cabin" dance sequence. By replacing Stowe's narration with Allen's dance, Jones exchanges Stowe's sentimental novel with his avant-garde dance aesthetic. Through dance, Jones delicately deconstructs the totality of written narratives, like Stowe's novel, which marginalizes African Americans in American history.

In the opening of "The Cabin" act, Jones not only satirizes the novel *Uncle Tom's Cabin* but also the thousands of stage adaptations of the novel whose popularity earned these shows the title "The World's Greatest Hit." Like the simple and inexpensive set designs of the vaudeville shows, a red-and-white checkered cabin frames the entire stage for "The Cabin" act. The procession of dancers enters and exits the stage, starting with Stowe's black characters Harry and Eliza dancing to "the raucous, rasping saxophones of the Julius Hemphill Sextet."[49] The music, like the costumes and the Jim Crow dancing, imitates the nineteenth-century pantomime music that often scored Tom shows. Furthermore, all the dancers, except Andréa Smith who plays Tom, wear blackface or whiteface masks. While the masks obscure and at times rearrange the racial identity of these dancers, they also point to the longstanding use of blackface by white actors in the theater versions of *Uncle Tom's Cabin*. Both the pro-slavery and anti-slavery Tom shows deployed blackface.

Fully purged of all anti-slavery content from their plots, the post–Civil War Tom shows reveled in caricatures of blacks who were subordinate to whites. A throwback to myths of the happy slave and romanticized plantations before black emancipation, these shows supported a larger post-Reconstruction racial fantasy that predicated itself on forgetting the Civil War and Reconstruction in the civic culture. In the post-slavery era, the American Tom shows drew on the already popular minstrel plays from Britain and completely replaced Stowe's description of "a large, broad-chested, powerfully-made man," with images of gray-haired, bumbling, self-hating, obeisant, blackface Tom. According to Robert Toll, "on stage, minstrelsy repeatedly acted out images which illustrated that there was no need to fight a war over slavery [and] no need to accept Negroes as equals."[50] By reanimating minstrelsy, Jones reminds his contemporary audience that the dominant theatrical representations of slave life in American culture originated in this racially degrading tradition. By doing so, *Last Supper* also refuses to reproduce what Lott describes as "the giddy pleasure that actors and audiences of all types experience in the performance of all stereotypes," especially those in blackface minstrelsy.[51] Through deliberate references to the blackface minstrel tradition, through setting, music, and costumes, Jones employs satire to recall and transform the audience's popular understandings of Uncle Tom. The satirical use of whiteface and blackface masks enables Jones to refer to the cross-racial democratic potentiality that Tom shows had for antebellum white audiences, while resisting the racial shame that reenactments of black subordination had for African Americans. In this way, *Last Supper* becomes a fascinating and ironic extension of Lott's influential claims about minstrelsy's possibilities for a cross-racial democracy but in a radically recontextualized way.

In "The Cabin," instead of portraying Tom as the slow-witted, gray-haired, and deferential man that the minstrel shows popularized, Jones admitted that he cast Andréa Smith in the role because he was "handsome, strapping, and gentle, with a rich, resounding voice and compelling stage presence. . . . Andréa was young in many senses of the word, and the openness and curiosity implied by his youth were necessary in re-creating such a worn, misunderstood icon as Uncle Tom."[52] By costuming Smith in an unbuttoned white shirt and then later making him bare-chested, Jones bestows Tom with a masculine sensuality that appears in Stowe's original text but that the nineteenth- and twentieth-century stage representations repressed. In addition, Tom is the only character in this scene that does not wear a mask and has a speaking role. Instead of invoking the familiar image of actors playing Tom in blackface, Smith-as-Tom is a bold, beautiful, and strong premiere danseur. And similar to Robert Alexander's animating Tom as the only character in *I Ain't Yo' Uncle* that has monologues and asides, Jones transforms Tom from vaudevillian spectacle to speaking subject and ultimately fulfills Baldwin's textual demand for Tom's full humanity.

In order to reclaim Tom, Reed casts Uncle Robin as a literary revision of Stowe's Tom, while Alexander authorizes Stowe's black characters to rewrite the novel altogether. Jones, on the other hand, only satirically and rhetorically exaggerates the character Stowe, while re-writing, or redancing, the novel's ultimate scene of suffering in which Simon Legree brutally sanctions Tom's murder. At first, Tom's fate in *Last Supper* mirrors his tragic end in *Uncle Tom's Cabin*: Legree disrobes Tom, hangs him upside down, and orders him to be whipped to death. In the *Last Supper* when Tom dies, Eva suddenly appears as an angel who summons Tom to heaven. As *Last Supper's* Stowe proselytizes that "glory is such that it can only come to us one at time," Jones's Tom, true to Stowe's vision, willingly departs and joins Eva in heaven. However, it is at this point when Tom accepts his heavenly fate that Jones stages a *coup de théâtre* and reconstructs Stowe's ending. Instead of following the chronological plot of the novel in which George, Eliza, and Topsy emi-grate to Liberia, Jones's whipping scene initiates the dancers to reverse their movements. Similar to watching a video as it plays backward, the dancers reverse their actions to the scene in which Legree is about to whip Tom. In what Jones describes as his "retrograde" scene, Legree, instead of beating Tom, retreats the blows from Tom's body, and in lieu of dying, Tom is resurrected.[53] Once Tom is brought to life, the scene returns to forward motion, and an endless stream of slaves, in-cluding Tom, confront Legree and refuse to submit to his whip. Legree attempts to subjugate them with his brute force, but the Lazarus-like characters merely return to the line, almost daring him to beat them.

In dance, reversals offer the experience of what the dance critic Brenda Gottschild-Dixon describes as "seeing a world in chaos—upside down—and to find one's center off-center."[54] During this off-centering, the background becomes the foreground, and Jones's object, as Fred Moten eloquently argues about black radical aesthetics, can and does resist subjugation.[55] Subsequently, Jones's reversal decenters the cul-tural authority of both Stowe's text and its vaudevillian adaptations and puts forth a new narrative of African American resistance and agency. According to Jones, this alternative ending is "the one we would like to have seen, in which Tom, instead of dying at the hands of the ag-gressor, stands up with all the other slaves and resists Simon Legree" (210). *Last Supper* not only "corrects" Stowe's ending, but also offers a counter-memory, like Reed's and Alexander's, in which Tom chooses his fate. For Jones, Tom's suffering embodies the late-twentieth-century tragedies of AIDS, racism, and sexism while Tom's unrelenting faith and eventual triumph over Legree serves as a model of racial reconciliation and transcendence. Jones's Uncle Tom is not merely a caricature of blackness but a symbol, like the Negro spirituals sung throughout the show, of human perseverance. Despite the fact that Tom lives in "a world that is a place of pain and suffering," he links enslaved African Americans and present-day AIDS patients through their mutual sense of grief, dying, and faith. However, since Tom's function is always symbolic, resurrecting Tom serves as a metaphor and a model of how to integrate the actual lives and histories of enslaved African Americans into the national memory. As Jayna Brown suggests, African American dance forms encode moments of historical memory, like that of slavery, onto the moving black body, while remembering how such historical shifts affect African Americans' lived experiences.[56] And just like history, dance can be choreographed, performed, and improvised. By reclaiming Uncle Tom—the most dispossessed and yet the most faithful believer in American democracy—Jones's *Last Supper* begins his search for utopia and desire for a democratic sublime, his Promised Land.

In the closing scene of "The Promised Land" the performer, Arthur Aviles, dances naked onstage. Shortly, he is joined in his nakedness by the other dancers, who include not only the company members but also an additional forty-five dancers, drawn from whatever community the piece is performed in. Jones uses local dancers and denizens because he wants to make a microcosm of the larger community in which "the fat, skinny, rich, poor, old, young, male, female, Asian, Spanish, gay, straight, black, Native American, and European" cover the stage "naked, singing together."[57] Unlike the performers in "The Cabin," whose minstrel-like masks obscure their racial and gender identities, the nudity in "The Promised Land" reveals and revels in these bodily distinctions. In a *New Yorker* interview with Henry Louis Gates Jr., Jones explains how nudity in *Last Supper* enabled him to achieve what we can call his democratic aesthetic: "It was a piece that had been about the things that separate people, and I thought, What is the most direct way that I could talk about unity, and the risk that we take on all levels with our bodies? Get a sixty-five-year-old grandmother to be naked with a twenty-year-old strapping black man. . . . Nudity became a metaphor for our true commonality."[58] Jones's "Promised Land" provides an alternative, albeit fictional, body politic that includes those citizens, African Americans, queer, or HIV-positive, while simultaneously engaging in the politics of recognition and a battle for equality that requires a revision of symbols and images. Furthermore, as these dancers move in and out of formations, leaning on and pushing each other at times and at times embracing and kissing each other, they model that sociopolitical tensions can be reconciled through an honest interrogation of the constructs of race, gender, and sexuality. As the piece ends with all the dancers ambling forward and back, singing nonsense syllables in childlike harmony, and turning and standing completely naked together to face the audience, Jones offers his audience Stowe's heaven on earth or—even better—democracy in America.

Finally, while *Last Supper* begins by caricaturing Stowe's sentimentalism, it deploys satire in pursuit of its larger goal of enacting American democracy. Like Fredric Jameson, who argues that utopian visions attempt to envisage a society "radically different" from the present, I suggest that Jones's satire enables him to confront a problematic American past, while his utopian strains encourage him to imagine a new futuristic, democratic project for himself and his audience. "The utopian idea," Jameson writes in *Marxism and Form*, "keeps alive the possibilities of a world qualitatively distinct from this one and takes the form of a stubborn negation of all that is."[59] *The Last Supper* opens with satire's affects of derisive humor and discomfort; it culminates, nonetheless, with another set of feeling politics: the sublime. Although he never uses the word "sublime," when Jones commented in an interview that he wanted the *Last Supper* "to elevate the struggle" so that "out of fighting we will triumph, that something great and beautiful will come out of it," his choice of words—"triumph," "great," and "beautiful"—reveals the sublime.[60] Rethinking Immanuel Kant's *Critique of Judgment* (1790), Jean-François Lyotard describes the sublime as the overwhelming feeling of awe and fear that comes over a person when s/he is confronted by an unknowable and unrepresentable object.[61] Here, Jones's search for utopia underscores the brutality of slavery while simultaneously positing democracy as beyond representation but nonetheless desirable. He transforms the closed, shadowy, plantation setting of "The Cabin" into an excessive display of difference: "*The Promised Land*, with its hordes of naked flesh coming wave after wave into the footlights, pubic patches, pert breast, sagging breasts, wrinkled knees, blissful eyes, furtive expressions of shame, is a visual manifestation of my profound sense of belonging."[62] Although it strives for democracy, the spectacular grandeur of "The Promised Land" and the beauty and discomfort of the naked human body recognize our human mortality and emphasize the fact that we do not always know what exists beyond the here and now. By exhibiting a sublime affect, "The Promised Land" overwhelms, fuses joy and terror, and confronts the cast and the audience with "the threat of the absolute unknown" — an interracial utopia unimaginable to Stowe, unlived by Jones, and unrecognizable to the audience.[63]

Unfortunately, because the sublime in "The Promised Land" can never be fully represented or known, its manifestation of democracy is limited: it can never permanently exist beyond the stage. Because of the particularities and temporality of Jones's choreography, or any choreography, for that matter, there is an inevitable limit to his vision. For "choreography," Susan Foster writes, "is not a permanent, structural capacity for representation, but rather a slowly changing constellation of representational conventions."[64] Like Jacques Derrida, who claims that democracy is an incomplete project, one that always "remains inaccessible, not just as a regulating ideal but also because it is structured like a promise," Jones acknowledges the constraints of trying to embody democracy onstage: "When 'Uncle Tom's Cabin' was over, I thought I had said everything I could say and now I was ready for the unknown," says Jones. "I was wrong. Those naked bodies were about making us all equal. But we aren't."[65] Inevitably, the sublime affect of *Last Supper* bears the intense difficulty of giving a permanent and tangible form to American democracy and duplicating racial equality in the present. Or to put it differently, the sublime as democracy, according to Amy J. Elias, "is a desired horizon that can never be reached but only approached in attempts to understand human origins and the meaning of lived existence."[66] By forcing the audience and the cast to confront a racial utopia that is lacking in their present, the nudity and harmony onstage unveils the limitations rather than the endless possibilities of contemporary American racial politics. Jones employs the African American counter-memory politics of revising and reversing Stowe's dehumanizing scenes of black suffering in order to integrate African Americans into the national narrative.

Just as *Flight to Canada* privileges civil rights leadership, Jones turns to Martin Luther King Jr.'s most famous speech, "I Have a Dream," to musically score this final dance sequence. Initially, when the audience hears King's words, they experience a sense of familiarity and perhaps commonality because they have the shared knowledge of the speech.

However, like the dance reversals in the opening sequences, "The Cabin," King's speech is literally played backward. Whereas the retrograde dance scene rewrites Stowe's ending by forestalling Tom's death, Jones's reversal of King's words achieves another effect. His juxtaposition of King's 1963 "I Have a Dream" racial optimism and the apocalyptic rhetoric of his last speech "I See The Promised Land," situates *Last Supper* in an African American critical patriotism that calls upon the mythos of democracy in order to demand real structural equality and full citizenship in the present. In Jones's quest to perform democracy, he gives the audience King's speech, an antecedent democratic text to encounter, interpret, and enact in their daily lives.

Through the journey from slavery to freedom, from *Uncle Tom's Cabin* to the Promised Land, *Last Supper* puts forth a new narrative of racial possibilities, one that mixes Stowe's vision of democracy with Baldwin's racial equality. Even as it reveals the impossibility of literalizing its interracial utopia under current political conditions, *Last Supper* simultaneously reinforces the need and desires for such democratic narratives and realities. From its move from the satirical to the sublime, however, Jones's performance also considers the limits of satire within the post–civil rights democratic aesthetic tradition. Despite its ability to challenge the status quo, satire does not provide a permanent template, utopian or otherwise, for a remodeled society. The pursuit of the sublime here, on the other hand, suggests that while racial equality may not last long here on earth, it does not only have to exist in heaven as Stowe's text suggests. In the end, Jones best describes the paradox of his democratic aesthetic in his book *Last Night on Earth*: "[*Last Supper*] was the largest work I ever made and a work that came out of my desire to sum up everything I believed," and, like his vision of democracy, "it was impossible for it to succeed, but it did not fail."[67]

ON LADYSHIP AND BONDAGE: KARA WALKER'S REVENGE

> i'm topsy turvy i'm wicked and i'm black
> all you yellow-ass niggers better watch your back.
> i'm wicked and i'm so so mean.
> i'm the baddest black nigger you ever seen.
> ROBERT ALEXANDER, *I Ain't Yo' Uncle*

Even though Stowe's Uncle Tom may have the most controversial legacy in American culture, Stowe's "poor, diabolic, excellent" Topsy is by far her most memorable character. Set "a race apart" from the other black characters, including the eternally pious Tom, Stowe's Topsy was the first famous "pickaninny" in American culture. Coming of age in the nineteenth century, the pickaninny image stereotyped black children as ill-fated, orphaned, bug-eyed, wild, and grinning like the devil. When asked about her parentage, Topsy replies, "I spect I grow'd. Don't think nobody never made me" (210). Impulsive, hardened to punishment, and utterly rebellious, Topsy claims an unnatural birth or, as Yarbrough notes, offers "a now-famous explanation of her own conception in such outrageously 'natural' terms that it approaches the atheistic absurd."[68] However, unlike as in Stowe's version, Topsy's unkempt countenance, matted hair, ragged clothes, and vulgar English onstage no longer are sympathetic traits but reconstituted as comic props. She is not a character to be reformed, civilized, or Christianized, but a happy, spritely character who always gloats in her tragedy. Describing one of the Topsys who played in the mining camps of the West in the 1870s, Harry Birdoff notes in *The World's Greatest Hit* that instead of remaining "the wild waif of Mrs. Stowe's imagination," Topsy became "the living embodiment of the 'wickedest nigger on earth.'"[69]

Despite her notoriety, the figure of Topsy has rarely been the main subject of African American criticism of *Uncle Tom's Cabin*.[70] This is true even though Topsy has always functioned as the comic relief or what Hartman describes as "low farce" in contrast to the sentimentalized dignity of Stowe's Uncle Tom.[71] In the essay "*Uncle Tom's Cabin*: Before and After the Jim Crow Era," Michele Wallace suggests that the overwhelming attention African Americans have paid to the metamorphosis of Tom's image rather than that of Topsy's stems from a cultural preoccupation with representations of black masculinity.[72] Wallace goes on to argue that because African American racial progress historically has been tied to recuperations of black manhood, the varied social movements of abolitionism, civil rights, and Black Power engaged Uncle Tom through acceptance, resistance, or alteration. Although Stowe borrowed many of Topsy's definitive traits from popular blackface minstrel shows, when most African American writers focused on defeating the racist iconography in Stowe's text, they did so by rejecting Uncle Tom and creating positive (or at least more radical) representations of black manhood.[73] For example, as James Baldwin and Richard Wright put forth even more radical objections to Stowe's Tom, they completely ignored, forgot, or refused to address Topsy.

Described by Stowe to be "diabolic" and "excellent," Topsy was the novel's most unruly black character. Because her rebelliousness was gendered female and more comical than revolutionary, the majority of pre–civil rights era African American counter-compositions, such as Douglass's "Heroic Slave," did not highlight Topsy as a potentially radical or subversive figure. For a later generation of African American intellectuals, like Alain Locke and Montgomery Gregory, Topsy was the paradigmatic icon of racial shame and degradation. So states Gregory in his essay "The Drama of Negro Life," published in Locke's *New Negro*: "Although *Uncle Tom's Cabin* passed into obscurity, 'Topsy' survived. She was blissfully ignorant of any ancestors, but she has given us a fearful progeny."[74] Her lineage included early-twentieth-century black women performers who were the notable exceptions to Topsy's absence in African American cultural production. In *Babylon Girls*, Jayna Brown thoughtfully demonstrates the ways in which black female dancers in the Harlem Renaissance era became a fruitful site for re-imagining the figure of Topsy within a subversive corporeal and kines-thetic rubric. By tapping into Topsy's disobedience, African American women performers, like Ethel Waters, were able to cast off their "harnesses" and reclaim their bodies in the face of a racialized domestic labor.[75] For Brown, Topsy's unruliness was not limited to Stowe's novel, but became a major trope for "black female expressiveness resilience" during this modern era. Taking up Brown's claim of the centrality of this trope, this section examines how Robert Alexander's *I Ain't Yo' Uncle* and Kara Walker's controversial installation *The End of Uncle Tom and the Grand Allegorical Tableau of Eva in Heaven* (1995) reconstruct the "poor, diabolic, excellent" as the vengeful heroines of their texts.[76]

Much like contemporary black women's representations of Sally Hemings, post–civil rights artists Alexander and Walker stand out in the long history of African American criticism of *Uncle Tom's Cabin* because they recast black female corporeality as integral to a post–civil rights memory of slavery and, for that matter, minstrelsy and segregation. And yet for Alexander and Walker, Topsy (unlike Sally Hemings) is not a historical person whose interiority needs to be fully recuperated. Instead of filling in the caricature of Topsy with a three-dimensionality that Baldwin sought, they use the satirical devices of absurdity, hyperbole, and excess to exaggerate the already exaggerated Topsy. Alexander ends up exploring the self-destructive consequences of Topsy's rage, and Walker explodes Topsy's fantasies of revenge. By doing so, these contemporary African American Topsy narratives not only enact new ways of reimagining the social agency of the enslaved, but also present negative affects, such as nihilism and shame, as both a byproduct of African American civic estrangement and a potential site of democratic collectives in the present.

In *I Ain't Yo' Uncle*, Alexander refashions Topsy as a race rebel in postindustrial Los Angeles. Unlike Tom, whose death in the play mirrors his fate in Stowe's novel, Topsy, adorned in 1990s hip-hop fashion and carrying a boom box, raps about her predicament: "I shot a bitch 'cause she looked at me wrong. I burned Uncle Tom's condo with the nigger still in it. I love to hear glass break. I love to watch shit burn" (90). Here, Topsy's lyrical prowess offers a counter-narrative to the Uncle Tom/Rodney King spectacle of black suffering that the play centralizes. In contrast to Tom's victimization and George's impotent insurrection, Alexander radically deviates from the novel *Uncle Tom's Cabin* when he substitutes Stowe's image of Topsy as a Christian missionary with that of a post–civil rights urban rioter. However, Topsy's defiance and her violence appear misdirected when, much like the black and Latino youths who rioted following the not-guilty verdict of the Rodney King trial, she takes out her anger by crashing, looting, and burning down the buildings in her own neighborhood. Alexander clearly grants his Topsy substantially more agency and more anger than she has in Stowe's text. Ironically, even though the targets of Topsy's anger are police brutality and American racism, her acts of black-on-black violence end up being self-sabotaging and nihilistic.

Describing the LA riots of 1992, Cornel West wrote in *Race Matters* that "for all its ugly, xenophobic resentment, its air of adolescent carnival, and its downright barbaric behavior, [the riots] signified the sense of powerlessness in American society."[77] Extending West's analysis to Alexander's play, Topsy's behavior responds to the crisis of postindustrial racial inequality with a violent expression of post–civil rights rage and civic unrest. Through what Houston Baker characterized as the "deep-bass black notes of rap expressivity" of the 1991 Los Angeles riots, Topsy interrupts Stowe's authorial control over Topsy's image

2. Kara Walker, *The End of Uncle Tom and the Grand Allegorical Tableau of Eva in Heaven* (1995).

by narrating her story through the musical idiom of rap.[78] And yet, as Topsy represents the vocal and political agency that hip-hop affords post–civil rights youth within a racist society, she simultaneously symbolizes the racial melancholia that undergirded the rioting. Topsy's resistance is ultimately self-destructive and ineffective because it provides no direct challenge to the police brutality, unemployment, drug epidemic, and incarceration that make up the underbelly of post–civil rights Los Angeles. In the end, while Topsy's rap is not a sentimental narrative of black suffering, her rebellion as nihilism becomes another affective excess that cannot generate sustainable racial equality or structural justice. Alexander's play then uses Topsy to critique the limits of nihilism and its external kin, rage, as transformative political affects.

This expression of suspended justice becomes the celebrated subject of Kara Walker's reconstruction of Topsy in *The End of Uncle Tom and the Grand Allegorical Tableau of Eva in Heaven*. Born in 1969, Kara Walker is the youngest artist and the only woman featured in this chapter. Best known for her room-size tableaux of black cut-paper silhouettes that examine the underside of America's racial and sexual tensions, Walker's early work and her particular emphasis on excessive violence and exaggerated racial iconography often put her at odds with a generation of African American artists, like Betye Saar, who gained prominence during the feminist and Black Power movements.[79] In this regard, it

Cut paper and adhesive on wall, approx. 156 × 420 inches (dimensions variable).
Image courtesy of Sikkema Jenkins and Co.

is worth mentioning—crucial, even—that Walker's work not only reveals the varied ways that post–civil rights artists engage with the sites
of slavery based upon their historicized identity formations, but also
asks us to consider whether "post–civil rights" is itself an outdated term
that, more than forty years later, encompasses a wide variety of dif-
fering historical transformations within black culture. While Reed is
positioned at one end of this epoch and speaks directly to Black Power
idioms immediately within his reach, Walker, more than anyone else
in this book, was born into the paradoxical privilege and pessimism
that constitutes post–civil rights black citizenship. She came of age in
the twilight of the Black Power movement and during the emergence
of the period marked by an unprecedented black middle class, black
feminism, multiculturalism, and hip-hop. As such, her work is another
reminder of the different ways that post–civil rights cultural producers
are remembering slavery at different points in time.

Playing with the sentimentality of the scene titled "St. Clare to Little
Eva in Heaven" from Aiken's 1852 stage adaption of the novel, Walker's
The End of Uncle Tom and the Grand Allegorical Tableau of Eva in Heaven
(above) is a large-scale silhouette that consists of four scenes filled
with aberrant sexuality, violence, and partial redemption. In the first
scene, a quartet of black females and a baby suckle each other while
a slave child holding a tambourine defecates in front of them. In the

second scene, a young, naked, male slave child holds an empty water bucket and faces a young mistress who is presumably the Eva of the title. Staring past the young boy and wearing a large petticoat dress, the young mistress holds an axe above her head with its blade turned backward. Immediately behind her, a young pickaninny figure menacingly threatens the mistress with a sharpened stick, which she angles underneath the petticoat at the mistress's bottom. In the third scene, a portly and deformed master anally penetrates a young slave child who braces her/himself against a wilting cornstalk. A young baby whom the master punctures with a sword lies underneath him. As a counterbalance to the plantation mansion of the first scene, in the background of the third scene a young man frantically runs from one slave cabin, presumably Uncle Tom's, to an outhouse with a female slave standing on the porch looking on. And in the final scene, despite being in heaven, a one-legged, prostrate Uncle Tom clasps his hands together and kneels in a deep prayer. His pulled-down pants expose a penis that mirrors the young slave boy's in both size and flaccidity. From his anus, an umbilical cord connects him to a toddler who writes behind him on the ground. The silhouette ends with two semi-transparent women raising their hands.

Similar to Reed, Alexander, and Jones, Kara Walker's silhouette *The End of Uncle Tom* uses satire to undermine Stowe's authorial control and upsets Stowe's sentimental depictions of black suffering by presenting what the critic Dan Cameron argues is "an orgy of redemption in which slaves turn on their masters and create even more elaborately violent episodes of sexual farce."[80] However, rather than refashion Uncle Tom as a figure of racial resistance, Walker exaggerates popular receptions of Tom and satirizes the sentimental, comedic, and race traitor versions of him. In *The End of Uncle Tom*, Walker illustrates Baldwin's critique of Stowe's emasculated and overly submissive Tom by portraying him as a semi-clad crouching person who is endowed with a flaccid penis and anal umbilical chord. By doing so, she undercuts Stowe's claims of martyrdom and reveals that Tom's celestial fate was even more tragic than the novel suggested. At the end of the novel *Uncle Tom's Cabin*, Tom presumably goes to heaven after Simon Legree whips him to death. Although Tom never experiences racial and political equality on earth, Stowe insinuates that he may be equal to Eva in heaven.

Walker's *The End of Uncle Tom* is topsy-turvy and inverts heaven into our earthly hell. Instead of creating a sublime vision of an interracial heaven as Jones might, Walker's heaven is a place plagued by racial and sexual violence of antebellum America. As Walker's Tom appears as both minstrel and mutant, he is more impotent and more servile than Stowe ever wrote. Tom's flaccid and poorly endowed penis and anal umbilical cord are reminiscent of the castrated Tom on the minstrel stage, and Walker, like Reed, signifies on the Black Power castigation of Tom as an emasculated race traitor. Whereas Reed critiques the racial essentialism of the Black Power movement by reconstructing Tom vis-à-vis Robin as race rebel, Walker resists the same racial reductionism by overstating Tom's piety and physical impotency. However, instead of refashioning Tom as a trickster or rebel, Walker disrobes him to symbolize her larger mission of stripping *Uncle Tom's Cabin* down to its most primitive racial elements. Because Walker is more interested in exploring the racial fantasies of Stowe's subtext, she refuses to rewrite the scenes of interracial intimacy of Tom and Eva that dominated the pictorial reproductions of the novel.[81] Instead, she exposes the sadomasochistic and homoerotic tensions upon which Stowe's sentimentality rests by directing the viewer's gaze to the interracial violence of Eva and Topsy.

Unlike Tom or Eva, Topsy is not a titular character in Walker's silhouette. In fact, the primary way to discern Topsy from other characters in the image is through her physical proximity to Eva and her uncanny resemblance to Stowe's depiction of her as the prototypical pickaninny with "black skin," "round, shining eyes," and "wooly hair," and "dressed in a single filthy, ragged garment" (207). In *Uncle Tom's Cabin*, Stowe depicts Eva and Topsy as having a loving friendship, as exemplified in the scene in which Eva declares: "O, Topsy, poor child, I love you! . . . I love you, because you haven't had any father, or mother, or friends—because you've been a poor abused child" (245). And yet despite Eva's benevolence, she can neither free Topsy nor help her escape. In fact, although there are traces of egalitarianism in their friendship, the legality of their relationship as master and slave always overshadows this hint of equality.[82] *The End of Uncle Tom* (Figure 2a) initially appears to be a complete distortion of Stowe's text, when Walker's Eva wields the axe backward at herself and Topsy advances toward Eva's skirt with a sharpened stick. However, much like Walker's exposure of Stowe's

2a. Installation detail of Kara Walker, *The End of Uncle Tom and the Grand Allegorical Tableau of Eva in Heaven* (1995). Cut paper and adhesive on wall, approx. 156 × 420 inches (dimension variable). Image courtesy of Sikkema Jenkins and Co.

heaven as an interracial orgy, her silhouette magnifies the sadomasochistic dynamic that simmers beneath the surface of Eva and Topsy's textual relationship. Because of their propertied relationship, Eva's "love" for Topsy in the novel is always defined by the sadomasochistic terms of master and slave, or domination and submission in which equality in love remains an unattainable ideal.[83] Thus by downplaying Eva's legal power over Topsy, Stowe's attempts not only render Eva more angelic, but also obscure the unequal power dynamic that inevitably undergirds their friendship. Such a denial on Stowe's part further empowers Eva's character. For Eva to be benevolent, Topsy becomes even more malevolent. For Eva to be pure, Topsy is comparably corrupt. Walker's prostrate image of Tom departs from Stowe's more dignified representation of him as "a large, broad-chested, powerfully-made man"; her image of Topsy, however, slightly exaggerates the original. This is partly because Stowe's original description of Topsy was already a full-blown caricature of blackness, one that borrowed heavily from the prevailing racist stereotypes of the minstrel stage.[84]

In this way, Stowe did not provide Topsy with a radical subjectivity, but portrayed her "as the Other" in which "the slave was the blank screen on which the writer could project any image that she pleased."[85] So instead of amplifying Topsy's racial alterity through her hair texture, sharpness of features, and stereotypes of demeanor, Walker's recasts the large-scale silhouette itself as her satirical genre. Walker takes a form like the silhouette, which in antebellum America reproduced racial taxonomies, and amplifies it further so that we can begin to see and deconstruct the exaggerated versions of the original. While visualizing and exploding Stowe's description of Topsy risks reproducing rather than resisting these images of nineteenth-century scientific racism, the enormity of Walker's silhouettes redirects our gaze from seeing Topsy as Stowe's permanently racialized Other.[86] The silhouette's sidelong glance is Walker's answer to the blank racial screen of the sentimental novel; as she once acknowledged, "It's the little look and it's full of suspicion, potential ill-will, or desire. It's a look unreliable women give."[87] In Walker's hands the silhouette is used as a forum of dissent, criticality, and revision. By redirecting our gaze to Topsy's, she forces us to come to terms with the fact that we are not only spectators to Stowe's diabolical vision and the interracial debauchery of minstrelsy, but rather active and consenting participants in the ongoing melodrama of race in post–civil rights America.

In *The End of Uncle Tom*, Topsy seeks to avenge her enslavement. Despite accusations that these images reiterate rather than deconstruct old stereotypes of African Americans, or are what the art critic Kristen Buck calls "Xeroxes" of the minstrel show, Walker animates the pickaninny figure as an agent who desires and attempts to kill her mistress, Eva.[88] And even though Tom and Eva are featured as the titular characters of Walker's text, Topsy appears to be the only image that is not defecating or disfigured. By depicting Topsy as an avenging object rather than simply a comical prop, *The End of Uncle Tom* unabashedly rejects those images of Topsy unconditionally loving Eva. In the novel, Topsy's unflinching loyalty to Eva can exist only if Topsy is in fact without interiority and agency, a pickaninny, so to speak. However, as Walker illustrates, behind Topsy's wicked grin Topsy not only recognizes Eva's authority over her but also attempts to completely usurp Eva's power. In the silhouette, Topsy's forestalled sadistic stab (for, like a true sadomasochistic encounter, the affliction of pain is delayed) reveals that Topsy is aware of and rejects her racial subjugation. Here, Topsy does not simply submit to the powerlessness foisted upon her by slavery, but violently enacts a narrative of revenge and freedom.

Her ambush of Eva ensures that she is neither property nor pickaninny and ties her to the long genealogy of subversive unruliness that Jayna Brown attributes to Harlem Renaissance black female performances of Topsy. Unlike the literary reparations that Robin and Raven receive in *Flight to Canada* to compensate for the exploitation they experience at the hands of Swille and Stowe, Topsy's revenge narrative here puts forth an even more radical but less forgiving resolution of America's racial melodrama. Reparations (and the process of remembering and reclamation) seek to integrate the past into the present, by acknowledging past trauma as a step toward a more inclusive future. Revenge, on the other hand, as an affective and material response to perceived harm or injustice, is, according to Michael Ignatieff, commonly regarded as a low and unworthy emotion, similar to what Sianne Ngai describes as "ugly feelings" because its deep moral hold on people is rarely understood.[89] But because revenge refuses immediate closure, the static nature of Walker's silhouette is a near-perfect genre. Revenge's moral good, Ignatieff acknowledges, is that it keeps the past alive, honoring the dead by taking up their cause where they left off.[90] Here, Topsy continues and ultimately avenges the plot of subjugation and sadomasochism into which she was born.

Much like satire being a weighty counterpart to sentimentality, revenge offers a viable alternative to suffering. As one of the few philosophers to have asserted the centrality of revenge in the pursuit of justice, Friedrich Nietzsche opined: "*The spirit of revenge*: my friends, that up to now, has been mankind's chief concern: and where there was suffering, there was always supposed to be punishment."[91] In many ways, Eva and Topsy's sadomasochistic psychodrama visualizes American racial discourses that espouse racial progress or color-blindness without admitting the ongoing structural racism or our continued dependence on racial hierarchies.[92] As Eva tries to destroy herself before being destroyed, she symbolizes the spectacle of whiteness and the simultaneous fear of losing white privilege and the impotence of racial guilt.

Hoping to stab Eva, Topsy represents the insurrectionary act of black freedom. However, if Walker is right when she states that *The End of Uncle Tom* is a manifestation of "our collective psyches," then the piece is also about countering our desires for a fantasy of racial harmony.[93] Through her use of black cutouts on a white background, Walker forces her viewers to see themselves through the reductive and artificial binary of white and black race relations. The silhouette, argues Christina Sharpe, "allows Walker to produce the admittedly historical impossible and yet theoretically necessary imaginative work of placing herself and the viewer into the material condition of the past that is not yet past.[94] However, when Walker visually delays Topsy's victory or Eva's defeat, she critiques the paralysis that exists within post–civil rights race relations. As Eva's masochism reveals the political ineffectiveness of white liberal guilt through Topsy, Walker also questions and to a certain degree limits the fantasy of racial revenge. Metaphorically, Topsy's and Eva's forestalled actions anticipate the import of race in the national subconscious. By transfixing the scene of interracial violence, Walker enables (or manipulates) the viewer to fill in the narrative based on his/her individual desire to have either Topsy redeem herself or Eva punish herself. Not quite breaking the fourth wall of theater, as in McCauley's *Sally's Rape*, or incorporating community members in the cast, as does Jones's *Last Supper*, the size of Walker's installation democratizes the form of the silhouette. The enormity of the images pulls in the audience, transforming us from spectators to subjects, from consumers of the images to active citizens in the cyclorama. This democratic aesthetic is the most unnerving of all, for Walker forces her viewers to acknowledge that on some level we all, both the powerful and the dispossessed, are tied together by the founding racial relationships of masochist/sadist, white/black, and master/slave.

As we leave her sadomasochistic representations of slavery, she reminds us of the complex and ugly affect of shame as well. Bearing a striking similarity to Baldwin's reading of Stowe's novel, critics like Betye Saar read the use of blackface minstrelsy in Walker's work as an uncritical reproduction of black degradation in the public sphere. As such, *The End of Uncle Tom* is always destructive, and its popularity among white patrons further perpetuates feelings of African American melancholia and non-belonging in the present. But such criticism also ignores how revenge and shame can serve as productive affects.

Unlike guilt that comes from individual authorship of a crime, shame emerges not from direct actions but from membership in a community implicated in these deeds. This is the difference between the emotion embedded in Eva's masochistic axe-wielding (guilt) and the affect experienced by the viewing audience who bear co-responsibility for the legacy of slavery in the present (shame). In this sense, shame is an affect that requires recognition of responsibility and, as W. James Booth argues, is part of the demand of memory-justice.[95] Walker's images revel in the national sin of slavery and serve as a reminder that our repression of both slavery's scenes of subjection and its sexual perversions is the basis of our national shame. Revealing our investment in racial binaries, in the black and white cutouts that shape our realities, Walker ends up integrating her audience. While Jones's democratic sublime represents our best aspirations, Walker's sadomasochism exhibits our greatest wrong. Thus, instead of revising Stowe's Heaven as Bill T. Jones does with a utopian vision, Walker creates a heaven that is plagued by violence, shame, and revenge. Here, we find interracial dissonance and African American revenge and characters forever caught in the cyclorama of their own racial desires and abjection. She reminds us that we may get to Jones's Promised Land, but only after we divest ourselves of the racial violence that paves the way. And perhaps then, when Americans reconcile the deep, dark sin of slavery into their national narratives — and only then, Walker shows — Topsy will stop growing.

WILL THERE BE ANY BLACK PEOPLE IN HEAVEN? THE REINCARNATION OF *UNCLE TOM'S CABIN*

As we have seen, Tom and to a lesser extent Topsy are the figures to which African American artists have returned in order both to critique racial oppression and to reframe the terms of American citizenship. Since the early twentieth century, there have been a variety of ways that the images of Uncle Tom and Topsy have been used. First, in plays and films that caricature black life; second, in an anti-racist African American discourse that rejects such caricatures in order to release African Americans from the "deleterious impression" made by these images; and third, in contemporary African American narratives that parody these caricatures in order to oppose and to reconstruct these racist images.[96] All these representations of Tom and Topsy reflect the changing American political and racial tensions of the post–civil rights period. The first and second categories clearly revealed the varied attempts to appropriate or reject Stowe's Tom and Topsy to support the larger political causes of either white supremacy or racial equality. However, in the more recent genre of African American satire, the political motivations are not as easily discerned. In their attempts to challenge racist stereotypes, these representations also risk reproducing the very same images they claim to dismantle. Unlike their literary predecessors of Baldwin and Wright, who completely rejected Tom and Topsy, these contemporary artists revel in the contradictions and the inconsistencies that beleaguered Stowe's characters.

Partly because they have the luxury of not having to abolish slavery and segregation, and partly because they live in the racial ambiguity of the post–civil rights era, Reed, Alexander, Jones, and Walker have the generic freedom to deviate from and distort the past. These artists return to images like Tom and Topsy because they seek to liberate "both the tradition of these representations of the black popular and high art forms and to liberate our people from residual, debilitating effects that the proliferation of those images undoubtedly had upon the collective unconscious of the African American people."[97] By neither forgetting slavery nor rejecting its caricatures, Reed, Alexander, Jones, and Walker all have engaged Tom and Topsy as symbols of both racial oppression and racial resistance. Thus, while Reed and Jones create a multicultural utopia and Alexander and Walker depict an interracial hell, they all provide Tom and Topsy with a subjectivity and interiority never seen before in American culture. In this way, these artists do not put forth static representations of slavery; rather, they participate in a long history of African American criticisms of Stowe's novel while also challenging their predecessors. Moving across genre, ideology, and gender, they use Tom or Topsy to produce multiple dissenting affects and discourses of critical patriotism. And yet, despite their differences, these varied efforts to imagine racial harmony reveal that a confrontation with the complex past of slavery is the only path toward a sustainable practice of American democracy.

Travel to Africa has all the benefits of travel to other places, but it also has something *special*.

SYLVIA BOONE, *West African Travels*

In West Africa, along the palm-lined coast of Ghana, are several forts and castles that constitute another symbol; unlike Plymouth Rock, they were points of departure, not arrival, places of despair rather than liberty. . . . And now together with Gorée Island in Senegal, far to the north of Ghana, they are the few physical remains of the traffic in human beings that brought many Americans, black Americans to the United States.

NATHAN HUGGINS, *Revelations*

THREE

A Race of Angels

(Trans)Nationalism,
African American Tourism,
and the Slave Forts

HARRIET BEECHER STOWE concludes *Uncle Tom's Cabin* with all her black characters save the loyal Uncle Tom — Topsy, Eliza, and George — emigrating to Liberia in West Africa. While all these characters are born in the United States, Stowe recognizes that due to the Fugitive Slave Act of 1850, they were neither citizens of the United States nor completely protected from reenslavement. As such, to resolve their precarious political identity, she relocates the only free black characters in the novel to "Africa." Stowe depicts their emigration to Africa as the ultimate fulfillment of their spiritual obligation to Christianize heathen Africans and their political goal of being active participants in a democratic nation-state. Many critics have noted that

Stowe's decision to transplant the novel's only free black characters to Africa risked endorsing the prevailing rhetoric of black inferiority and racial segregation in the United States. However, while her use of "Africa" provided an ambiguous image of racial freedom for African Americans, it also drew upon one of the most dominant tropes in the African American expressive tradition in which "Africa" appears as a site of racial equality, black mobility, and democracy for disenfranchised African Americans. And while the majority of African Americans never endorsed returning to Africa, Africa historically has served as one of the chief terrains on which African Americans have negotiated their conflicted relationship to the United States.[1]

While antebellum emigrationists of the 1860s like Martin Delany and civil rights era expatriates such as W. E. B. Du Bois framed their "returns" to West Africa as a form of racial and national freedom, during the post–civil rights era the Back to Africa discourse has undergone a significant transformation. Now, ad campaigns for "coming home" tourism have replaced repatriation rhetoric. In response to their overarching feeling of civic estrangement, African Americans once again posit "Africa" as an alternative to the United States. Rather than accept their absence from the myths of civic identity, many post–civil rights African Americans regard the slave fort, specifically two of the most popular transatlantic symbols of the slave trade, La Maison des Esclaves (the House of Slaves) at Gorée Island, Senegal, and Cape Coast Castle at Cape Coast, Ghana, as monuments of the "African diaspora" and a symbol of the origins, genealogy, and history denied to them in the United States.[2] As a result of grounding the slave fort as a constitutive marker of African American identity, heritage tourists belong to the "imagined community" of the African diaspora that temporarily compensates for the feelings of civic disenfranchisement in the United States. National yearning now becomes diasporic membership, civic alienation replaced by transnational citizenship. In this way, African diasporic discourses directly compensate for those traits of racial melancholia or what Eng and Han describe as the continual estrangement from the ideals of whiteness, the ultimate object of American citizenship.[3] At the same time, however, by principally constituting and engaging Africa through the historical narrative of slavery, contemporary African Americans risk producing images and narratives of Senegal and Ghana that merely reinforce their disillusion with the United States. Thus while African American heritage tourists partially resolve their civic alienation by imagining the slave forts as an originary site, unlike their forebears, they do not construct "Africa" as viable political home-land. Instead, as David Scott points out, within post–civil rights cul-tural imaginary, such countries remain fixed in a pre-colonial past in which the terms "slave fort" and "Africa" are interchangeable signifiers for African diaspora political identities.[4]

I am particularly interested in how post–civil rights African Ameri-can photographers Chester Higgins and Carrie Mae Weems and film-maker Haile Gerima continue to deploy a democratic aesthetic in order to subvert the racial exclusivity of American civic myths and estab-lish new forms of diasporic solidarity through tourism. By doing so, Higgins's and Weems's photographs, "Dakar, Senegal, 1972. The Door of No Return in the House of Slaves" from the *Middle Passage* series and "Elmina Cape Coast Ile de Gorée" from *The Slave Coast* series, and Gerima's film *Sankofa* assert a narrative of lineage and origins that pre-dates the founding of the United States. On one hand, these images not only reframe the language of civic belonging in the transnational dis-course of the African diaspora, but also simultaneously and inevitably challenge the racial hegemony of American national memory. On the other hand, these visual representations risk reinforcing a touristic gaze of what I understand to be "African American exceptionalism." As used here, African American exceptionalism describes an interpretative pro-cess and ideological project in which African Americans "map" their unique history of American slavery, segregation, and post–civil rights racism onto the racial histories of non-U.S. black subjects. Here, heri-tage tourism works as a form of African American exceptionalism that posits and arrests "Africa" solely as a site of slavery and thereby denies the specificity and contemporaneity of West African nation-states. In these accounts of mourning and homecoming, modern-day Senegal and Ghana are neither engaged nor integrated. These countries, and by extension much of postcolonial West Africa, now loom as the exclusive mnemonic properties of the African American heritage tourist.

COMING HOME TOURS: CIVIC ESTRANGEMENT AND IMAGINING THE AFRICAN DIASPORA

Similar to the Pan-Africanist Back to Africa discourses of the emigra-tion and the expatriate movements, the post–civil rights African Ameri-can Back to Africa discourse argues for a transnational affiliation with

Africa. By invoking an analogous sense of continuity and lineage to that of Pan-Africanism, the contemporary rhetoric assumes that African Americans should travel to West Africa, claim it as their lost homeland, and declare "the right of return." Nevertheless, post–civil rights African American travel narratives do not align returning to West Africa with a larger international movement for racial freedom. In sharp contrast to the earlier emigration of the nineteenth century and the expatriation movements of the mid-twentieth century, the majority of post–civil rights African Americans now travel to the West African countries of Ghana and Senegal as heritage tourists. Instead of proclaiming a Pan-Africanist sensibility in which West Africa is a surrogate homeland, contemporary African Americans now view Africa through the lens of the African diaspora and consider their travel there as part of an obligatory process of self-identification and cultural affirmation. In striking contrast to the Pan-Africanist pledge of African "unity," the concept of the "African diaspora" specifically refers to a "global vision" of blackness that draws on "transatlantic histories of movement, the movement of fugitive slaves and imperial civilizations, the colonized and colonizers, and black colonial subjects and the agents of empire."[5] Once the signifier for legal citizenship, racial equality, and black sovereignty, "Africa" is now primarily reconstructed as the originary site of displacement for all New World blacks. Rather than romanticizing their return to West Africa as an extension of black solidarity or a commitment to nation-building, these heritage tourists do not privilege all of Africa as a geographical site to which they should return, but give preference to the slave forts of Cape Coast Castle and Elmina in Ghana and Gorée Island in Senegal. As such, the contemporary Back to Africa movement does not posit Africa as a place that affords African Americans racial freedoms that are, as Kevin Gaines notes, now "impossible in America."[6] Today, returning to Africa primarily means visiting what Edouard Glissant calls the "point of entanglement [intrication]," those sites at which their ancestors began the torturous journey to the New World.[7]

In her literary travel narrative *Lose Your Mother*, Saidiya Hartman writes that despite the unexceptional nature of being a tourist who "with the willingness and the cash could retrace as many slave routes as her heart desired," there was something "particular, perhaps even peculiar" about the advent of her generation of post–civil rights African Americans' tourism to the slave forts in Ghana. Unlike previous gen-

erations of African Americans who sought patrimony and patriotism
with African nations, for Hartman and her contemporaries, "the holding cell had supplanted the ancestral village. The slave trade loomed
larger for me than any memory of a glorious past or sense of belonging
in the present."[8] While it is difficult to date exactly when the affects and
discourse changed from Back to Africa and repatriation to commercial
tourism, I would argue that we can locate the beginnings of the shift in
the mid-1970s. More specifically, it is the intersection of five distinct factors that sparked the first big wave of African American heritage tourists to the slave forts. The first was the 1966 political coup in Ghana and
the economic instability of independent Tanzania, Guinea, and other
African nations of interests for African American expatriates. Second,
partly inspired by the success of Alex Haley's novel *Roots* (1976) and
the attendant mini-series (1977), there was an increased enthusiasm for
what David Lowenthal describes as "the zeal for genealogy" among
African Americans to locate their African ancestors.[9] Third, there continued to be no heritage sites in the United States commemorating the
histories of enslaved African Americans. Fourth, the designation of the
slave forts at Gorée Island in Senegal (1978) and Elmina and Cape Coast
Castles in Ghana (1979) as "world heritage sites" by the United Nations
Educational, Scientific, and Cultural Organization (UNESCO) brought
these areas wider recognition. And fifth, an increase in the standard of
living of a newly expanding African American middle class meant that
for the first time there were those with the financial means to engage
in large-scale international tourism.[10]

Thus by turning to the transnational African diaspora as an alternate
civic community, African American heritage tourists appear to make,
in the words of Benedict Anderson, "less and less attestations of citizenship, let alone of loyalty to a protective nation-state."[11] As transnational
figures who invoke the diaspora and claim Africa as a site of origin,
these heritage tourists appear to completely subvert the definition of
national identity and traverse beyond the American nation-state.[12] And
yet there remains a paradox. As Michelle Stephens suggests in *Black Empire*, "While discourses of nation and diaspora are often to seen in opposition to each other, involving bounded versus unbounded notions of
both geography and the self, both can still mobilize imaginings of the
self that operate on affective and sentimental level, a level most commonly seen to operate outside the direct jurisdiction of the state in the

realm of culture."[13] For Stephens, culture becomes a site at which we can locate those accommodations, alliances, and creative tensions between the nation-state and the disapora. In regards to the advent of the African American heritage tourists, her argument is particularly instructive. On one hand, the appearance of African American heritage tourists who embark on these transnational pilgrimages reflects the need to locate multiple sites of origins, thereby resisting the totality of national myths. In lieu of their ongoing segregation from American civic myths, "Africa" becomes a desired and seemingly authentic source of cultural identity. On the other hand, as tourists, they travel with the expectations of visiting "authentic" sites.[14] And they assume that these slave forts are none other than the most authentic and historically significant monuments of the slave trade. Unaware of or overlooking controversies surrounding commercialization, historicity, or present-day functionalities, contemporary African American heritage tourists risk representing "Africa" only through the lens of American slavery and freedom. By returning to the slave fort and perceiving this return as a rite of passage, African American heritage tourists supplement the conspicuous absence of symbols of slavery in the United States with the image of the slave fort. Because they visit Africa with the intention of remembering slavery, African American heritage tourists are less likely to be interested in narratives about these slave forts that incorporate their recent uses as administrative offices, training colleges, or police stations than Ghanaian or Senegalese citizens.[15] Instead, these forts and by extension Africa are tangible markers of African American experiences of slavery, segregation, and racism.

I focus on photographs from Carrie Mae Weems's *Slave Coast* (1993) and Chester Higgins's *Middle Passage* (1994) series, and Haile Gerima's film *Sankofa* (1993) because their representations of the slave forts are emblematic of the links between tourism, travel, and visual practices. Historically, travel narratives about Africa were nineteenth-century written travelogues by European and white American explorers and missionaries; however, by the beginning of the twentieth century, as more and more people began to travel and photograph their objects of interests, travel narratives became visual and travel itself became more touristic. This was so much so that in the late twentieth century, photography and film supplanted the written text as the primary medium of the travel narrative and, with the exception of Saidiya Hartman's *Lose Your Mother* (2007), Keith Richburg's *Out of America* (1997), Eddy L. Harris's *Native Stranger* (1992), and Maya Angelou's *All God's Children Need Traveling Shoes* (1986), most post–civil rights African American travel narratives reflect this generic shift. Because Chester Higgins is best known for the commercial success of his portrait photography in exhibits such as *Crowns and Feeling the Spirit* and his *New York Times* photojournalism, I find his "The House of Slaves" a useful image against which to contrast the work of Carrie Mae Weems's. Their different historical contexts, genre, and gender provide valuable points of distinctions, while their status as post–civil rights African Americans suggest a shared history of civic estrangement and exclusion. As a result, Higgins and Weems offer us a spectrum through which we can better understand how contemporary heritage tourism visually constructs and memorializes the slave fort. By including Gerima's *Sankofa* in my analysis of the visual reconstructions of the slave forts, I not only incorporate what remains one of the seminal cinematic representations of slavery in American independent film history, but also consider how cinematography as well as photography can challenge and reproduce what John Urry describes as a "tourist gaze" in which the slave fort emerges as an authentic yet displaced symbol of an African American prodigal returns to Africa.

SENEGAL IN BLACK AND WHITE: CHESTER HIGGINS, CARRIE MAE WEEMS, AND LA MAISON DES ESCLAVES

I had been to the slave castle once before at Gorée Island. . . . At one point during my tour I walked into the room designated for the "crippled and infirmed." And despite my tendency toward ironic detachment in places hollowed by history, to my enormous surprise, I found myself crying uncontrollably.

HENRY LOUIS GATES JR., *Wonders of the African World: The Slave Kingdoms*

Unlike the slave forts in Ghana, there have been a number of controversies surrounding the House of Slaves regarding its role as a major transit stop in the slave trade. In 1995 the historian Philip Curtin sparked a heated debated when he wrote, "Gorée was never important in the slave trade," a sentiment further underscored in 1996 when Emmanuel de Roux published an article entitled "Le mythe de la Maison des Esclaves qui résiste à la réalité" in the French national newspaper, *Le Monde*.[16] While this debate played out among French and Senegalese historians and newspapers, it had nominal impact on the African American heritage tourist industry. Despite the controversy, the House of Slaves remains one of the most highly visited and most sacred monuments of the slave trade, as Henry Louis Gates Jr.'s melancholic epigraph attests. Thus it comes as no surprise that in the absence of national heritage sites that commemorate enslaved African Americans in the United States, Higgins and Weems traveled to Gorée Island to locate physical monuments of the slave trade and thereby engage in a formal remembrance of the lives and experiences of their enslaved ancestors. By privileging and reconstructing the House of Slaves at Gorée Island as the visual symbol of the entire slave trade, Higgins and Weems are able to remember slavery and reclaim Africa as an originary site of African American identity. And as they reclaim Gorée Island as a starting point of the slave trade and therefore the genesis of African American culture, Higgins and Weems create a democratic aesthetic in which they initiate new myths of belongings and beginnings for post–civil rights African Americans. By asserting their allegiance and membership in the larger "imagined community" of the African diaspora, African American artists resist their civic estrangement in the United States. However, like any other myth of civic belonging, the myth of the African diaspora excludes those interpretations of the past and experiences in the present that disrupt the historical authenticity of such myths.

Recalling his first journey to Africa, Higgins wrote, "I was full of anticipation. Finally, I was to discover for myself the parallel black reality I had nourished in my imagination. . . . On that first trip, I began a life-long study of the mannerisms, culture, and traditions of African people; mirror images of the people of my childhood."[17] For the last thirty years, Higgins has traveled to Africa several times and used his camera "to discover, confront, examine, and depict—through dispersions and connection—the existence of people of African descent."[18] The culmination of this search resulted in Higgins's book *Feeling the Spirit: Searching the World for the People of Africa* (1994), which documents what he describes as the "historical ruptures" and "divisions" among "the peoples of Africa" initially caused by slavery, segregation, and apartheid and now sustained by racism and ethnic conflict.[19] While a shared, ongoing history of displacement, divisions, and rifts in identity was the genesis of the present-day discourse on the African diaspora, Higgins is quoted as saying that the goal of *Feeling the Spirit* was not to highlight the moments of separation but to reveal "the affinities between residents of Africa and their far-flung relatives dispersed by slavery."[20] As he described the book, "*Feeling the Spirit* is about dispersion and connections. Today, African people live on four transatlantic continents in many different nations. We are a diverse people. Although we are separated by geography, national boundaries, and language, we are still similar in the ways that bind us together. In our diversity we are much alike."[21] Higgins's photographs provide a visual narrative of an African diaspora that, as Paul Gilroy articulates in *The Black Atlantic*, challenges "both the structures of the nation-state and the constraints of ethnicity and national particularity."[22] But his praise of the African diaspora "diversity" plays on a seemingly unique American rhetoric of racial and ethnic plurality and democracy. In this semantic attempt to move beyond the nation-state and connect to a larger transnational black community, Higgins's language simultaneously grounds his status as a critical patriot who does not repudiate but reifies, does not dismantle but reengages the meta-discourse of American democracy.

Like national civic myths that transmit the fiction of collective histories to its citizenry, the myth of the African diaspora also requires tropes of unity and continuity. Both myth-making processes either forget or marginalize aspects of the past in order to sustain doctrines of coherence and consensus. In an effort to protect and perpetuate the ideology of an uncompromised American democracy, American civic myths mandate the excision of colonialism and slavery from the national memory. While narratives of the African diaspora often attempt to address the racial exclusivity of national myths, they do so by inventing oppositional narratives of transnational racial solidarity. Instead of prescribing national allegiance, such myths of transnationalism dissolve the nation-state by emphasizing commonalties that transcend geographical, linguistic, or even ethnic difference. For example, in an effort to reveal how "in our diversity we are much alike," Higgins arranges his collection of photographs "by sticking different places and parts of the Diaspora right next to each other."[23] Instead of portraying his individual subjects in the context of their national or ethnic backgrounds, Higgins erases or, as he writes, "eliminates" their borders in order to reconcile the divisions constituted by forced movement and displacement.[24] Keeping in the spirit of Stuart Hall's brilliant analysis of Jamaican-born photographer Armet Francis in the essay "Cultural Identity and the Diaspora," I also would argue that in *Feeling the Spirit*, Higgins endeavors to reconstruct visually "the underlying unity of the black people whom slavery and colonization distributed across the African Diaspora. His text is an act of imaginary unification."[25]

Although Higgins has traveled to Gorée Island twelve or more times, I examine his construction of the African diaspora in one of his earlier black-and-white photographs of Gorée Island, "The Door of No Return in the House of Slaves" (Figure 3) because I think it is representative of his larger vision of the African diaspora. In the *Middle Passage* series of the book, Higgins begins his visual narrative at the House of Slaves at Gorée Island, but he then follows these photographs with a documentation of the people of Africa, who (given that the subtitle of the book is *The People of Africa*) presumably constitute the African diaspora. In this collection of photographs, Higgins moves the viewer from the House of Slaves to the African burial ground in Manhattan to the former slave cabins in South Carolina to a memorial service in honor of the millions of enslaved Africans who died in the Middle Passage at Coney Island, New York; from the Celebration of the Oath of Bois Caiman in Haiti, which commemorates the beginning of the Haitian revolution, to the Sisterhood of the Good Death ceremony, which acknowledges the end of slavery in Brazil. Like the arrangement of photographs throughout *Feeling the Spirit*, Higgins did not arbitrarily place the photographs of the *Middle Passage* series alongside each other, but bound them together by the joint history of African captivity, the middle passage, and New World racial discrimination. Higgins's placement of these photographs allows him to create a visual coherence in which the genealogy of the African diaspora begins at the slave fort and culminates in New World ceremonies that remember the histories and rebellions of enslaved Africans. Furthermore, by representing the House of Slaves as the nascent point for all members of the African diaspora, Higgins supplements their histories of separation and scattering with "an imaginary fullness or plentitude."[26] By reconfiguring the slave fort as the symbol of departure and the site to which diasporic blacks should return, Higgins's "Middle Passage" series is a visual text that brings what Bayo Holsey describes as a "redemptive quality to enslavement," in which returning to Africa becomes both a transnational act of resistance and a triumph over slavery's past.[27]

3. Chester Higgins, *Dakar, Senegal, 1972. The Door of No Return in the House of Slaves* (1972). Gelatin silver print. Reproduced in Chester Higgins, *Feeling the Spirit: Searching the World for the People of Africa* (New York: Bantam, 1994). Image courtesy of Chester Higgins. © Chester Higgins Jr. / chesterhiggins.com.

For Higgins, "the structure of [the House of Slaves] stands as a hor-rifying physical reminder that human beings are capable of enslaving each other."[28] The interior of the House of Slaves holds "the terror in the cramped, awful dungeons where Europeans enacted unspeakable crimes against African men, women, and children, trying to strip them of their humanity."[29] As such, the slave fort becomes the symbol of the forced separation and loss of identity that enslaved Africans experi-enced on the shores of West Africa, on the slave ships, and in the New World. In order to keep the aspects of "authenticity" that make Gorée Island both a world heritage site and a popular tourist destination, both Higgins and Weems use the authoritative gaze of black-and-white pho-tography and privilege absence to make the viewer remember the his-tories and experiences of those enslaved Africans who unknowingly departed for the New World. In addition to removing color to fix an image in the remote past, Vilém Flusser has argued that black-and-white photographs bear the badge of authenticity because they cre-ate the illusion that the world, when broken into black and white and thus perfectly opposable elements, becomes more "accessible to logical analysis."[30] In *Spectral Evidence*, Ulrich Baer applies Flusser's philosophy of black-and-white photography to readings of contemporary photo-graphs of Holocaust landscapes in which "the abstractions of *true* and *false* and *good* and *evil*, which predate the invention of photography, seem to find their representational correlates in black and white photo-graphs."[31] Much like the dichotomy of Kara Walker's black-and-white cutouts, Flusser's arguments can be extended to these photographs of the slave forts in which the abstractions of slavery and freedom also cor-respond to the polarity embedded in black-and-white photography.

Historically, "The Door of No Return" was the last view of Africa that enslaved Africans had as they embarked on the slave ships for the New World. In the photograph "The Door of No Return in the House of Slaves," Higgins reinforces the sense of separation by foregrounding the silhouette of a young, black woman against the background of the seemingly mysterious, unending Atlantic Ocean. As a result, the door represents the "process and the condition" of the African diaspora — the coerced transference of cultures, languages, and bodies from the Old World to the New.[32] Here, because of the astounding darkness envel-oping the silhouette, the doorway becomes the most significant object for the viewers. Even though our gaze naturally is drawn to the camera's focus point of the horizon in the Atlantic Ocean (which in fact simulates the last view that enslaved Africans had before boarding the ships), the darkness of the silhouette and the doorway pulls us closer toward the Door of No Return. In this way, the overwhelming darkness also literalizes Glissant's theory of opacity. For Glissant, opacity not only opposes what he sees as a colonial discourse of transparency, but is the apt metaphor to describe New World slave resistance and histories as well. Transparency, Glissant argues in *Le Discours Antillais*, has been the privilege of colonial power to define the colonized subject, as Other, slave, and ahistorical. Opacity, then, is a refusal of transparency, a counter-narrative in which camouflaged resistance, much like the forest-covering maroon communities in the slave-holding Caribbean, rejects the objectifying gaze of the European colonialists.[33] Moreover, because the removal from Africa for enslaved Africans was so violent and absolute, opacity is the primary prism through which we can understand the unknowable chaos and fragmented darkness that make up New World black histories. In Higgins's photograph, since the doorway is occupied by the young woman who stands at the intersection of both the darkness and the blinding light or between Africa and the New World, there are no objects competing for the viewer's attention. She thus embodies this break between Africa and the daunting currents of the Atlantic Ocean. Her body, the doorframe, and the actual frame of the photograph not only literalize the threshold between the Old World and the New, but the totalizing darkness of her background manifests Glissant's opacity, reminding the viewer of black resistance against the unnatural laws of racial slavery.

And yet, despite functioning as a formative site of separation for enslaved Africans, Higgins portrays the slave fort as the ultimate site of reunification—the place that stripped Africans of their humanity but one to which we must return in order to restore our memories of Africa as home. By creating a silhouette, Higgins provides a visual image of continuity and unity within the African diaspora. Paradoxically, this figure's anonymity is a stand-in for the lost histories and voices of "some 10 million African men, women, and children [who] passed through the dungeons in the House of Slaves on their way to the slave labor markets." Her ambiguity also represents the fluidity of transnational identities.[34] Similar to Walker's silhouette *The End of Uncle of Tom*, the purpose of Higgins's silhouette is to outline shapes and forms only; there are no discernable markers of her ethnicity or nationality. Because we cannot locate her particular site of origin, we cannot essentialize her nationality as African American, Jamaican, Brazilian, or Senegalese. However, unlike Walker's satirical gaze, which foregrounds the silhouette as an exaggeration of racial caricature rather than black interiority itself, Higgins's figure becomes what Joseph Roach describes as "surrogation" and is a stand-in for the missing voices of those enslaved, dead, and forgotten throughout the entire African diaspora.[35] While the silhouette forces the viewer to remember the thousands of Africans who forcibly left their homes and families in Africa, the young woman also inhabits the space between Africa and the Atlantic Ocean, or, as James Clifford writes, "the co-presence of here and there" that creates the African diaspora consciousness.[36] Her darkness suggests that she is from anywhere in the black world, but her non-specificity claims nowhere. As such, she truly becomes Higgins's "citizen of the world" in which African diaspora myths of similarity and belonging subsume markers of difference.[37]

Much like the contemporary black feminist narratives on Sally Hemings, Higgins's text reminds us of the centrality of black female corporeality to slavery's scenes of subjection and the genealogy of that subjection as well. But in addition to being a prodigal daughter, the feminized triangular shape of the silhouette also suggests a recentering of Africa as both the beginning of the "triangle" slave trade and the "founding mother" of the African diaspora. To quote Hall again, the imaginary coherence of the African diaspora is restored by figuring Africa as "the mother of these different civilizations . . . for Africa is the missing term, the great aporia, which lies at the centre of our cultural identity and gives it a meaning which, until recently it lacked."[38] As such, in order to reconcile the ongoing sense of fragmentation and historical displacement that defines the post–civil rights African American identity, Higgins depicts "The Door of No Return" as the monument to which African Americans must return and the silhouette as a nascent point. And it is only through the process of reclaiming and memorializing this slave fort that African Americans will be able to supplement narratives of dispersal with Pan-African fictions of healing and wholeness.

Like Chester Higgins, photographer Carrie Mae Weems returned to West Africa in order "to gain a first-hand understanding of the way that

Africa had impacted both her and America."[39] In 1993, immediately after finishing *Sea Island Series*, in which she examined the legacy of slavery in the United States by capturing the landscape of the coastal islands of the American South, Weems decided that she wanted to visit what she called "the vestiges of slavery: the slave ports, forts, castles, along the coast of Ghana, Elmina, Cape Coast, and Ile de Gorée."[40] While in *Sea Island Series* Weems focused on the remnants or traces of slavery in the United States, like praise houses, graveyards, and abandoned slave quarters, Weems traveled to West Africa to locate the remnants of the transatlantic slave trade that she could not find in the American South. By documenting both the coasts upon which enslaved Africans arrived in the New World, such as Charleston, South Carolina, and the forts from which they left Africa for the New World, Weems also turns to Africa in order to create an alternative transnational discourse of origins and belonging. Thomas Piche describes Weems's *Africa Series* as a myth-making process in which she "creates a fiction out of the truths she encounters rather than finds a truth deep within fictions. Rather than looking for Africa [as she did in *Sea Island Series*], she goes to Africa."[41] And yet, while Weems does create a myth of the African diaspora that allows her both to claim Africa as a site of origin and resist the racial exclusivity of American nationalism, she, unlike Higgins, emphasizes the moments of rupture and discontinuity that compose the African diaspora.

I would argue that these thematic distinctions are in fact ideological differences informed by the time of production of these photographs. Originating in 1972 and on the heels of the civil rights movement, Higgins's "The Door of No Return at the House of Slaves" emblematizes a Black Power vision of the African diaspora in which international black solidarity and racial unity supplant fidelity to and faith in the American nation-state. Weems's *Slave Coast Series* also upholds the African diaspora as an alternative imagined community. While the need for black oppositional narratives to American civic myths has remained constant throughout the post–civil rights era, there is no singular or hegemonic remembrance or configuration of the African diaspora. Unlike "an act of imaginary reunification" that Higgins's photograph inscribes, Weems's project is greatly influenced by post-structuralist and multicultural identity politics debates that took place in the 1980s and early 1990s. Following suit, Weems's images are ones that we can think of in terms of what Brent Edwards calls "differences within unity."[42] This diversity of diasporic cultural identity then elides claims of racial purity or biological solidarity, but rather, like the diasporic aesthetic that Weems represents at Gorée Island, is both a story of common histories and a narrative of fragmentation and difference.

Weems's myth of an African diaspora, in which inflections of difference are as important or even more important than those of sameness, is embodied in the silver gelatin print "Elmina Cape Coast Ile de Goree" (Figure 4) from *Slave Coast Series*. Although the title and accompanying text suggest that the triptych includes all three forts, the actual photograph features three different views of the House of Slaves at Gorée Island. By conflating all three forts into one, Weems deemphasizes their respective locations in the nation-states of Senegal and Ghana and consolidates them into one singular image of the slave trade and beginning of the African diaspora. However, even though her text provides a narrative of wholeness and oneness, the accompanying photograph completely undermines the sense of continuity and unity that she puts forth in her text. "Elmina Cape Coast Ile de Goree" is a vertical triptych of the famous staircase of "The House of Slaves." In the first photograph, there is a close-up frontal shot of the entire staircase with a miniaturized view of "The Door of No Return" as the focal point. Unlike Higgins's photograph, because there are no people in Weems's reconstruction of "The Door of No Return," the actual architecture ends up reproducing the ominous air of the slave trade. Instead of having a silhouette remind the viewer of the ghostly traces of the slave trade, Weems simply situates the darkness that surrounds the Door of No Return between the bright sunlight that comes from the inner courtyard and from the Atlantic Ocean to emphasize the historical significance of the port. Shrouded by light not overwhelming darkness, the Door of No Return appears so small, so seemingly benign, that it makes its actual role as the final gateway between Africa and New World slavery even more disturbing and dehumanizing.

Furthermore, through her manipulation of the architecture of Gorée Island, Weems tries to re-create the melancholic affects caused by the confinement, dismemberment, and displacement of the slave trade itself. In contrast to the wide-angle shot of the staircase in the first image of the triptych, the second and third images are side-angle shots of the staircase. The second photograph features only the top of the left

ELMINA
CAPE COAST
ILE DE GOREE

4. Carrie Mae Weems, *Elmina Cape Coast Ile de Goree*, from *The Slave Coast Series* (1993). Gelatin silver print. Image courtesy of P.P.O.W. and Carrie Mae Weems.

side of the staircase, while the third of the triptychs appears to be the view taken from the top of the staircase in the second photograph — revealing only the bottom part of the right staircase and the quarters reserved for enslaved men that stands right behind it. The vertical placement of the photographs forces the viewer's eye to travel along the staircase, while the side-angle shots upset the sequential order of such travel. Instead of traveling up and down the staircase in one fluid motion as in the first photograph, the second and third photographs discourage the viewer from re-creating a narrative of wholeness and stability. Instead, these images stacked on top of each other suggest the ruptures and discontinuities that constitute Weems's image of the African diaspora. They materialize what Edwards refers to as "décalage" or the necessary and inevitable negotiation of the gaps, discrepancies, and misrecognitions that exist among and between members of the African diaspora. Riffing off Leopold Senghor's décalage, Edwards uses the visual image of the joint as a point of separation and linkage to describe the unevenness and divergences that alongside moments of collaborations constitute diaspora practices.[43] Instead of representing the diaspora as singular and intact, Weems breaks up the staircase to suggest a sense of transformation and movement. She re-creates the House of Slaves as a point of origin that parented unwanted mobility and coerced travel and that harkens back to the mass exodus out of the Door of No Return and the attendant tortuous journey of the Middle Passage. Here, both the gaps of the triptych, the vertical placement of the prints, and the actual images contained in the photographs produce an image of the African diaspora, a décalage of sorts, that both deconstructs the myth of reunification and privileges sites of cultural difference.

Reappropriating the slave fort as the originary point of identity, Weems reaffirms African American claims of historical connection to Africa and legitimates their membership in the African diaspora. As a result, the fragmentation of the staircase can be read as both the visual recognition of cultural difference and the commemoration of diversity. The focus on the staircase, as opposed to the Door of No Return, indicates both movement and flexibility. Weems emphasizes that despite the literal rigidity of the structure of the slave fort or, better yet, the durability of American racism, the African American traveler can return to Africa in order to reclaim the slave fort and reshape its historical meaning. While the side-angle shots suggest discontinuity, they also hint at plurality. These photographs allow the viewer to understand the House of Slaves and the memory of slavery from multiple perspectives and viewpoints, thereby resisting the impulse toward authoritative understandings of the past. By providing the viewer with these varying images of the slave fort, Weems also reminds us of the diversity of all those who left these shores for the New World. Like Higgins's photograph, Weems's triptych is a surrogate for missing bodies and the forgotten histories of enslaved Africans. However, instead of using a solitary figure of black female corporeality to remember and fill in the void left by slavery, Weems replaces their absence with multiple perspectives, thereby mirroring the heterogeneity and diversity that initiated and continue to make up the African diaspora. In her capturing of difference through the depiction of several viewpoints, Weems's triptych contains a civic myth of the African diaspora that embodies the philosophical underpinnings of democracy denied to African Americans in the United States.

When Higgins and Weems each reconstruct the House of Slaves as a metaphor of the African diaspora, they create, to borrow a phrase from Smadar Lavie, "a frame of analysis that resists and transcend national boundaries."[44] In many ways, the medium of photography and its play with surface and shadows, realism and the unrepresentable, and the self and the other embody what Victor Turner defined as "liminality," or a state of being in which subjects are "neither here nor there; they are betwixt and between."[45] Their depictions of the House of Slaves construct alternative civic myths that challenge American national memory while recentering these fictions with an African American historical framework. The fort resides in Africa and yet becomes American. As such, Higgins and Weems reproduce a narrative of returning to Africa in which "Africa" is always seen not as it is at present, but through "the backwards glance or hindsight."[46] In order to remember the House of Slaves as it once was, as a site of trauma for thousands of enslaved Africans, "Africa" and the slave fort itself can be signifiers only of historical violence and loss. Unfortunately, in order to visually reproduce and preserve the House of Slaves as a heritage site, Higgins and Weems reconstruct the present-day House of Slaves only as an extension of the past and not as co-equals. They seem to position Gorée Island, and by extension all of Senegal, in what Sandra Richards describes as "a chronological period in which time has either stopped, or the past is identical to the present."⁴⁷ Thus, unlike the preceding Back to Africa movements in which African American emigrants and expatriates engaged the African politics of their respective periods because "Africa" represented a potential site for political sovereignty and racial equality, the post–civil rights discourse does not invoke "Africa" as a substitute homeland. The repositioning of Africa as an extension of remembering American slavery within the African American consciousness is a direct consequence of the post–civil rights African American political position of legal citizenship and civic estrangement. In order to compensate for their exclusion from civic narratives, they reconstitute "Africa" as a site of a shared history.

Not at all coincidentally, Higgins and Weems shoot in black and white. Although their images are taken outside the United States, both Higgins and Weems borrow from the American social documentary tradition in which black-and-white photography conveys a sense of authenticity. Black-and-white photography tends to invoke a sense of gravitas, stillness, and the past. For example, a color photograph of the House of Slaves reveals that the imposing staircase and the adjoining walls in the courtyard, which is a brilliant white in Weems's photograph, is actually a fading terra-cotta color. These rust-hued stairs lead up to doors that are not black but sage green, framed by pale yellow walls. In contrast to the stillness and the solemnness that Weems's black-and-white photograph conveys and the absolute blackness of Higgins's picture, the bright colors of the actual House of Slaves imbue the landscape with a sense of energy, warmth, and movement. If they were to capture the realism of the House of Slaves through color photography, Higgins and Weems risk disrupting the tourist gaze of Gorée Island as both "sacred" and "heritage." So in order to re-create the sense of haunting and sanctity that they felt and that other African American heritage tourists expect to experience at Gorée Island, Higgins and Weems transport the House of Slaves from its present-day color and warmth and attempt to put it back in its "authentic" role as a slave fort.

By erasing the color of the building, Higgins and Weems do not re-create Gorée Island as it once was, for it never was a white building in a darkened landscape, but reconstruct Gorée as a sacred site, a visual shrine to their enslaved ancestors. Instead of privileging the feelings of discontinuity and discomfort that viewers might have with an image of a brightly lit and somewhat welcoming tropical building, Higgins and Weems visually restructure the fort as a permanent reflection of or a monument to the past. Like the opposing elements of slavery and resistance or slavery and freedom, black-and-white photography renders the intangibility of these concepts real and accessible to the viewer. While color distracts and would most likely make us forget the feeling of loss associated with slavery, black-and-white forces the viewer to reconcile the strict binaries through which we interpret the picture, but more importantly they symbolize the rigid laws of citizenship and nonbelonging under which enslaved Africans lived.

According to Cheryl Finley, Gorée Island normally is "teeming with life, visited annually by thousands of pilgrims from the Diaspora and tourists around the globe."[48] And even though the House of Slaves at Gorée Island is one of the most lucrative tourist sites in Senegal, especially among African Americans, in the photographs of Higgins and Weems, the bodies of tourists are conspicuously absent. In addition to the dearth of tourists, Higgins and Weems also erase the presence of the Senegalese inhabitants who live at Gorée Island and the fishermen and the House of Slaves employees who work on the island. Because of their deliberate emphasis on absence, they represent the House of Slaves as a silent witness to the trauma and the forgotten histories of the millions of Africans forced to travel to the New World. Not only do the missing bodies of tourists and the local denizens constitute the space of absence in their photographs, but so does the erasure of all markers of present-day Senegal. Their pictures try to induce the viewer to remember slavery through voids, erasures, and absences. Much like the effects of their black-and-white photography, they recover the traumatic experiences of enslaved Africans at the House of Slaves by removing any signs of life or contemporaneity. Ironically, this displacement of a post-colonial Senegalese present is fraught with contradictions for the diasporic project to which these photographs lay claim. In an effort to move past the borders of and an allegiance to the U.S. nation-state, these artists nevertheless succumb to a discourse and aesthetic that, as George Elliott Clarke writes, "Americanizes blackness."[49] The singularity of the tourist gaze here privileges an African American melancholic and redemptive sojourn to Senegal, like those described by Gates above, rather than accounts for the disappointments, disjunctures, and yearnings that exist between African Americans and their Senegalese hosts, or even among Senegal's own citizens.

Unlike Weems's photograph, which creates absence through invoking and disrupting the tradition of landscape art, Higgins's "The

Door of No Return at the House of Slaves" creates absence through a reenactment of solitude. Given our point of view, the Door of No Return is foreboding and unwelcoming, the darkness is dwarfing and atomizing, and the ocean restless and weary. Thus by removing competing objects and thereby contending narratives, Higgins's landscape in "The Door of No Return at the House of Slaves" simply serves as a symbol of slavery and nothing else. Although the photograph is taken in Senegal, there are no markers of national identity or time period. In fact, we know it is Senegal because Higgins's caption informs us as much. But for the most part, contemporary Senegalese culture is absent and replaced with an image of a slave fort that is exclusively locked into the parameters of American slavery and African American return. Through the juxtaposition of light and darkness and the invocation of absence through the loneliness of the silhouette, Higgins reproduces the feelings of desertion, dismemberment, and lack produced by the transatlantic slave trade and the Middle Passage. However, by foregrounding absence, Higgins either disentangles us from the present or renders the present filled with lack. Either way, the viewer does not have a sense of postcolonial Gorée Island. As a result, the transnational stories of the diaspora, of which modern Senegal is inevitably apart, are sacrificed and replaced with a myth of the African diaspora that transcends the racial limitations of American national memory but recenters those African American perspectives of slavery that are forgotten in United States.

Instead of re-creating absence through juxtaposition, Weems's "Elmina Cape Coast Ile de Goree" omits any people or objects that would compromise the historical significance of the House of Slaves. In an interview about her trip to West Africa, Weems admits: "It wasn't the experience I expected, it was much more complicated than claiming roots, I felt methodical and emotionally distant. I had to deal with my emotions later."[50] For Weems, the House of Slaves was not simply a site to reclaim, but one that contains and yields the indescribable feelings of a deep melancholia and loss, the effects of civic estrangement. Wrestling with this emotional distance, Weems chose to photograph only the architecture of the House of Slaves. In lieu of using the gendered imagery of Mother Africa (Higgins) or prodigal New World daughter (Gerima) to remember slavery, "Elmina Cape Coast Ile de Gorée" engages in what Kimberly Brown describes as Weems's "refusal of the corporeal," an aesthetic prominently showcased in her later photograph series, "Roaming" (2006). Here, through displaying the emptiness of the House of Slaves, Weems's photograph attempts to produce not the lack imposed by enslavement, but, like Glissant's opacity, the inability to express fully the history of terror that slavery created. Likewise, for Weems to reconstruct the feelings of loss and abandonment that she associated with the slave trade, she reenacts the actions of the slave traders themselves and exorcises the entire fort of the bodies and remnants of the enslaved Africans. In order to acknowledge their presence, she accents their absence.

Although Higgins and Weems both reconstruct the House of Slaves as a metaphor for the African diaspora—Higgins as a site of "imaginary reunification" and Weems as a "differences within unity"—their representational concerns originate with the need to locate heritage sites that memorialize American slavery. And in spite of some of their ideological distinctions, both photographers effectively create a democratic aesthetic and simultaneously undermine the transnational myth of the African diaspora to which their photographs lay claim. These photographs reveal Higgins's and Weems's reappropriation of the Senegalese slave fort as a generative marker of identity that transcends and visually supplements the racial exclusivity of American civic myths of belonging and historical commonality. By sanctifying the House of Slaves as the constitutive site of the African diaspora only, their photographs also erase or marginalize those histories and present-day realities that move beyond African American prodigal claims. Within the context of heritage tourism, travel to the interior lands of Senegal is tangential and the present-day government of Senegal in and of itself can be secondary or, as the anthropologist Paulla Ebron notes, "seem irrelevant, even antithetical" to the larger and more personal mission of self-discovery and re-memory.[51] In such moments, the myth of the African diaspora, despite protestations otherwise, risks becoming an exclusively and undeniably African American national space.

BACK TO DARKNESS AND TO PEACE:
HAILE GERIMA, CAPE COAST CASTLE,
AND THE MYTHOPOEIA OF RETURN

In West Africa, along the palm-lined coast of Ghana, are several forts and castle that constitute another symbol; unlike Plymouth Rock, they were points of departure, not arrival, places of despair rather than liberty. They were the embarkation points for hundreds of thousands of men, women, and children who came to America in chains. And now together with Gorée Island in Senegal, far to the north of Ghana, they are the few physical remains of the traffic in human beings that brought many Americans, black Americans to the United States.

NATHAN HUGGINS, "American Myths and Afro-American Claims"

In 1993 the Ethiopian-born filmmaker Haile Gerima released *Sankofa*, an independent film set in the Cape Coast slave fort of modern Ghana and an unidentified plantation in the nineteenth-century New World. Gerima spent twenty years researching, writing, and filming this feature-length work, whose title comes from the Akan word meaning "to remember the past to go forward." For Gerima, *Sankofa* was a conscious "re-coup" of cinematic representation of American slavery from the dominant narratives of the Hollywood classics *The Birth of a Nation* (1915) and *Gone With the Wind* (1939).[52] Unlike "the happy slaves" of the minstrel adaptations of *Uncle Tom's Cabin* or the pro-slavery romance films such as *Gone With the Wind*, Gerima wanted *Sankofa* to portray "an African race opposed to this whole idea, by making the history of slavery full of resistance, full of rebellion. Resistance and rebellion—the plantation school of thought believed it was always provoked by outsiders, that Africans were not capable of having that human need."[53] Because the histories of enslaved African Americans have been forgotten or erased in the national memory, Gerima believes that African American films must "create monuments, healing symbols, Nat Turners: they have to convey their variety and the truth of their history" in order to revise or fill in the prevailing historical narratives.[54]

Gerima created *Sankofa* in order to assert alternative myths and symbols of belonging: "Instead of feeding them the myth of Lincoln, just bring Nat Turner. You have a statue of Jefferson; next to him put Nat Turner or Harriet Tubman."[55] In *Sankofa*, Gerima highlights the slave fort as a monument that commemorates enslaved Africans and puts forth slave insurrectionists as iconic figures. Interestingly enough, much like Chester Higgins and Carrie Mae Weems, Gerima transforms the slave fort from an originary site of the slave trade to an ancestral memorial to which only African diasporic blacks have "the right of return." Gerima not only supplants memorials like Plymouth Rock with the slave fort, but also creates a visual genealogy that provides his post–civil rights African American audience with alternative myths of belonging and healing. In lieu of the national amnesia regarding slavery, *Sankofa* recasts the slave fort and more specifically Cape Coast Castle in Ghana as the constitutive site of African American identity and the ultimate homecoming for the African American returnee. Cape Coast Castle emerges as the site in which his African American female protagonist, Mona, works through her racial anxiety and reclaims her history. By reconstructing Cape Coast Castle only as a site of slavery, *Sankofa* privileges the perspective of an African American heritage tourist over all other interpretations and contemporary uses of the fort, thereby positing American blackness as the pivot point, even when diasporic discourses seem to be engaged.

Sankofa opens and ends in the courtyard and the dungeons of the Cape Coast Castle in present-day Ghana. In the first scene we see an old Ghanaian divine drummer (Kofi Ghanaba), whom we later learn is named Sankofa, covered in white ceremonial powder, chanting incantations, and playing the drums to summon the spirit of his ancestors. The scene immediately shifts from the drummer to Mona (Oyafunmike Ogunlano), an African American model dressed in a kinte cloth hat, blonde wig, and tiger-stripe swimsuit; she is standing on the steps of the building to pose for a white American male fashion photographer. The camera then cuts away to a group of white tourists who are distinguished by their 35mm cameras, shorts, and baseball caps. As they follow and listen to the Ghanaian tour guide's lecture about the pivotal role Cape Coast Castle played in the slave trade, Sankofa abruptly appears, interrupts the tour, and proceeds to chastise the tourists, the fashion photographer, and Mona for desecrating the ground on which his "people were snatched and taken by the white man." He brandishes his staff and shoos away the white tourists: "Get away from here. Leave this ground." Conversely, Sankofa commands Mona to reclaim Cape Coast Castle and "go back to your past. To your source."[56] Although Mona does not know the historical significance of the slave fort, she remains transfixed by Sankofa's utterance.

In the next scene, Mona does not return to the photo shoot but instead (now donning her natural kinky hair and a loose brown robe) stealthily follows the group of white tourists into the slave dungeons of Cape Coast Castle. There, while the tour guide's speech fades in the background, Mona perceives the sound of a heavy door slammed shut and pitch-blackness suddenly surrounding her. When the lights come back on, Mona unexpectedly finds herself in the same room in which a group of chained African men, women, and children encircle her. Demanding to be released, Mona bangs on the door. Once the door opens, the night sky confronts her and a crowd of white men, whose antiquated dress and torch lights suggests they are slave traders, drag Mona back into the tunnel. Despite her protestations, "You are making a mistake. I am not African. I am American. I am not a slave," the men rip off her clothing and violently brand her chest. As she screams, the non-diegetic music changes from West African drumming and chants to a live recording of Aretha Franklin singing the gospel hymn "Precious Lord," a sonic shift that marks her initiation into the peculiar institution of slavery and a founding aesthetic of black survival. When Mona falls to the ground from shock and loses consciousness, the group of chained African men pick up her limp body. Once again, the room turns black, and when the next scene fades in, we have been transported to a sugarcane plantation in the New World, where the majority of the film takes place.

The film is narrated by Shola, a nineteenth-century slave woman on the Lafayette plantation. The same actress plays Shola and the twentieth-century Mona, both of whom are ignorant of their connection with "Africa." Ruth Mayer notes that the women "turn out to be complementary figures—interacting indirectly and along twisted lines."[57] However, after enduring severe sexual and physical abuse from her slave owners, Shola undergoes a psychological awakening and, as the film progresses, begins to use Akan rituals and religious symbols as a "means of personal empowerment, subversion, and resistance."[58] On the plantation, Shola refuses further subjugation by joining a group of slave insurrectionists who burn the plantation, murder several overseers, and escape to the hills. As Shola runs away from the plantation (only to be eventually caught), she begins to narrate an excited tale of tricking her captors and flying back to Africa. Capturing her fantastical story through a high-angle shot, in the next scene the camera fluidly pans over the cane fields, over the Atlantic Ocean, and then back to Cape Coast Castle. Then, in a flash-forward to the late twentieth century, *Sankofa* ends with an image of Mona's joining an African diaspora reunion. Nude, screaming, and stumbling out of the slave dungeon, Mona emerges from underground only to fall into the arms of an older, maternal African woman who dresses her in a white dress and blue headscarf. Ignoring the white fashion photographer who interrogates her about her absence, the automaton-like Mona walks toward Sankofa's beating drums. In contrast to the group of white tourists who open the film, *Sankofa* ends with close-ups of black men and women whose clothing, hairstyles, and skin complexions suggest they come from varied places in the African diaspora. As this group sits and dutifully listens to Sankofa's drumming and songs of homecoming, Mona looks at Sankofa and joins them.

Even though much of *Sankofa* takes place on the nineteenth-century sugarcane plantation in the New World, Gerima uses the slave fort, specifically Cape Coast Castle, to not only frame his film but to provide a cinematic monument for post–civil rights African Americans. In the beginning of *Sankofa*, Cape Coast Castle represents a site of fragmentation and loss, but by the end of the film the fort symbolizes the spiritual plentitude and diasporic wholeness of "Africa." In *Sankofa*, Cape Coast Castle undergoes a hermeneutical transfiguration from a locus of oppression to a site of belonging and racial reunification. When we are first introduced to Mona at Cape Coast Castle, she appears unaware of its historical and cultural significance. Instead of standing in a reflective posture like the silhouette in Higgins's photograph, she uses the slave fort as a backdrop for a fashion photo shoot. However, through Mona's ignorance, Gerima reveals the negative consequences of forgetting the histories and contributions of enslaved African Americans. Not only does she desecrate the fort by using it as a background for her fashion pictures, but she poses for photographs that inevitably reproduce racial stereotypes. Her tiger-stripe bathing suit implies African primitivism and alludes to the hegemonic representations of Africa in Tarzan films. Additionally, when the white male photographer demands that she "be more sexy" on the steps of Cape Coast Castle, he invokes and reinforces eighteenth- and nineteenth-century images of black female hyper-sexuality. Finally, as Mona wears a blonde wig, she appears to have internalized standards of beauty that privilege whiteness over blackness. Quite similar to black feminist reconstructions of Sally Hemings and Topsy, the Mona/Shola dyad in *Sankofa* is an explicit reminder of the pivotal role black female corporeality plays in our post–civil rights remembering of slavery. Initially, as Mona stands parallel to her white photographer on the steps of the fort, she symbolizes the national forgetting of slavery, a modern amnesiac who must undergo a violent journey of decline and racial redemption.

And yet, according to Kara Keeling, "*Sankofa* provides an opportunity to examine the possibilities for the production of a black cultural nationalist subject prescribed in the female body."[59] Instead of filling in the subjectivity of enslaved black women's narratives as the playwright Robbie McCauley does or flattening out the black female body as Kara Walker does, Gerima fully subsumes the African American female body into his diasporic mythology of forced dispersal and eventual reunification. As such, though she can never be Mother Africa, the founding figure of the diaspora, she emerges as its prodigal daughter whose ideological transformation from amnesiac to returnee fulfills longstanding Black Nationalist tropes of black women's corporeality. The emphasis on "womb-centered definition of black women," according to Madhu Dubey, renders black women's bodies as contested sites that need to be recuperated and reclaimed by the black community.[60] In this discourse, the black woman's body symbolizes the traumatized past but, more important, is often imagined as a figure of cultural recovery and an embodiment of lost origins and a mythically unchanged Africa.

Within the first few minutes of the film, Gerima plays out this gendered racial script by setting up the paradox that his film will try to resolve — even though Mona is a legal citizen of the United States, she remains culturally inferior. Through Mona, *Sankofa* reveals that the price African Americans pay for forgetting slavery in order to culturally assimilate is far too high. The cost is not merely forgetting the past, but a blind acceptance of the post–civil rights racial paradox in which African Americans are legal citizens but civically estranged. The opening sequence reveals the paradox, but it is in the bowels of Cape Coast Castle that Mona finds the solution. While *Sankofa* concludes by representing the slave fort as a locus of black solidarity, in the scene in which the nineteenth-century slave traders drag Mona back into the bowels of Cape Coast Castle, the fort actually reverts to its original function as a slave port. In these slave dungeons, Mona learns the narrative of racial captivity and coercion that engendered the prosperity of New World plantations. Additionally, she locates the site and the moment in which the African diaspora was born. Although they are still in Africa, the chained men and women who surround Mona have already lost their individuality and freedom. While Mona screams, their muteness sym-

bolizes an erasure of their former ethnic languages, cultures, and identities. In the slave trade, these differences were ignored and conflated
into the ubiquitous racial category of "blackness." As Mona attests her
American citizenship in the slave dungeons in order to avoid enslavement by yelling "I am not an African. I am American," her national
allegiance offers her no protection from the transnational racism of
the slave trade. Similarly, the previous exchange between Mona and
the photographer on the slave fort steps reveals that her "Americaness"
cannot shield her from the racial stereotypes of the white male photographer's gaze. Both in the past and the present, the "blackness" of
African Americans appears to trump their national belonging. In this
scene, despite her protestations and much like her ancestors, Mona personifies the fragmentation and dehumanization that accompanied the
creation of the African diaspora. As the traders brand her and she loses
consciousness, Gerima re-creates a "scene of subjection" in which she
is initiated into enslavement and symbolically loses her subjectivity and
individuality.

As the story progresses and Mona becomes more and more conscious of her past, *Sankofa* substitutes the sense of loss and historical
amnesia that plagues Mona with images of collective remembrance and
wholeness. When Mona emerges from the bowels of the Cape Coast
Castle, she appears to be what Sylvia Kandé describes as a "Born again
African," who, after being enslaved and reconnecting to her past, embraces the larger community of the African diaspora.[61] However, by
recentering Africa as the place at which Mona not only salvages her
past and her present self, *Sankofa*, much like Higgins's "The Door of
No Return in the House of Slaves," concludes with an imaginary reunification of the African diaspora and depicts Africa as the primary place
that African Americans should reclaim and find redemption. Moreover,
Sankofa suggests that Mona's journey or what Gerima calls "awakening
consciousness" cannot occur in her birth country of the United States.[62]
As such, not only does Mona have to leave the United States, but she
has to culminate her journey at the historical site of origin, Africa. More
important, unlike her experiences in the United States in which she
can consider herself as "American" only by forgetting slavery, *Sankofa*
re-creates an African diasporic community in which Mona neither for-
sakes her pasts nor exists on the margins. In fact, by engaging the past
and repossessing this site of slavery, Mona engages in a ritual reenact-

ment in which she overcomes the national amnesia of slavery and her former feelings of civic estrangement. By confronting the legacy of slavery and deconstructing the illusion of American historical narratives, African Americans who recuperate and return to their ancestral pasts now can claim an alternative "source." And *Sankofa* implies, by reclaiming "Africa" as a figurative birthplace, that African Americans can redefine their imagined community and supplement the racial exclusivity of the American nation-state with the transnational racial solidarity of the African diaspora, as Mona does.

While Higgins and Weems sacralize the House of Slaves as a monument to the slave trade by shooting in black and white and removing all traces of tourism in their photographs, Gerima creates the same sense of reverence by rendering the slave fort the mnemonic property of the African American heritage tourist. Even though *Sankofa* produces "the diversified aesthetic of the African Diaspora" through its secondary characters, Sankofa, Nunu, Shango, Joe, and Lucy, who presumably come from Ghana, Jamaica, and the United States, the primary character in the film, Mona, is undeniably African American.[63] Not only can we discern her national identity from her speech and her clothing, but the content of the narrative reflects the particularities of an African American political identity. In his director's statement for *Sankofa*, Gerima proclaims that he hopes "the film will stimulate the necessary thought processes needed to engage in meaningful discussion and debate about the present-day 'slavery' in which we as Africans find ourselves."[64] When Gerima asserts that the goal of *Sankofa* is to promote dialogue about slavery among "Africans," he appears to be keeping in line with his larger African diasporic vision of healing and reconciliation.

However, when interviewer Pamela Woolford asks him to clarify what he defines as "present-day slavery," Gerima quickly slips into an Americanist narrative: "I think America is constructed to this day around a very plantation arrangement. I think especially African Americans and white Americans — their relationship is from the old tradition of ownership, guidance, responsibility. These are still the problem of this country. . . . Knowledge of this history is necessary to change the climate of this country."[65] Though Gerima initially defines "present-day slavery" as a phenomenon that affects all "Africans," he locates his solution to this problem within the very specific context of American race relations. Furthermore, Gerima's tension between his African diasporic project and his Americanist narrative is not limited to his director's statement, but exists throughout and is inseparable from his represen- tations of slavery in *Sankofa*. While Mona's transfiguration from what Peter Ukpokodu describes as "an erstwhile flighty, fashionable, ma- terialistic, class-conscious girl of vanity" into "a more mature, pensive, knowledgeable Mona" is the focal point of the entire film, the neces- sity of conversion makes sense only within the context of Mona's inter- action with the white American photographer before her "fall" into slavery and after her emergence from the slave dungeons heightens the racial contrast.[66] At the beginning of *Sankofa*, Mona's blind acceptance of the sexual overtures of the fashion photographer on the steps of the slave fort epitomizes her state of ignorance and her racial oppression. Conversely, her outright refusal to speak to him, much less pose for him, at the end of the film symbolizes her enlightenment and her racial resistance. Her self-discovery can be understood only within the con- text of the politically and racially overdetermined relationship between Mona and this white American photographer. As such, despite his best intentions, *Sankofa* projects a narrative of belonging and return that re- sponds to civic estrangement with a democratic aesthetic stepped in African American exceptionalism. Here, in the absence of national be- longing, diasporic yearning becomes swallowed by an American racial rhetoric in which the histories of slavery, segregation, and post–civil rights racism become implicated and interpolated in the present lives of non-American black subjects.

I have suggested that by memorializing Cape Coast Castle as a site of slavery only, *Sankofa* avoids competing narratives (and uses) of the slave fort and repositions the African American prodigal daughter, Mona, as one of the rightful inheritors of the slave fort. This monumentalization, nevertheless, rubs against the grain of local memorialization practices. Over the last ten years, as Bayo Holsley's *Routes of Remembrance* de- tails, the Ghanaian government and many African American activists have publicly disagreed about the conservation strategy of and exhi- bitions featured at Cape Coast Castle. In these debates, Ghanaian offi- cials have wanted to modernize the facilities, paint the walls a brighter color, and add displays about archeology, trade, European contact, the freedom struggle, education, religion, and the cultural and economic life of the central region today, in order to redress what they felt was a one-dimensional view of the forts and castles in the central region's history—namely, that of slavery. Some African Americans argued that such conservation efforts would create an artificial appearance or effect that inevitably would compromise or cover up the sordid history of the slave fort. Furthermore, for other African Americans, the attempts to focus on other functions of the fort did not suggest a more inclusive historical presentation but rather another way to deemphasize the significance of "their" ancestors. The histories of these forts before and after the slave trade become secondary or inconsequential to the process of remembering slavery and returning home. The consequence of such elisions is not simply mnemonic, but structure contemporary relationships between African American heritage tourists and their Ghanaian environs and denizens. According to Holsley, pilgrimages to Cape Coast Castle might provide "an alternative sense of belonging to counter-balance the alienation that many have in the United States. Such stories, however, suggest a happy ending in diaspora's return to Ghana and do not cite the contemporary struggles in which Ghanaians are engaged nor reveal the ways in which Ghanaians dispute narratives of a seamless homecoming. The connection to Ghana is then not nested on a shared struggle but rather solely on ancestral links."[67] This retrospective affiliation not only points to the ways in which tourism has become the primary form of engagement for post–civil rights African Americans, but also shows the troubling limits of the democratic aesthetic when exported abroad.

Finally, *Sankofa* uses racial alterity in order to judge and delineate the differences between commercial tourism and heritage tourism. The film begins with a group of white tourists whose appearance and behavior immediately mark them as cultural outsiders. When the drummer Sankofa approaches them, he rebukes them for defiling the memory of his enslaved ancestors. Instead of seeing them as tourists who see themselves as implicated in or heirs to the legacy of slavery as well, the film casts them as ignorant consumers of the slave fort. As commercial tourists with cameras and sun-visors, they represent interlopers and therefore have no historical claim to the fort. Similarly, both Mona and the fashion photographer appear as consumers who blaspheme the history of the fort because they are using the fort as the setting for their photo shoot. Nevertheless, unlike his condemnation of the white tourists, the character Sankofa does not admonish Mona for visiting the fort but for being unaware of its historical and ancestral significance for her. By the conclusion of *Sankofa*, Mona has metamorphosed from tourist to a cultural insider. Likewise, the group of white tourists has disappeared and Gerima replaces their illegitimate presence with a group of black men and women who presumably are from all over the African diaspora. Through these juxtapositions, *Sankofa* conflates commercial tourists as white Americans or Europeans and suggests that the only rightful claimants of the fort are members of the African diaspora. And yet, the film undercuts its own narrative of the African diaspora because it is Mona's African Americaness that becomes fundamental to Gerima's cinematic tale of remembrance and redemption. For Mona is emblematic of the thousands of disproportionately African American heritage tourists who annually travel to Elmina, Gorée Island, or Cape Coast Castle and expect to see an authentic site of slavery. In reality, the controversy about Cape Coast Castle takes place between Ghanaian historians and tourist officials and African American tourists; but in *Sankofa* the mnemonic debate is between the descendants of enslaved Africans and white tourists. By reclaiming Cape Coast Castle from white tourists, Mona literally and African Americans synecdochically can assert a mnemonic authority that neither fully subverts American civic myths nor incorporates contemporary (at times competing) Ghanaian uses and interpretations of the fort. When the film ends, Mona has finally found her African diasporic community that not only supplements her feelings of civic estrangement in the United States, but also approximates the slave fort Cape Coast Castle in Ghana (for a brief moment) as her authentic home.

Heritage tourism continues to be the most popular reason for African Americans to travel to Africa. They rarely linger there, but the visit itself enables black heritage tourists "to briefly escape American racism and experience racial dignity at its source."[68] Travel to the slave forts helps African Americans resist civic estrangement by both forgoing allegiances to the nation-state and by reinstating national hegemony. Not only do they reframe the language of belonging in the transnational discourse of the African diaspora, but by doing so they challenge the racial authority of American civic myths and national memory. And yet, travel to Africa to see sites of slavery risks rendering "Africa" to be only a site of slavery. In these narratives of homecoming and mourning, modern-day West Africa is neither engaged nor integrated. Ironically, as the democratic aesthetic resists civic invisibility of African Americans in the United States, heritage tourism to the slave forts often produces a visual rhetoric that results in a displacement of contemporary Ghana and Senegal. Revealing that the democratic aesthetic is predicated more on a commemoration of slavery's past than on having a vision of the future or establishing an alternative homeland in an emancipated African postcolonial present, these contemporary narratives overwrite most affective or ascriptive forms of diasporic citizenship and suggest that national belonging is the desired and inevitable outcome for African American returns to the homeland.

ON THE OCCASION OF THEIR VISIT: SLAVE FORTS AND THE AMERICAN PRESIDENCY

> We cannot push time backward through the door of no return. We have lived our history. America's struggle to overcome slavery and its legacy forms one of the most difficult chapters of that history. Yet, it is also one of the most heroic; a triumphant of courage, persistence, and dignity. The long journey of African Americans proves that the spirit can never be enslaved.
>
> PRESIDENT BILL CLINTON at Gorée Island, April 2, 1998

> Down through the years, African Americans have upheld the ideals of America by exposing laws and habits contradicting those ideals. The rights of African Americans were not the gift of those in authority. Those rights were granted by the Author of Life, and regained by the persistence and courage of African Americans, themselves.
>
> PRESIDENT GEORGE W. BUSH at Gorée Island, July 8, 2003

On the warm afternoon of July 11, 2009, President Barack Obama's twenty-four-hour tour of Ghana culminated with a visit to the famous slave fort at Cape Coast Castle. Accompanied by his wife, Michelle Obama, their daughters, Malia and Sasha, and his mother-in-law, Marian Robinson, Obama's sojourn to the slave fort was not entirely unprecedented. In 1998, President Bill Clinton's trip to Gorée Island was the first trip by an American president to this paradigmatic site of the transatlantic slave trade—a trip, it should be mentioned, that caused much furor at home because only a few days before, Clinton awkwardly confessed in Mukono, Uganda, that "European Americans received the fruits of the slave trade . . . and we were wrong in that."[69] Almost immediately, Clinton and his aides bemoaned that his admission would result in a demand for a national apology and claims for reparations for slavery. In response to this brouhaha, Clinton's speech at Gorée Island was a clever sleight of hand, in which he acknowledged America's slave past while evading its impact on contemporary U.S. race relations. Phrases like "we have *lived* that history" and "one of the most difficult chapter of *that* history" situated slavery and its legacy in a bygone past. In the end, Clinton's "apology" became part of a project to delete chattel slavery from the national memory—to forget it, in other words.

Even though Clinton might have rhetorically evaded the long-term remnants of slavery in the United States, his trip to Gorée Island simultaneously initiated a new ritual for the American presidency. Five years later, when President Bush visited Senegal, his trip was not clouded by fears of a national apology, but it did suggest that, like the African American heritage tourist, travel to the slave fort was an essential rite of passage for American presidents who sought to engage Africa and symbolically include African Americans in such gestures. However, unlike Clinton, who bemoaned the horror of the transatlantic slave trade while delicately dancing around America's own peculiar institution, Bush was much more explicit in his critique of the founding dyad of American democracy and slavery when he described the United States as "a republic founded on equality for all [that] became a prison for millions."[70] This mutuality of slavery and freedom, according to Bush, generated a genealogy of a particular form of critical patriotism in which "enslaved Africans heard the ringing promises of the Declaration of Independence and asked the self-evident question, then why not me?" By including enslaved African Americans in the founding narrative, Bush's speech appears to be in line with the democratic aesthetic produced in many post–civil rights African American representations of slavery. However, because this acknowledgment took place outside the United States and because of his conservative policies on race and economic equality, few considered Bush's rhetoric anything more than a symbolic speech-act. Ironically, even though Clinton and Bush generated different receptions at home for their trips to Gorée Island, neither president engaged the theme of slavery again once they returned to the United States. As such, Gorée Island emerged as a site of American presidential mediation and memorialization, a faraway, occasional place in which the ghosts of slavery remained, outside and beyond the purview of an American racial present.

It is within this historical context of apologies and admissions, however, that we should situate Obama's visit to Cape Coast Castle in July 2009. Departing from the standard tour of the House of Slaves in Senegal, Obama's choice of Ghana appeared particularly fitting for an American president still riding the wave of optimism that surrounded his own election as well as that of Ghana's newly elected democratic leader, John Atta Mills. Moreover, Ghana has a different history of pan-Africanism from Senegal. This relationship peaked when Ghanain leader Kwame Nkrumah offered dual citizenship to African American expatriates such as W. E. B. Du Bois and Maya Angelou in the 1960s, and Ghana became a primary destination for African American expatriates. And yet, when Obama emerged from the dungeons of Cape Coast Castle, he quickly framed his visit within a universal narrative of global trauma in general and that of the Holocaust in particular. Like Buchenwald, Obama noted, Cape Coast Castle "reminds us of the capacity of human beings to commit great evil."[71] By comparing his trip to Cape Coast Castle to his previous visit to the Buchenwald concentration camp, one of the first and largest concentration camps on German soil, Obama recognized that the slave fort similarly invokes a discourse of diaspora for African Americans, as Buchenwald does for the thousands of Jewish American tourists who travel there every year. By traveling with his immediate family, "with Michelle and our children" who are descendants of enslaved African Americans, Obama's trip also became part of a genealogy of ancestry and return to which the previous American presidents do not claim. "As Americans, and as African Americans," he went on to say, "obviously there's a special sense that on one hand this is a place of profound sadness; on the other hand, it is here where the journey of much of the African American experience began." Like Clinton and Bush, Obama establishes the slave fort as a constitutive site for African American identity; however, he departs from his predecessors when he simultaneously invokes the fort as "the portal through which the diaspora began" and frames Cape Coast Castle as a liminal space of two imagined communities, the betwixt and between of African Americans and the African diaspora. In this way, Obama cements a relationship between African Americans and Ghana that heritage tourism is built on, one in which, as Kevin Gaines notes, "the identification of Africa can be regarded not as a rejection of America but instead a crucial foundation for expressions of American citizenship."[72]

While travel to Cape Coast Castle could also have been a moment for the first Kenyan American president to also identify with Ghana's independence movements and its post-colonial present, the Ghanaian government seemed intent on celebrating the slave fort as the property of the African American heritage tourist. Unveiled at the Obamas' visit was a white marble plaque that now guards the doorway to the male slave dungeons: "This Plaque Was Unveiled By *President Barack Obama* and by *First Lady Michelle Obama* of the United States of America on the Occasion of Their Visit to Cape Coast Castle on the 11TH Day of July 2009." Placed directly across from the UNESCO plaque that vows to uphold the memories of those "ancestors" who have died, this new plaque further establishes the genealogy of New World slavery and American democracy, an almost exclusively African American and now an exceptionally American one, that begins at the slave fort and ends in the American White House. Despite the fact that Obama is not a descendent of enslaved Africans, as an American president and black American citizen he conterminously embodies a liberal narrative of American democracy and progress and the contradictory legacy of racial slavery. Unfortunately, Obama's implicit critique of the invisibility of slavery from the national rhetoric was short-lived, for like his presidential predecessors Obama returned home to the United States with no further mention of American slavery as the founding trauma of African American political identity. Moreover, the sense of optimism rather than racial melancholia to which Obama's speech appealed was easily undercut by the tumultuous nature of American politics and the very real and desperate material reality that Ghanaian citizens and African Americans faced during the rising global recession in 2009. For deeper in the male dungeons of Cape Coast Castle, the very same bowels in which Mona gets trapped in *Sankofa*, there is a sign that was put back in its place after Obama's trip. The words ask us to consider the cost of remembering slavery in the present. The black and white placard at the foot of the ancestral shrine reads: "President Obama! My Ancestors were Sold into Slavery. Where Are You on Reparations?"

I served you faithfully for thirty-two years and Mandy twenty years. At $25 a month for me, and $2 a week for Mandy, our earnings would amount to $11,680. Add to this the interest for the time our wages has been kept back and deduct what you paid for our clothing and three doctor's visits to me, and pulling a tooth for Mandy, and the balance will show what we are in justice entitled to. Please send the money by Adams Express, in care of V. Winters, esq, Dayton, Ohio. If you fail to pay us for faithful labors in the past we can have little faith in your promises in the future.

> Letter from JOURDAN ANDERSON to his former master,
> Colonel P. H. Anderson, Dayton, Ohio (1865)

You hear these white people talk about they've pulled themselves up by their own bootstraps. Well they took our boots, no less our straps, and then after they made us a citizen, honey, what did they turn around and do? They passed black codes in order to take from us all the benefits of citizenship.

> Reminiscences of AUDLEY MOORE (Queen Mother Moore),
> *Black Women Oral History Project* (1978)

FOUR

What Have We Done to Weigh So Little on Their Scale?

Mnemonic Restitution and the Aesthetics of Racial Reparations

IN DAVID REMNICK'S BOOK *The Bridge: The Life and Rise of Barack Obama* (2010), one of the president's former law students at the University of Chicago remarks on Obama's ambivalent feelings on reparations: "He told us what he thought about reparations. He agreed entirely with the theory of reparations. But in practice he didn't think it was really workable." The former student went on to say, "You could tell he let the cat out of the bag and felt uncomfortable. To agree with reparations in theory means we go past apology and say we can actually change the dynamics of the country based on other situations where you saw reparations."[1] A passing remark in Remnick's six-hundred-page book, this report of Obama's equivocal thoughts about reparations for slavery might have been little noticed if not for Henry Louis Gates Jr.'s *New York Times* op-ed piece on April 23, 2010, "Ending the Slavery Blame-Game." Gates notes that Obama's unlikely position as "African-American and president" gave him "the unique opportunity to reshape the debate over one of the most contentious issues of America's racial legacy: reparations."[2] Gates rightly pointed out the controversial nature of the slavery reparations debate in the United States. Within African American politics, the reparations movement has often revealed deep-seated class divisions. According to Adjoa Aiyetoro and Adrienne Davis, until very recently African American elites and their institutions have "largely rejected, belittled, or distanced themselves from racial reparations, perhaps as a strategy of racial respectability."[3] Among the larger American constituency, opinion polls continue to reveal a huge racial divide in popular attitudes toward reparations. In the most comprehensive poll to date conducted in 2004, more than half of black respondents agreed that they were entitled to some form of restitution for their ancestors' uncompensated labor, while more than 95 percent of white Americans rejected such a claim.[4] In stark contrast to the increasing interest in reparations among elite and non-elite African Americans in the early-twenty-first century, the interracial divide has remained constant. According to James T. Campbell, "In the long annals of American politics, one would be hard-pressed to find any issue on which white Americans exhibited such intense agreement."[5] As such, it is Obama's particular ancestry as a child of a black Kenyan father and a white American mother that makes him, according to Gates, "a leader who is uniquely positioned to bridge the great reparations divide." Through his unique racial and political lens, Obama would not only be able to acknowledge the interracial collaborations of the eighteenth- and nineteenth-century slave traders and owners, but as a result be more likely to hold all parties, European colonial powers, the United States, and the African kingdoms that participated in the transatlantic slave trade morally accountable and financially responsible.

As expected, Gates's thesis that African kingdoms such as the Asante in what is now Ghana and the Fon of Dahomey (now Benin) equally benefitted from the slave trade with their European and American counterparts created quite a stir. Highlighting the significance of the domestic slave trade in the United States, Eric Foner retorted that it was "Americans, not Africans, who created in the South the largest, most powerful slave system the modern world has known, a system whose profits accrued not only to slaveholders but also to factory owners and merchants in the North."[6] Likewise, Herb Boyd argued that "the United States was the greatest beneficiary, and thus should be the main compensator."[7] The lengthiest critique, however, came from Barbara Ransby, who contextualized both Gates's editorial and the ongoing legacy of slavery in the present. Situating Gates's essay as a form of "post-racial" discourse, Ransby argues that equating African complicity in the slave trade with European and American gains absolves Americans of the "financial responsibility" and the attendant affects, like "guilt" and "shame," that are produced by the "horrific legacy of slavery in the Americas."[8] For Ransby, Gates's post-racialism ignores the long history of reparations as a social justice movement and denies how slavery continues to shape racial inequalities today. By tracing the long arm of slavery to the twenty-first-century carceral state, Ransby changes the terms of the reparations debate from the diasporic back to the domestic, from the birth of the slave trade to its enduring legacy in the present, and from the "post-racial" to the racially biased penal system. Despite these significant rhetorical and ideological distinctions, what is striking about the Gates–Ransby public exchange is how it momentarily resurrected the reparations discourse that dominated the early part of the decade but appeared eclipsed by the election of the first African American president.

Nearly a decade before Gates's op-ed piece, Randall Robinson published his treatise *The Debt: What America Owes Blacks*. While Robinson's book did not catalyze the large coalition of pro-reparations grassroots organizers, legislators, attorneys, and academics that had been organizing since the late 1980s, his endorsement of reparations meant that it could no longer be read as a Black Nationalist fringe issue.[9] Taking the debate to popular culture, comedians Dave Chappelle and Chris Rock did skits on black people receiving pay checks as reparations, Aaron Sorkin's popular television show *The West Wing* dedicated an entire episode to the debate, and in November 2000 *Harper's* published a

"Forum" on the issue that featured the opinions of well-known litigation attorneys. Concurrently, a cottage industry of reparations antago-
nists, including Shelby Steele, Armstrong Williams, and David Horowitz, mounted a formidable anti-reparations protest. These debates
about how best to remember the past and understand its impact on the
present began to serve as an essential bridge between the more formal
demands for reparations and the growing call for a national remembrance of slavery. Unlike more traditional scholarship on reparations
produced almost exclusively by legal scholars or political scientists, this
chapter underlines the pivotal role that aesthetics have always played
within debates about reparations for slavery and racial equality. Influenced by and in conversation with the artists I have featured throughout this book, contemporary reparations advocates also value the politics of recognition as a form of restitution and have privileged what
W. James Booth calls "memory-justice" as a key strategy within their
twenty-first-century reparations discourse.[10] Considering the aesthetic
arm of the reparations for slavery movement, my approach is less preoccupied with proving the viability of reparations claims and more
interested in situating the contemporary African American reparations
discourse within the broader post–civil rights movement to reclaim
sites of slavery and reimagine democracy. By looking at the contemporary reparations campaign as part of the dominant poetics and politics
of post–civil rights African American culture, we can understand that
the issue, as Robin Kelley writes, "was never entirely, or even primarily,
about money. The demand for reparations was about social justice, reconciliation, *reconstructing* the internal life of black America, and elimi-
nating institutional racism."[11]

It is true that similar to their postbellum predecessors who tried to
overcome the economic disempowerment caused by slavery through
seeking a redistribution of material resources, post–civil rights African Americans invoke reparations as a form of economic citizenship
to which by birthright they should have access. When asked what the
freed people needed in 1862, Frederick Douglass answered, "We ask
nothing at the hands of the American people but simple justice and an
equal chance to live."[12] Douglass's response underscored the freedmen's
belief that owning land would be an act of restitution ("simple justice")
and a benefit of citizenship ("equal chance to live"). For those who had
previously been "propertied" themselves, reparations in the form of

land redistribution would secure those aspects of citizenship, both legal and economic, that slavery had denied them. Regarding notions of economic citizenship, I turn to Alice Kessler-Harris's *In Pursuit of Equity*, in which she explains how the right to work and the idea of economic freedom were gendered and racialized in the early twentieth century. Invoking the axiom that individual economic freedom enables political participation, Kessler-Harris, like Judith Shklar, argues that "the right to earn wages" was and continues to be a provision for "full participation in the polity."[13] Applying this notion of economic citizenship to post–civil rights African Americans, reparations advocates argue that because slavery unjustly deprived their forebears the rights and benefits of labor, the descendants of slaves inherited a secondary economic citizenship and therefore never had access "to the full play of power and influence that defines participation in a democratic society."[14] By historicizing African American reparations demands as part of a long social movement for economic justice, the contemporary reparations discourse argues that material restitution is a belated redress for the legacy of economic disenfranchisement and functions as a pre-condition for racial democracy.

But in addition to arguing for more traditional forms of reparations such as a redistribution of material resources, the post–civil rights reparations texts on which I focus—the lawsuits of *Cato v. United States* (1995) and *re African-American Slave Descendants Litigation* (2004), Randall Robinson's *The Debt*, and Mary Frances Berry's *My Face Is Black Is True* (2005)—concurrently ask for what I call "mnemonic restitution" in order to challenge the purposeful and "polite" national amnesia around slavery, as well as those practices of racism that uphold the civic estrangement of all blacks, naturalized or native born, that live in the United States. Clearly, there are major differences, in terms of reception and performance, between the filing of a lawsuit and the publication of a book. The legal reparations have a direct instrumental demand, such as material payments to the plaintiffs, which differ from historiographic intervention. Keeping these distinctions in mind, I focus primarily on their rhetoric of redress because the discourse of mnemonic restitution is what distinguishes reparations as a post–civil rights phenomenon. In these briefs and books, demands of mnemonic restitution become a way to lay claim to the nation through revising the historical record to include rather than excise slavery from the national consciousness and therefore fully recognize past and present African Americans in the civic myth and culture of the nation. Moreover, by requesting national slavery museums, formal apologies, historic commissions, and the public accounting of private corporations and institutions that benefited from American slavery, these narratives centralize the politics of recognition and the remembrance of slavery as a form of reparations. The demand for mnemonic restitution, then, like the civic estrangement it seeks to resolve, is not only ascriptive in its quest for belonging, but is driven by the attendant affect of yearning as well.

Since race, gender, ethnicity, class, and religion have historically determined who is to be included and excluded from the American national community, a contest over history becomes a contest of citizenship. These "ascriptive" aspects of U.S. citizenship not only mean having access to political power and protection of personal liberties but being included in the myths of civic identity or common histories, language, rituals, and customs with the majority of American citizens. Heavily influenced by post–Second World War demands from European Jews for both moral and material symbols of German atonement, the contemporary African Americans reparations rhetoric also posits an integral relationship between democracy, economic justice, and memory.[15] Like Jewish Holocaust survivors, contemporary African American reparation demands appeal to both the politics of remuneration and the politics of recognition for reparations, and, according to Elazar Barkan, "enable the victims to claim a share of the economic pie, and, perhaps even more important to legitimize their side of history."[16] In the case of Jewish Holocaust victims, defining and distributing reparations in the form of mnemonic claims was not only fundamental to the Federal Republic of Germany's desire to atone and to refashion its new national identity against that of Nazism, but it was also essential to the needs of Jewish victims and their descendants to mourn and collectively move forward. Despite its limitations, the German–Jewish reparations agreement remains the most extensive and most successful reparations program to date. Using this model of material and mnemonic justice, contemporary African American reparations advocates now package their restitution claims to include acts of national remembrance and consider it essential to their strategy of gaining the long overdue rights and privileges of civic membership.

Comparing contemporary African American reparations demands

to that of South Africa's Truth and Reconciliation Commission, Wole Soyinka noted that contemporary African Americans who sought to align their reparations claims with post-colonial African nations did so because they do not have full citizenship in the United States:

> If the slaves had been accompanied by a different quality of social integration into American society . . . the children of the black Diaspora, from their state of infinite contentment would have told the kinfolk on the other side to shut up, reminding them that their ancestors share the responsibility for selling them off to European slavers, that any compensation, in any case, should be made strictly to the descendants of those who endured the horrors of passage and the degradations of plantation.[17]

Citing an African American discourse of diasporic affiliation rather than Gates's African accountability, Soyinka suggests that transnational reparations rhetoric is the inevitable result of the ongoing social segregation of African Americans. Unlike its predecessor of legal segregation, social segregation speaks to the admixture of economic and civic disenfranchisement that African Americans continue to experience despite legal desegregation. Affectively, it is a form of "racial melancholia" in which African Americans who are continually estranged from the nation wrestle with feelings of disillusionment, mourning, and yearning, as well as the material effects of black economic vulnerability. Most post–civil rights African Americans who seek reparations direct their political grievances to the place and space in which their social segregation is born; as such, they remain steadfastly nationalistic in their political desires and disappointments, thus less likely to be diasporic in their claims and grievances.

Mnemonic restitution not only seeks a democratizing of American history and civic membership but is affective as well. Keeping in line with David Eng's distinction between political reparations and psychic reparations in *Feeling Kinship*, mnemonic restitution repairs the past and also promises to change our relationship with history itself.[18] Instead of casting the past as a bygone era, contemporary reparations advocates highlight the cost that forgetting slavery and ignoring black suffering has had on all blacks presently living their lives in the United States.[19] By demanding an apology or acknowledgment (as the lawsuits proffer) or revising the historical record (as Robinson and Berry do), they construct a lineage between slavery and our present and also seek to repair the massive racial disparities in which post–civil rights blacks are overrepresented in jail and among the nation's poor and underrepresented in politics and power. Cast in this light, contemporary African American reparations activists not only combine economic justice and memory-justice, but display a deep, ethical commitment to creating an alternative racial framework for the future. Moreover, while mnemonic restitution requires a collective working through of the difficult affects of grief, remorse, and shame associated with the trauma of slavery, it also imagines that new racially inclusive collectivities can thrive in the wake of such remembrances. This is so much the case that advocates think of reparations as essential to the process of reconciling the paradox of legal citizenship, economic disenfranchisement, and civic estrangement that has come to determine contemporary African American political identity.

Through close readings of contemporary reparations discourse, we gain insight into how legal citizenship (the right to vote), economic equality (the right to earn), and the even more intangible component of citizenship and civic membership (the right to recognition) all work together to define the parameters of national identity. As a result, we can understand the unprecedented emphasis on memory justice in contemporary reparations discourse as a strategic response to those ascriptive and affective forms of citizenship, like civic estrangement, that are still denied to African Americans. As a result, we can distinguish the modern reparations discourse not by its desire or call for distributive democracy, but rather, like the other contemporary narratives on slavery, by its return to the constitutive moment of black non-citizenship and absolute exclusion—slavery—as the primary vehicle to enable African Americans to be recognized and represented in the civic sphere.

TO BE FREE OF THE BADGES AND INDICIA OF SLAVERY: REPARATIONS LAWSUITS AND THE DEMAND FOR ACKNOWLEDGMENT

In their original bill, which they filed for themselves and others similarly interested, appellants, H. N. Johnson, C. B. Williams, Rebecca Bowers, and Minnie Thompson, alleged that within the years 1859 to 1868 they and their ancestors "were subject to a system of involuntary servitude" in states of the South, and that as a result of such servitude many million bales of cotton were produced.

JUDGE JUSTICE ROBB, *Johnson v. McAdoo* (1916)

Since the freedmen's land movement in 1865, African Americans have engaged in what Vincene Verdun calls different waves of reparations activism that have included petitioning, legislation, and, to a lesser-known extent, individual and class-action lawsuits.[20] Filed in 1916, *Johnson v. McAdoo* is the first known reparations lawsuit. Four African American plaintiffs represented by Cornelius J. Jones filed suit against U.S. Treasury Secretary William G. McAdoo in the District of Columbia Circuit Court for $68 million.[21] The complaint argued that the revenues and proceeds gained from the Internal Revenue Tax on Raw Cotton actually belonged to them because they were the laborers who picked the cotton but did not have access to their wages. As the Treasury Department vacillated from denying the existence of the cotton tax revenue to claiming that the aforementioned revenue was legally theirs, the district court eventually dismissed the suit by invoking the legal doctrine of sovereign immunity.[22] While this early reparations lawsuit stands out because it sought redistributive democracy for those who "were subject to a system of involuntary servitude," its emphasis on material restitution to legitimate demands for economic citizenship resurfaced in the reparations discourse of the late-twentieth-century cases *Cato v. United States* and *re African-American Litigation*. These lawsuits, however, do not simply add remembrance rhetoric to *Johnson v. McAdoo*, but also are responses to the limits of civil rights legislations that promised racial equality. While assaults against affirmative action are vicious attacks against policies that have provided unprecedented access for African Americans, desegregation and affirmative action in and of themselves have not led to full citizenship; instead, class divisions have led to essentially two black Americas. Grappling with that post–civil rights legislative disillusionment, the contemporary reparation movement—especially with its attention on incarceration and mass poverty—yearns to complete the unfinished project of democracy for African Americans.

Even though *Cato v. United States* now acts as a singular precedent for future federal reparations lawsuits, originally it was one of twelve complaints filed against the federal government for reparations for slavery. The plaintiffs, Jewel, Joyce, Howard, and Edward Cato of Oakland, California, sought compensation "for damages due to the enslavement of African Americans and subsequent discrimination against them, for an acknowledgement of discrimination, and for an apology."[23] In order to circumvent some of the legal doctrines that led to the immediate dismissal of *Johnson v. McAdoo*, the complainants of *Cato* referred to the Native American land claims case of *Oneida Indian Nation of New York v. State of New York* (1982) as a precedent to circumvent the statute of limitations and argued that the Thirteenth Amendment "created a national right for African Americans to be free of the badges and indicia of slavery" in order to challenge sovereign immunity. Despite these legal maneuvers, both the trial court and the appellate court dismissed the complaint and ruled that legislation rather than litigation was the most appropriate forum through which the plaintiffs should express their grievances and claims for restitution.[24] Regardless of the appellate court's eventual dismissal of *Cato v. United States*, the complaint itself offers remarkable insight into the three main areas in which remembrance has primacy within the African American reparations movement: the ritual of legal redress; the therapeutic language of trauma, loss, and healing; and the demand for a national apology for and acknowledgment of slavery.

Beginning with *Johnson v. McAdoo*, different waves of reparations lawsuits reveal an almost ritualistic preoccupation with writing the histories and contributions of enslaved African Americans into the official record. Filed against the backdrop of a post–Civil War reconciliation that excised slavery and African Americans from the narratives of reunification, the Johnson litigants sought redress on behalf of former slaves through the cotton tax and shone a light on the connections between black labor, land, and citizenship. The vast scale of their claims not only limited the degree to which a complete amnesia of slave labor could occur, but also institutionalized these memories into the public and juridical realms and fashioned itself as a originary source for the later (legal) representations of slavery. In some ways, the plaintiffs of *Cato* and *re African-American Litigation* are similar to the nineteenth-century slaves who turned to the courts to sue for freedom, negotiate labor contracts, and ultimately construct themselves as legal and political actors in a system that often denied their very humanity.[25] Through the posterity gained by entering one's grievance into the public record, the post–civil rights plaintiffs, those surrogates for former slaves, use litigation to keep the contributions of enslaved African Americans alive and to challenge the national amnesia about slavery. But the historiographic intervention is only one component of the democratic aesthetic here. "More than any other nation," James Campbell writes, "the historical redress debate in the United States has been waged in the language of torts."[26] Unlike the notable South African Truth and Reconciliation Commission, American reparations advocates almost always privilege the juridical realm as a way of influencing policy and accessing justice.

In doing so, the plaintiffs not only participate in the long history of black reparations activism, but also embody one of the most popular and public of American democratic performances: lobbying in court. As the most famous test case, *Brown v. Board of Education* (1954), shows, judicial rulings are important because they guide rulings in future cases and can represent a major policy victory for particular group interests. By filing the suit, the *Cato* plaintiffs asserted their legal right as citizens to launch a complaint of injury against the federal government. Thus, in both the formal language of tort reform and the forum of the courtroom, these lawsuits deploy a democratic practice that is rhetorical and performative and makes policy. In this sense, the reparations lawsuits should be distinguished from all the other aesthetic texts at which I have looked. In addition to their pursuit of memory-justice, these suits make claims on the law and use the performance of democracy in order to safeguard future black citizens from the harms of an inherited economic and civic injustice.

Following the tradition of *Johnson vs. McAdoo*, *Cato* sought monetary reparations from the federal government and argued that enslaved Africans and their present-day descendants should receive "$100,000,000 for forced ancestral indoctrination into a foreign society; kidnapping of ancestors from Africa; forced labor; breakup of families; removal of traditional family values; deprivations of freedom; and imposition of oppression, intimidation, mis-education, and lack of information about various aspects of their indigenous character."[27] Using the tort model, which allows persons to recover for all harm imposed by the assault, the *Cato* brief proffers a grand narrative of racial oppression in which slavery, despite its abolition, continues to overdetermine the life choices of post–civil rights African Americans. Here, slavery is not simply an institution of the past, but more similar to Pierre Nora's notion of memory as "a perpetually actual phenomenon, a bond tying us to the eternal present."[28] Therefore, in order to legitimate material restitution claims in the present for a past injury, the litigants invoke memory-language, interchange the past injustice with the present institutional racism, and fold individual trauma into collective victimization.

By highlighting mnemonic loss within its claims for monetary material restitution, the *Cato* suit invokes a psychoanalytic discourse of trauma and repair similarly enacted by authors such as Toni Morrison (*Beloved*) and Randall Robinson (*The Debt*). The plaintiffs seek restitution for "ancestral indoctrination into a foreign society; breakup of families; removal of traditional values; and mis-education and lack of information about various aspects of their indigenous character."[29] In this litany of past injustices, slavery is not only an institution that deprived enslaved African Americans of their right to control their labor and earn wages from it, but also a social structure that imported them into a foreign society while stripping them of their African pasts. Arguing that the wrongful act of slavery continues to affect the descendants of slaves, the litigants articulate an initial forced amnesia and an ongoing failure of memory as the foundation for their material claims. By filing a lawsuit and then foregrounding amnesia as a harm done within their brief, the *Cato* litigants counter the civic non-recognition or politics of forgetting with their textual remembrances.

Beyond drafting their reparations demands in the exclusive language of material restitution, the *Cato* complaint requested that the court "order an acknowledgement of the injustice of slavery in the United States and in the 13 American colonies between 1619–1865, as well as of the existence of discrimination against freed slaves and the descendants from the end of the Civil War to the present" and "an apology from the United States."[30] Unlike the claim for $100,000,000, these latter claims are not for material restitution for unpaid labor or unjust impoverishment. Instead, *Cato's* claims rest upon the German–Jewish reparations agreements in which remembrance and atonement are essential features of restitution. Furthermore, while acknowledgments and apologies appear to be indistinguishable, they actually function as distinct reparative acts. By seeking an acknowledgment of slavery, segregation, and ongoing racial discrimination from the federal government, the plaintiffs attempted to receive mnemonic restitution for their exclusion from national memory while simultaneously initiating the larger process of racial reconciliation. Additionally, when they asked the court to order the federal government to formally recognize its own culpability in the racial oppression of African Americans, the very need and nature of the complaint suggests that the United States has yet fully to admit either its history of racial subjugation or acknowledge the contributions and experiences of those African Americans who endured it. According to Trudy Govier, "The absence of acknowledgement is fundamentally undermining to those efforts to escape the vicious cycle of history. To further appreciate the destructive impact, we have only to look at such lack of acknowledgement from the perspectives of victims. . . . To acknowledge wrongdoing is to accept responsibility for it, and the acceptance of such responsibility is likely to have practical implications and costs."[31] By failing to remember those citizens whose historical realities run against the narrative of a seamless American democracy, the United States not only renders pre–civil rights African Americans to be historically insignificant but, as Govier notes, risks reproducing the racial paradigm created by slavery and perpetuated by segregation. As the *Cato* complainants pursued a national acknowledgment of American slavery and racial discrimination, they did so to assert their right to recognition and write enslaved African Americans back into the national narrative.

Reconstructions of the historical record, moreover, are implicit in national acknowledgments. The legal scholar Roy Brooks notes that clarifying the historical record "provides the factual foundation for apology," which is a necessary feature for racial reconciliation and atonement.[32] Similarly, Melissa Nobles asserts that official apologies to indigenous people in places like Australia, New Zealand, and Canada have helped assuage feelings of civic alienation and betrayal while advancing the process of national reconciliation.[33] In the United States, such apology politics surfaced when President Bill Clinton toured sub-Saharan Africa in 1998 and invoked the language of atonement at Gorée Island. Such an apology, Jeffrey Blustein explains, "if sincere, transforms the meaning of the past by expressing the responsible party's acknowledgement of the legitimacy of the victim's claim and the wrongness of the prior conduct. . . . Past wrong doing is repaired, and its significance retrospectively altered."[34] When the *Cato* litigants appealed for a national apology, they underscored the unresolved dispute between the individual plaintiff (a surrogate for all enslaved African Americans and their descendants) and the defendant, the United States. By asking for an apology as part of their reparations demands, the complainants not only referred to the original wrongful act of slavery but implied that the federal government had yet to acknowledge fully "the fact of the harm, accept some degree of responsibility, and promise not to repeat the offense."[35] Accordingly, this desire for both historical acknowledgment and a national apology in the late twentieth century further suggests that non-recognition or forgetting has become a significant marker of racial disadvantage and secondary citizenship. By demanding an act of public contrition, the *Cato* plaintiffs sought to resolve the post–civil rights African American paradox of legal citizenship and civic estrangement by replacing their marginalization from the historical record with an official remembrance of the lives and contributions of enslaved African Americans. The past is democratized and reconstructed: it no longer represents exclusion but constitutes a new site of shared authority. But because the litigants' claims are also on material (and not just mnemonic) grounds, the suit is also doing more. Unlike the plays, films, photographs, novels, and historical texts that I have considered in which historical intervention is a form of mnemonic restitution, this lawsuit is not aesthetic but a direct appeal to the law. Instrumentalist in purpose, it is ostensibly more far-reaching in its democratic strategy and victories.

After the court's dismissal of *Cato v. United States* in 1995, Deadria Farmer-Paellmann noted, "It was unlikely that the federal government would ever give African Americans permission to sue itself for slavery reparations."[36] By 1997, after recognizing the inherent difficulty of suing the government and reading a footnote in Vincene Verdun's 1993 *Tulane Law Review* article entitled "If the Shoe Fits, Wear It: An Analysis of Reparations to African Americans," Farmer-Paellmann began researching "who else owes reparations besides the government" and "started looking at corporations and private estates."[37] By deviating from the public action suits of *Johnson v. McAdoo* and *Cato v. United States* but still making claims on the law itself, Farmer-Paellmann tried to circumvent the sovereign immunity doctrine that heretofore limited the public litigations. Instead of seeking restitution for slavery from the federal government, she filed *Farmer-Paellmann v. FleetBoston* in the Eastern District of New York on March 26, 2002. By the end of the year, Farmer-Paellmann and the Restitution Study Group—a New York non-profit legal group—had filed nine reparations lawsuits around the country. The cases included twenty plaintiffs who demanded restitution from twenty private corporations in the banking, insurance, textile, railroad, and tobacco industries whose predecessors-in-interest financially benefited from and supported the institution of slavery.[38] In 2004, the consolidation of these complaints under the larger rubric of *African-American Slave Descendants Litigation*, filed in the North District of Illinois, resulted in a lengthy judicial opinion that dismissed the case on the grounds of standing, the political question doctrine, and the statute of limitation. Subsequent refilings and appeals were similarly dismissed.

In the *African-American Slave Descendants Litigation* lawsuit, the plaintiffs raised several distinct claims of conspiracy, piracy, and human rights violation that refer to wrongful actions of forced displacement, coerced labor, and lifetime enslavement.[39] The remaining claims of conversion and unjust enrichment seek restitution for the adverse impacts that slavery has had on present-day African Americans. Like *Cato v. United States*, these plaintiffs perceive intergenerational African American economic and social disempowerment as a direct by-product of American slavery and segregation. Specifically, the plaintiffs argue that the defendants not only failed "to account for/and or return to Plaintiffs and Plaintiffs class the value of their ancestor's slave labor" but that because of "the profits and benefits" derived from slavery, the defendants have been and continued to be unjustly enriched at the expense of enslaved African Americans and their descendants. Unjust enrichment often is the legal basis of restitution claims and refers to "the unjust retention of a benefit to the loss of another or the retention of money or property of another against the fundamental principles of justice or equity and good conscience."[40] Extending the unjust enrichment beyond the individual to the collective group of African Americans, the complainants of *African American Slave Descendants Litigation* have a causal argument in which they contend that when these corporations financially benefited from slavery while withholding said monies from enslaved African Americans, these private companies were able to reap the benefits from their initial profits long after the abolition of slavery.

Unlike these corporations, the majority of African Americans were unable, because of slavery, segregation, and institutional economic racism, to either inherit wealth from their predecessors or transfer wealth to their descendants. Consequently, as the corporations gained from the continuous compounding of their original investments in slave labor, generations of African Americans disproportionately constituted the American socioeconomic underclass. In the complaint, the plaintiffs note that they seek restitution in order to address the fact that "26 percent of African American people in the United States live in poverty compared to 8 percent of whites," and that "African Americans are more likely to go to jail, be there longer, and if their crime is eligible, to receive the death penalty. They lag behind whites according to every social yardstick: literacy, life expectancy, income, and education." [41] Unlike the monetary sum demanded in *Johnson* and *Cato*, these litigants do not seek a large financial sum but first ask the judge to order an "accounting" so they can better determine the amount of money these corporations gained by profiting from unpaid slave labor. Following the opportunity to look at the financial records of these corporations and their predecessors, the plaintiffs then demand "the imposition of a constructive trust," "the restitution of the value of their descendants' slave labor," "the restitution of the value of their unjust enrichment based on the slave labor," and "a disgorgement of illicit profits." [42]

While the demand for accounting has clear financial consequences for both parties, the claim also has significant mnemonic implications. By publicly forgetting the profits or gains made during slavery, these corporations continue to uphold images and narratives of an American past that exclude and omit pre–civil rights African American contributions and experiences. Legally, a judicial order for an accounting requires that the defendants disclose their financial records to the plaintiffs. Here, the plaintiffs demand that "a fair and just accounting be made for profits derived from the slave trade." They have been unable to assess the corporate records because "the defendants have failed to provide the plaintiffs with said records and have failed to comply with the plaintiffs' demands." In response, the complainants demand a judgment: "(1) requiring the defendants make a full disclosure of all their corporate records that reveal any evidence of slave labor or their profiting from the same; (2) seeking the appointment of an independent historic commission to serve as a depository for corporate records related to slavery; and (3) directing defendants to account to plaintiffs for any profits they derived from slavery." [43] Instead of striving for acknowledgment and thereby revising the official historical record through the act of a national apology, these plaintiffs sought acknowledgment by demanding an accounting and public disclosure from the defendants of the profits gained from slavery. According to the legal scholar Keith Hylton in "Slavery and Tort Law," to include a demand for an accounting is an unusual claim in tort suits, and "the fact that the reparations plaintiffs included a separate demand for an accounting suggests that there is something special about this part of the lawsuit."[44] Financially, to provide an accounting means to supply a written record of business transactions, assets, liabilities, and funds paid or received for a person or business. In this lawsuit, the plaintiffs claim that the defendants have not made their records a matter of public record or been forthcoming with the plaintiffs' request to survey these records. By withholding these records, these corporations ensure that the descendants of slaves have no way to discover the defendants' ill-gotten gains.[45] Their nondisclosure also enables these private institutions to deny any corporate responsibility.

But the call for the accounting is also an appeal to the politics of recognition. A public accounting "would also require disclosing information on how firms profited from the violence against African Americans during and after slavery."[46] Such an accounting would revise the historical record because it requires that these corporations admit their predecessors' active participation in American slavery and acknowledge that they inherited monies from slavery-era profits. Furthermore, these public disclosures would signify a formal remembrance of slavery and an integration of the history of American slavery into these corporate narratives. However, while the lawsuits demand an accounting from a limited number of defendants and therefore would only reveal a small portion of the slavery-derived profits, there are more far-reaching mnemonic consequences to such actions. First, it would increase the public understanding about the extent of wealth amassed by private corporations from the labor of black slaves. Given the national amnesia over slavery, the release of these records would provide deeper and more nuanced histories of the role that private companies (and perhaps the federal government) played in sustaining slavery. Additionally, it could also lead to a more fruitful application of the legal theory of unjust enrichment and substantiate African American claims that white Americans unfairly and continually benefit from the profits gained from slavery while the descendants of African American slaves inherit a place at the bottom of the socioeconomic hierarchy.

The plaintiffs sought a formal remembering of slavery through an accounting as well as through the establishment of an independent historic commission that would serve as a public archive of these corporate records. Historic commissions are both loci of historical authority and purveyors of historical narratives. Quite similar to the heritage museums in Ghana and Independence Mall in Philadelphia, historic commissions are memory institutions that ensure that documents, places, and practices "that are in danger of disappearing because they are no longer occupied or functioning will survive."[47] By requesting that an independent historic commission serve as a depository of these financial records, the plaintiffs seek to recognize the import of American slavery in the foundation of these corporations. Since these firms actually sought to keep their financial histories sealed, the historic commission would be a public archive whose sole purpose would be to safeguard and prepare historical documents for civic use and research. While the release of these records would not necessarily lead to a national remembering of individual enslaved African Americans, it does symbolize a formal integration of their collective experiences into the national consciousness and a rendering of the financial consequences of slavery to be a matter of public record. By acknowledging their predecessor's role in American slavery, these corporations would not only be displaying a gesture of goodwill toward the descendants of enslaved African Americans, but also actively institutionalize the remembrance of slavery as a condition for racial reconciliation.

Nevertheless, Farmer-Paellmann's lawsuits did not receive much support from the two main reparations groups, the grassroots National Coalition of Blacks for Reparations in America (N'COBRA), founded in 1987, and the Reparations Coordinating Committee (RCC), created in 2000 by Harvard law professor Charles Ogletree. Publicly critiquing her strategy in the *New York Times*, Ogletree sought to redirect the debate from corporate culpability to national responsibility: "The broader reparations movement seeks to explore the historical role that other private institutions and government played during slavery and the era of legal racial discrimination that followed."[48] Unlike the Cato litigants or Farmer-Paellmann, Ogletree is not seeking monetary restitution, but he believes bringing the federal government into litigation is important because "a full and deep conversation on slavery and its legacy has never taken place in America; reparations litigation will show what slavery meant, how it was profitable and how it has continued to affect the opportunities of millions of black Americans." N'COBRA released a similar statement in which the group "applauded" the corporate litigation, but it disagreed with efforts that did not "stress the central role the federal government played in the enslavement of Africans."[49] Both RCC and N'COBRA believed that excluding the federal government would be a great tactical loss: it would end up sacrificing much needed conversations and debates about slavery within the civic sphere. And yet despite these differences in strategies, N'COBRA, the RCC, Farmer-Paellmann, and the *Cato* plaintiffs all privileged mnemonic restitution in their tort claims because they framed it as justice for both the dead and the living. In order to address the intergenerational economic disempowerment of African Americans, the complainants sought a clarification of corporate profits and gains from slavery, segregation, and ongoing racial discrimination. In an attempt to confront the hegemony of national memory and those authoritative narratives of American history that forget American slavery, the plaintiffs set aside and privileged a formal remembrance of slavery in their demands. In the end, these lawsuits construct a democratic aesthetic that was never simply about money, but always about African Americans gaining full access to the three dimensions of citizenship.

THE BLANK CHECK OF HISTORY: RANDALL ROBINSON, MARY FRANCES BERRY, AND MEMORY DEBTS

> To have a museum chronicling the great crime that was African slavery in the United States of America would be to acknowledge that the evil was *here*. Americans prefer to picture the evil that was *there*, and from which the United States—a unique nation, one without any certifiable wicked leaders throughout its entire history—is exempt.
>
> SUSAN SONTAG, *Regarding the Pain of Others*

As these reparations lawsuits institutionalize and therefore democratize the national memory through juridical performances, their rhetoric of legal redress, and their formal demands for historical revision, Randall Robinson's *The Debt: What America Owes to Blacks* (2001) and Mary Frances Berry's *My Face Is Black Is True* (2005) also serve as models of mnemonic restitution. As such, while material restitution and economic citizenship might act as the societal wish-fulfillment of these texts, they posit "history" as a form of reparations to reconcile the post–civil rights African American crisis of representation, recognition, and membership in the public sphere. In order to resolve this narrative crisis (absence of formal signs and symbols of an African American past) and political yearning (civic estrangement), Robinson and Berry fill in what Jacques Le Goff calls the "archives of silence," which produce meta-narratives for post–civil rights African American economic and political estrangement and locate an alternative genealogy for African American claims of national belonging.[50]

In *The Debt*, social justice advocate and TransAfrica founder Randall Robinson endorses reparations for slavery as the way to supplement what he believes the United States owes multiple generations of African Americans for its institutionalized policies of racial discrimination and socioeconomic oppression. In his estimation, because the United States never compensated the former slaves for "two hundred and forty six years of massive wrongs and social injuries,"[51] the freedmen left slavery with such a severe socioeconomic disadvantage that their descendants continued to be "victims *ad infinitum*, long after the active stage of the crime [of slavery] has ended" (216). Robinson goes on to note that the adverse impact of slavery and segregation on contemporary African Americans is not only socioeconomic but also cultural. As such, his endorsement of reparations is less about legal citizenship than a direct challenge to the complicated socioeconomic and civic realities that contemporary African Americans inherited from their pre–civil rights ancestors. In response to this post–civil rights African American paradox of legal belonging and civic estrangement, Robinson puts forth a two-part reparations demand. The first aspect of his reparations demand is materially based and the second component is mnemonic. Ironically, despite its title, *The Debt* spends very little time discussing forms of financial restitution.[52] Instead, he constructs a non-tort model of restorative justice in which his claims for both material and mnemonic restitution stem from the non-recognition of enslaved African Americans in the official record.

More than insisting upon restitution for the "loss" of wealth and economic opportunities that defined African American poverty for most of the twentieth century, like the psychoanalytic language of trauma and loss in the *Cato* suit, Robinson demands reparations in order to heal the "psychic" damage that contemporary African Americans inherited from their forebears. To Robinson, reparations do not simply refer "to the transfer of material items or resources at all but to an admission of wrongdoing, a recognition of its effects, and, in some cases, an acceptance of responsibility for those effects and an obligation to its victims."[53] In contrast to what he sees as the more easily calculated economic injuries of racial oppression, Robinson contends that slavery relegated African Americans to being a people without myths and memory, thereby relegating them to becoming "history's amnesiacs" (16) who "alone are presumed pastless, left to cobble self-esteem from a vacuum of stolen history" (28). Here, economic wrongs need to be distinguished from psychological harm. For Robinson, it was the original wrongdoing of slavery that denied African Americans access to both African and American civic myths: "Maliciously shorn of his natural identity for so long, he can too easily get lost in another's. In any case, in America, there is little space *before*. *Before* the Mayflower. . . . *Before* that Dutch man-o'-war docked at Jamestown Landing in August 1619 with twenty Africans in its belly. . . . *Before* the Middle Passage. . . . And when *before* is on view, invariably it is white. Sight lines to the *before* that I require, that I crave, are blocked" (14).

Because slavery required Africans to endure what Orlando Patterson calls "social death," natal and cultural alienation were indispensable to their process of Americanization.[54] American slavery forced Africans to lose their "religions, languages, customs, histories, cultures, children, mothers, and fathers" (208). Unfortunately, as enslaved Africans grew geographically and chronologically distant from their indigenous languages, cultures, and religions, American slaveholders and politicians simultaneously denied them access to American citizenship, political protections, and civic myths. As a result, African American political identity stemmed from the systematic negation of their African cultural identities and from their legal exclusion from the American polity. For Robinson, since there has never been a nationalized effort to integrate the histories and images of enslaved African Americans in the civic landscape, contemporary African Americans remain victims because the "majority culture wronged us dramatically, emptied our memories, undermined our self-esteem, implanted us with palatable voices, and stripped us along the way of the sheerest corona of self-definition" (28).

For Robinson, this contemporary absence of African Americans from the civic landscape does not simply constitute harm to the individual psyches of African Americans, but also sustains a collective and national amnesia as well. He begins *The Debt* narrating a tour of the U.S. Capitol: "I looked straight up and immediately saw the callous irony, wondering if the slaves who had helped erect the structure might have bristled as quickly as I" (1). What Robinson notes as "callous irony" is both the appropriation of slave labor to build the massive Capitol and their glaring invisibility in its facade. When enslaved African Americans "cut the logs, laid the stones and baked the brick" of the building in the late eighteenth century, the Capitol acted as the literal and architectural home of American democracy. As such, the glaring disregard for black labor on the building's exterior corresponded to and further legitimated their status as non-citizens. However, Robinson's "bristle" is not simply a response to the fact that slaves built the massive structure, but that their contribution remains unrecognized more than two hundred years later. The ongoing erasure of enslaved African Americans from the history of the U.S. Capitol does not mirror the legal disenfranchisement of African Americans, but it does continue to echo their symbolic erasure from civic myths.

Following Robinson's critique of the Capitol, he goes on to describe the racial iconography of the *Frieze of American History*, which is located around the inside of the base of the dome. The "Frieze" is a painted panorama that includes scenes entitled "The Landing of Columbus," "The Landing of the Pilgrims," "Oglethorpe and the Indians," "The Declaration of Independence," "The Discovery of Gold in California," and "The Birth of Aviation." The only scene that even directly refers to American slavery is called "Peace at the End of the Civil War" and features a Confederate soldier and a white Union soldier shaking hands. Staring at the *Frieze* Robinson notes, "Although the practice of slavery lay heavily athwart the new country for most of the depicted age, the frieze presents nothing at all from this long, scarring period. No Douglass. No Tubman. No slavery. No blacks, period" (2). Although the "Frieze" alludes to the Civil War, its imagery of the Confederate and Union soldiers symbolizes the post–Civil War reunion of the South and North that came at the expense of African Americans' civil and political liberties. Ironically, through omitting images of freedmen and black soldiers, the "Frieze" acts as a monument that upholds the national memory and perpetuates a narrative of a seamless American democracy.

By forgetting slavery (and segregation, for that matter), the "Frieze" erases images of the past that directly conflict with the dominant narrative of celebrating American history and innovation. Whereas the racism that informed the initial design of the "Frieze" could contextualize the original absence of black Civil War soldiers, freedmen, or icons like Frederick Douglass and Harriet Tubman, the ongoing present-day omission of these icons and lack of historical revision underscores the contemporary exclusion of pre–civil rights African American narratives from the American pictorial landscape. Consequently, the Capitol and the "Frieze" continue to be "on proud display for the world's regards" as "the pictorial symbols of American democracy" (3). Robinson notes that despite the fact that "slavery lay across American history like a monstrous cleaving sword," the Capitol "steadfastly refuses to divulge its complicity, or even slavery's occurrence." Instead, "it gave full lie to its own gold-spun half-truth. . . . It kept from us all—black, brown, white—the chance to begin again as co-owners of a national democratic idea. It blinded us to our past and, with the same stroke, to any common future" (7).

Instead of walking on the Washington Mall with the sense of authority or pride that comes with civic membership, Robinson, like his forebears, can only see his invisibility. While the Mall is alleged to be "America's iconographic ideal of itself" (6), Robinson observes its absences: "No statues. No monuments. No legends. No Lore. No tonic of dark immortality to brace the soul. No explanations from the masters of global information. Only silence to my needs" (38). Robinson's narrative suggests that this national blindness about slavery has not only disinherited African Americans from founding narratives and civic myths, but has also compromised the American democratic ethos. The inconsistency of these narratives puts both African Americans and the larger nation at risk: "White people do not *own* the idea of America, and should they continue to deny others a place in the idea's iconograph, those others, who fifty years from now will form the majority of America's citizens, will be inspired to punish them for it" (174). Robinson notes that the United States could achieve true democracy once it "dramatically reconfigure[s] its symbolized picture of itself, to itself. Its national parks, museums, monuments, statues, artworks must be recast in a way to include all Americans." (174).

By doing so, the United States not only "opens itself to a fair telling of all its people's histories, and accepts full responsibility for the hardships it has occasioned for so many" (173), but also can amend its past injustices by reconstructing images and interpretations of the past that include the massive contributions of African Americans. By situating the acknowledgment of enslaved African Americans in the national memory as an essential component of his reparations demands, Robinson seeks mnemonic restitution for past and present civic estrangement. In a radical departure from pre–civil rights African American reparations demands, here the formal remembrance and atonement of slavery are equally as important as the redistribution of material resources. Because slavery was the root cause of African American legal, economic, and cultural impoverishment, "solutions to our racial problem are possible, but only if our society can be brought to face up to the massive crime of slavery and all it has wrought" (7). Robinson shapes a pro-reparations argument to gain the rights and privileges of civic membership.

While Robinson notes that reparations should entail the integration of multiple histories, he suggests the specific program called "a Year of Black Presence" as a form of mnemonic restitution: "Every black church, organization, and institution would commit to choose one-day of the 130-odd days that the Congress is in session and bring on that day one thousand African Americans to walk the halls of Congress in support of compensation measures designed to close the economic and psychic gap between whites and blacks in America" (247). In stark contrast to the glaring invisibility of African Americans from the façade of its building, the Year of Black Presence would mandate that "Congress, for one year, would never stop seeing our faces, never stop hearing our demands, never be relieved of our presence" (247). As such, African Americans could exercise their legal rights as citizens to petition the federal government, but also use their bodies to fill in the voids and the forgotten histories of enslaved Africans in the national landscape. Robinson proclaims that contemporary African Americans must use black corporeality, the one "asset" they have in "abundance," to win the battles over memory and poverty. By asking African Americans to appeal to Congress, Robinson underscores his larger democratic aesthetic. Instead of rejecting the monumentality of American civic myths and memorials such as the U.S. Capitol, Robinson's "Day of Black Presence" requires that African Americans physically inhabit the symbol of American democracy—the halls of Congress—thereby refashioning this national symbol into a site of slavery. By doing so, post–civil rights African Americans would concomitantly assert their rights as legal citizens to claim the symbols of the nation-state, while simultaneously performing and perhaps guaranteeing their right to recognition and civic belonging.

While *The Debt* calls for distributive democracy within the moral framework of the remembrance and recognition of slavery, in *My Face Is Black Is True*, the historian Mary Frances Berry, the former chairwoman of the United States Commission on Civil Rights, turns to historical writing itself as a contested site of meaning and memory in order to legitimate post–civil rights African American demands for economic and civic citizenship. Detailing the story of Callie House and the Ex-Slave Mutual Relief, Bounty, and Pension Association, Berry provides a historical antecedent for the contemporary African American reparations movements, which enables us to understand this post–civil rights redress, not as arbitrary but as part of a long history of enslaved African Americans seeking recompense and recognition for their unpaid labor. By doing so, Berry's narrative renders historiographic intervention as a form of mnemonic restitution while also memorializing the Ex-Slave Pension Association as the moral foundation upon which African Americans, like Farmer-Paellmann's lawsuits, could mandate their later claims for material restitution.

By placing the "the marginalized, the overlooked, and the rejected" histories of former slaves at the center of her narrative, Berry reconstructs the long history of African American demands for citizenship as emphasizing reparations.[55] Inspired by the counter-memory of African American oral histories, Berry privileged the oral history accounts of the Ex-Slave Pension Association into her article "Reparations for Freedmen, 1890–1916: Fraudulent Practices or Justice Deferred" (1972) for the *Journal of Negro History*.[56] In order to publish this first historical narrative on Callie House and the Ex-Slave Pension Association, Berry solely relied on the official records of House's court transcript in the National Archives. This lack of evidence underscores two compelling realities about the National Archives: it reveals the ways in which it serves as officiators and depositories of national histories, and it reflects how such national histories are synonymous with civic myths, determining who belongs to the nation and who deserves to be consigned to the dustbins of history. Due to the absence of primary source material on House, Berry spent a great deal of the article refuting the official record and the charges of fraud brought against the Ex-Slave Pension Association by the federal government in 1917, but she was unable to remove the full cloak of suspicion haunting House's legacy. Instead, Berry concluded the article by admitting that she needed to conduct "further investigation" and "must await other evidence, if it indeed exists."[57]

Because there are no first-person accounts from the ex-slave petitioners themselves, Berry's later historical monograph on House is even a more radical intervention. *My Face Is Black Is True* creates a counter-archive that "reconstructs the lives of people who leave no diaries, or accessible materials."[58] This archive did not require Berry to invent a useable past, but rather reread "the footprints they left" in the racialized rhetoric of the government records, the exculpatory materials from the court trial against the Ex-Slave Pension Association, and mainstream and African American newspapers accounts. While this excavation of history in and of itself serves a formal recognition of the enslaved African Americans, Berry issues her text as a new archive for the contemporary reparations movement. Berry returned to her research on the Ex-Slave Pension Association movement because she was inspired by the success of Robinson's *The Debt* and the renewed interest in reparations for slavery. To counter the loud critiques that contemporary African American claims for redress were without merit or precedent, Berry revealed that African Americans have been demanding reparations since Emancipation and that they understood the symbiotic relationship between receiving compensation for unpaid labor and the path toward full citizenship.

Through Berry's retrospective reading of African American reparations movements, the multidimensionality of both American citizenship and African American restitution demands becomes even clearer. More specifically, by emphasizing how House deliberately framed the reparations discourse as proof of African American loyalty to the Union during the Civil War, Berry underscores the inextricable link between economic enfranchisement, citizenship, and critical patriotism. Berry notes that reparations activism created "a democratic structure in which local people had control and a voice, at a time when blacks were practically disenfranchised" and enabled them "to exercise their citizenship rights to gain a new law at a time when disenfranchisement had closed other avenues for political action" (179). Under the leadership of House, an ex-slave and washerwoman, the Ex-Slave Pension Association began in 1890 and had at its peak about 300,000 members in cities and rural communities throughout the South. Comprising ex-slaves and their families between 1890 and 1917, the organization repeatedly petitioned Congress to distribute a monthly federal allowance or pension to former slaves. Through these petitions, the members of the Ex-Slave Pension Association asked for restitution not only because "generation after generation of Colored people served this country as slaves for two hundred and forty-four years or more," but because, as "citizens of the United States," they believed "it was just and right to grant the ex-slave pensions."[59] In 1899, as the Ex-Slave Pension Association began pamphleteering in southern black communities, the majority of African Americans no longer believed that they would receive land and were highly doubtful they would ever receive any form of compensation for their slave labor. Consequently, more than simply convincing the former slaves that they had a right to articulate their hardships to their representatives through petitions, House and the Ex-Slave Association premised their reparations campaign, as *Johnson vs. McAdoo* later would, on what Judith Shklar defines as the symbol of national belonging, the opportunity to earn.[60]

In order to dispute the charges that the contemporary reparations advocates are frauds who capriciously seek monies, Berry reveals through House that this originary reparations movement understood that individual economic freedom was paramount to political participation. She depicts House as a leader who truly believed that "these old African American men and women, aging, ill, and impoverished from hard work and ill treatment during slavery—many of whom were the relatives of the middle class—deserved recognition" (61). Through the Ex-Slave Pension Association, House argued that the federal government should no longer view slave labor as expendable but comparable to other forms of compensated labor and therefore should compensate them for their past work by assisting them in their retirement. In a letter that she included as part of the Ex-Slave Pension Association Convention proceedings in 1899, House wrote:

> I have been a promoter of the Ex-slave bill and an advocate of the National Ex-Slave Mutual Relief, Bounty, and Pension Association. For the past twenty-five months I have been among strangers laboring to the

best of my ability for the rights which my race is justly entitled to. It is my firm belief that honest labor should be rewarded, regardless of the skin color of the man or woman who performs that labor. I am in favor of the principles embodied in the Mason Bill because they are just, and should the Bill receive the consideration it richly merits, it will, in my opinion, be but a question of time when those of our race who have borne the burden and heat of the day, will receive some recompense for honest labor performed during the dark and bitter days of slavery. (78)

By repeatedly defining their labor as "honest" and by stating that "regardless of skin color," the government should remunerate the former slaves, House equated the black laborer with the white laborer in order to justify black demands for restitution. In a radical protest against the second-class citizenship imposed on African Americans, House publicly redefined the former slave as someone who had the inalienable right to control and to earn for his or her labor. Nonetheless, it was not simply the work expended during slavery that House believed should be compensated, but the work during the Civil War itself in which African Americans functioned as unpaid laundresses, nurses, and manual laborers for the Union Army. In House's estimation, these African Americans not only continued to work without compensation, but did so with an unfaltering sense of civic duty.

The government not only denied African Americans their earned pensions, but consciously denied all blacks, former slaves and freedmen alike, the same treatment granted white Union soldiers who "served ninety days from the battlefield" and were guaranteed both pay and pension. Therefore, while the pensions offered former slaves a financial remuneration, they also, in the words of the historian Elizabeth Regosin, "represented an essential right of American citizens, the right to compensation for services rendered to the country."[61] If we can read House's pension association as a campaign for economic citizenship, then House's process of petitioning could be considered part of an antecedent affect of yearning for recognition and civic membership. According to Berry, by "trying to put the name of every ex-slave on a petition asking Congress to pass a bill providing pensions" (60), House literally recognized and provided a public space for the names, identities, and histories of hundreds of thousands of former slaves. When the former slaves placed their signatures on these petitions, they not only expressed their commitment to the legislative process, but also challenged the prevailing national forgetting of African American experiences in and resistances to American slavery. Through its varied national chapters, the movement created a space in which the former slaves could share their personal memories of slavery with each other. From state to state, the members of the Ex-Slave Pension Association substantiated their claims for pensions by testifying about their experiences in slavery. As such, by becoming members, attending meetings, and signing petitions that validated their restitutionary demands, these former slaves prevented a complete erasure of their contributions.

Furthermore, because the Ex-Slave Pension Association was a national movement that directed their appeals toward the federal government, Berry reminds us that their activities helped keep the memory of slavery alive in the national landscape. In the early years of their movement, the pension reparations campaign peaked. By seeking compensation for their labor during slavery, the members of the Ex-Slave Pension Association blatantly challenged the racialization of national memory while proffering an interpretation of the past that included the voices and experiences of the former slaves. As the national memory paralleled and reinforced the political and civic segregation of African Americans, the Ex-Slave Association used the testimonies of ex-slaves in order to assert and reap the legal benefits of their citizenship and to counter their invisibility in the national memory. Berry concludes *My Face Is Black Is True* by rearticulating her two-fold argument about political genealogy and historical precedent. First, she underlines how the federal government conspired to deny African Americans monies earned and rights guaranteed them by law through racial intimidation, false charges, and coercion. As the movement grew, so did government persecution of the organization through the U.S. Postal Service. Eventually, the government not only refused to pass the pensions bill and invoked sovereign immunity in *Johnson vs. McAdoo*, but also, in a move that anticipates Marcus Garvey's eventual downfall, prosecuted and incarcerated House for mail fraud in 1917. Berry's emphasis on the government's successful repression of this labor movement solidifies her narrative of an ongoing demand for recognition and compensation for slave labor by African Americans on one hand, and the capacious nature of American citizenship on the other. Berry's book answers David Blight's grave question: "Was the best chance at slave reparations in American history missed in Callie House's failed or crushed movement?"[62] If not for the government's segregationist pension policies, African Americans would have gained some of the benefits of their work and the rights of national belonging.

Second, Berry's epilogue "The Reparations Movement Still Lives" casts House as the foremother of the post–civil rights reparations movement. By doing so, Berry is in dialogue with those black feminist projects that reconstruct black women's resistance in our contemporary understandings of slavery as well as our history of black freedom. While Berry does not use House, as Robin Kelley cogently argues, "to look at gender" and "consider things like women's unpaid labor, reproduction, sexual abuses, and ways to make restitution for these distinctive forms of exploitation,"[63] she does cast House as a "racial outlaw," with specific gendered implications. This not only places black women's political labor as the foundation of the modern-day reparations campaign, but at the center of black radical discourse. Berry achieves this genealogical intervention by tracing how the varied restitution discourses of Marcus Garvey and the United Negro Improvement Association (UNIA) in 1929, "Queen Mother" Moore's "The Reparations Committee of Descendants of United States Slaves" (1959), and James Forman's "The Black Manifesto" (1969) served not as discrete political movements, but as simultaneous reiterations and remembrances of the desires and "discontent" of Ex-Slave Pension Association members themselves. "African Americans in later generations have made progress," Berry states in closing, "but the underlying issue of appropriate payment is still unresolved. Mrs. House tried and failed to gain reparations for those African Americans still alive, who were the first generations to survive slavery" (251).

By reconstructing this lineage, Berry also circumvents legal arguments about the descendants of slaves having been affected by the institution of slavery and the moral debates about ahistoricity.[64] Instead of focusing on cumulative damage to justify the need for reparations, Berry's excavation of history underscores how the government denied African American citizens their rightful mnemonic and material claims and therefore bequeathed secondary economic and civic citizenships to multiple generations. Unlike the tort-model and its attendant performative elements, Berry's text underlines the long history of reparations, a call for historicity that contextualizes prior articulations of the "possibility" (251) for full citizenship of African Americans. By deliberately

denying the former slaves both the right to earn and their right to recognition, the United States failed to manifest the promise of American
democracy and ensured that African Americans continue to have an
estranged and inferior membership in the polity. For Berry, "those who
act in the cause today pay homage to their struggle and to the spirit of
Callie House," and they render their demands for citizenship as a pair-
ing of the mnemonic and material reparations.

WHY SORRY MIGHT NOT BE ENOUGH: THE COST OF REMEMBERING AND THE LIMITS OF MNEMONIC RESTITUTION

Truth as a prelude to reconciliation, that seems logical enough; but Truth as
the sole exaction or condition for Reconciliation? That's what constitutes a
stumbling block.

WOLE SOYINKA, *The Burden of Memory, the Muse of Forgiveness*

Despite the ongoing political resistance from legislators, conservative
scholars, and the majority of white Americans, there have been some
recent gains for reparations advocates. None of these successes has resulted in the redistribution of material resources to African Americans,
but only as acts of mnemonic restitution.

In the lawsuit *African-American Slave Descendants Litigation*, the plaintiffs called for a formal accounting of corporate records in order to
ascertain how companies originally profited and continue to benefit
from American chattel slavery. While the court ruled against the plaintiffs' request, there are now several laws around the country that require private corporations to reveal these records publicly. In October
2000, California passed a slavery-era disclosure law requiring insurance
companies to report on their role during slavery. Sponsored by State
Senator Tom Hayden, the law became the model for similar legislation
passed in more than a dozen states around the country. While none
of these corporations had distributed any material restitution to African Americans, the pressure from state and local governments and the
public disclosure of their companies' participation in slavery have com-
pelled many corporations to apologize. In 2003, a Chicago ordinance
required companies that did business with the city to disclose whether
they or any of their corpoate predecessors had profited from slavery.

In 2005 the chairman and chief executive of Wachovia, G. Kennedy Thompson, disclosed that the Georgia Railroad and Banking Company and the Bank of Charleston—institutions that ultimately became part of Wachovia through acquisitions—had owned slaves. More specifically, Georgia Railroad and Banking Company owned at least 162 slaves and the Bank of Charleston accepted at least 529 slaves as collateral on mortgaged properties or loans. The Bank of Charleston also acquired an undetermined number of people when customers defaulted on their loans. In response, Thompson issued the following written statement: "On behalf of Wachovia Corporation, I apologize to all Americans, and especially to African Americans and people of African descent . . . We know we can't change the past, and we can't make up for the wrongs of slavery, but we can learn from our past and begin a dialogue about slavery and the experience of African Americans in our country." [65]

Partly in response to Robinson's demand for mnemonic restitution and the non-recognition of enslaved African Americans in the U.S. Capitol Building, in 2005 members of the House of Representatives established a task force to study the history of and memorialize the slave labor used in the construction of the Capitol. Rep. John Lewis (D-Ga.), who with a former Republican member of Congress from Oklahoma, J. C. Watts, launched the task force, is quoted as saying, "I don't think the story of the Capitol would be fully told until we have something depicting the lives of the people who helped build it." [66] By integrating the history and contributions of those enslaved African Americans who never received compensation for building the U.S. Capitol, the task force engaged in a deliberate democratizing of American history. This was taken a step further in July 2008 when the House of Representatives passed a resolution apologizing to African Americans for slavery and the era of Jim Crow, a stance considered unthinkable only a decade earlier when President Bill Clinton made a similar gesture. Indeed, the resolution was the first time a branch of the federal government had apologized for slavery. Citing the trips to Gorée Island by Presidents Clinton and Bush as precedents for national acknowledgments of "the racism against persons of African descent" engendered by slavery and segregation, the resolution did not discuss material restitution despite its "commitment to rectify the lingering consequences of the misdeeds committed against African Americans under slavery and Jim Crow." [67] In addition to an acknowledgment, the resolution also offered a national apology—one quite similar to that sought by the *Cato* plaintiffs in 1995. Both the acknowledgment and the apology served to "move forward and seek reconciliation, justice, and harmony for all of its citizens." This recognition, much like the recent acknowledgments by Brown University, Emory University, and the University of Alabama as former slaveholding institutions, however, did little to address the present-day impact of racial inequality. In this way, the emphasis on national contrition is a double-edged sword, enabling the federal government to acknowledge this founding sin without a proposal for a radically different racial future or an engagement with the racial inequities that thrive in the post-slavery era. In short, the living suddenly risks becoming more invisible than the dead.

While reparations activists characterize mnemonic reparations as an apology, a revision of the historical record, and a public accounting of corporate records—all essential aspects of the reparations movement—they also understand that these symbolic changes must be accompanied by a structural transformation of the American economy. As such, in order for remembrance to begin the process of racial reconciliation and national healing, it has to correspond to tangible effects in both the legal and economic spheres of citizenship, much like those agreed upon in the post–Second World War German-Jewish restitution packages. In other words, the crisis of recognition that initially generated these contemporary representations of slavery was never simply about symbolic integration, be it the formation of a U.S.-based slavery heritage museum or the election of the first African American president, but often about shifting the conversation about racial equality from suffrage to economic, juridical, and civic enfranchisement. As Anne Cheng warns, while the public airing of grievance might promise public recognition, it is not without its potentials, for it "cannot really grant subjecthood to the disenfranchised since, strictly speaking, to be 'recognized' is still to occupy an object position."[68] The cost of recognition might be too high: it still requires that the dominant culture serve as the arbitrator of belonging, visibility, and remembrance. Not only might this ensure that African Americans remain guests at their own negotiation table, but it also asks the federal government and multinational corporations to contradict their own founding narratives of liberal progress and their "underlying ambivalence towards difference."[69] It also suggests that the art might be able to do the work of mnemonic restitution better than the state or rather that a novel, like Reed's *Flight to Canada*, can enact mnemonic restitution more effectively than a legal brief and acknowledgment by the state ever can. Thus, while the remembrance of slavery by the state, private corporations, and universities might lead to recognition, a central tenet of citizenship, it has yet to materialize into full racial freedom.

The central argument of this chapter and this book is that the recognition of slavery in the civic sphere will expand the parameters of African American citizenship. Post–civil rights African American artists, writers, and intellectuals consciously returned to sites of slavery to both contest the systemic erasure or non-recognition of blacks from the civic landscape and to model the tenets of a more flexible and radical democratic future. However, by examining the advantages and limitations of mnemonic restitution within the larger discourse of remembrance, recognition, and citizenship, we can better ascertain the effectiveness of these reparations narratives on American citizenship itself. In some ways, the revival of the reparations movement indicates what Ralph Ellison would describe as the "changing same" of racial African American economic, political, and social disenfranchisement. The resurfacing of slavery as one of the central leitmotifs in African American cultural production underscores the capaciousness and durability of American civic myths. These reconstructions of slavery have always corresponded to both those economic and symbolic markers of American citizenship that constitute racial exclusion, as well as to those African American desires to assert the rights and to claim the benefits of their legal citizenship. Recognizing the multidimensionality of American citizenship, contemporary African American reparations advocates nevertheless do not demand recognition in order to extricate African Americans from the nation, but rather to ensure that African Americans are fully integrated into the "We the People" that defines the American nation-state.[70] Consequently, the contemporary reparations movement has had to shape its demands, not exclusively in terms of material restitution but also to resolve African American civic estrangement. It has been about shifting the political discourse on citizenship from that of legal rights to that of civic membership and economic justice. Resisting romantic narratives of liberal progress, contemporary reparations advocates are critical patriots who neither encourage idolatry of the nation's past nor emphasize a blind loyalty to the state. They turn to the past not simply to come to terms with it, but to imagine a utopian future. Whether or not African Americans will ever receive reparations for slavery remains up for debate, but the reparations debate itself continues to reveal the economic despair and the political potential that define post–civil rights America.

There is no place you or I can go, to think about or not think about, to summon the presences of, or recollect the absences of slaves. . . . There is no suitable memorial, or plaque, or wreath, or wall, or park, or skyscraper lobby. There's no 300-foot tower, there's no small bench by the road. There is not even a tree scored, an initial that I can visit or you can visit in Charleston or Savannah or New York or Providence or better still on the banks of the Mississippi. And because such a place doesn't exist . . . the book had to.

TONI MORRISON, "A Bench by the Road"

The President's House, Freedom, and Slavery in the Age of Obama

ON THE WARM MORNING of March 18, 2008, Senator Barack Obama invoked the quintessential American credo of "We the People" in order to quell the political fallout generated by the controversial statements of his pastor, the Reverend Jeremiah Wright, about 9/11 and U.S. foreign policy. By opening with the foundational prose of the U.S. Constitution in what became known as his "race speech," delivered in Philadelphia across from both Independence Hall and the Liberty Bell, Obama thoroughly embraced the symbolic and the comforting refrain of American civic myths to navigate the muddy waters of presidential politics. But even as Obama reproduced the nationalist rhetoric of the timeless promise of American ideals codified in the shared past and parchment of American democracy, he simultaneously deployed a more radical mnemonic strategy. Rather than simply invoke the mythology of American Freedom by way of elision or selective forgetting, Obama instead acknowledged the racial logics of the U.S. past and simultaneously put forth a sobering counter-myth: "The document they produced was eventually signed but ultimately unfinished. It was stained by this nation's original sin of slavery."[1] While many pundits and politicians lauded this racial exegesis as sweeping and groundbreaking, they failed to recognize how resonant Obama's speech was with another controversy about the Liberty Bell, slavery, and presidential politics that had been brewing in Philadelphia since 2002. Directly across from the site of Obama's speech, along with Independence Hall and the Liberty Bell, stood the original "White House," the executive mansion of President George Washington and the home of the enslaved African Americans who worked for him.

After a long and highly public debate about whether or not a federal site should acknowledge America's foremost symbol of democracy (Washington) and its foremost national sin (slavery), the original "White House" opened with the title "The President's House: Freedom and Slavery in the Making of a New Nation" in December 2010 after an $11.2 million restoration project. The controversy began in 2002 when the public historian Edward Lawler published an article entitled "The President's House in Philadelphia: The Rediscovery of a Lost Landmark."[2] Lawler was writing in response to the expansive Liberty Bell Center project, a $13 million memorial spurred by the Independence National Historical Park (INHP), a local branch of the National Park Service, to move the Liberty Bell to the heart of the Independence Visitor Center Park. As a potentially lucrative site of American heritage tourism, the INHP superintendent and staff considered the Liberty Bell "the greatest relic of America's heroic age."[3] More than a holdover from another age, the Liberty Bell stood as a tangible symbol of "America's unvaunted qualities: independence, freedom, unalienable rights, and equality."[4] While Lawler commended the spirit of the project, his ninety-page report detailed the history that would be obscured by the construction of the new pavilion. The site of this new construction was once the location of a modest mansion belonging to the widow of William Masters, a mayor of Philadelphia in the mid-eighteenth century and one of the city's largest slaveholders. Moreover, and perhaps more dramatically, the mansion was home to both George Washington and John Adams during their respective tenures as presidents of the young United States. Despite such history, the President's House was demolished in 1952 in order to create the Independence Mall. When the INHP proposed the Liberty Bell Center project in 2002, the plan did not include a restoration of this building, but rather the placement of a public restroom at the same location.

In an effort to stave off the threat of historical obscurity that the Liberty Bell Center project posed to the President's House, Lawler argued for the National Park Service to unearth the original foundation of the Washington-Adams mansion rather than pave over it. He also described the probable layout of Washington's home, highlighting its slave quarters. Similar to the historical interventions that Annette Gordon-Reed's conjectures advance in *Thomas Jefferson and Sally Hemings*, Lawler's conjectured floor plans helped to fill in the missing history of American slavery in the early years of the republic. His blueprints not only reveal that Washington confined his slaves to a small room on the first floor of the home, but also suggests that Washington went to great lengths to skirt the gradual abolition of slavery in Pennsylvania, rotating the home's enslaved African Americans every six months. Initially, the INHP contested Lawler's conclusions—especially those about the slave quarters—and refused to incorporate a memorial of the forgotten President's House in its designs for the Liberty Bell Center. A former INHP staff member, Jill Ogline, articulated her own misgivings and those of the National Park Service when she wrote, "[To acknowledge] the Liberty Bell's proximity to a site upon which enslaved people toiled . . . [and to integrate] that story of enslavement into the bell's narrative of freedom might be the greatest dissonance ever to be interpreted at a national historic site."[5] Ogline was not wrong to note that this curious dissonance, the uncomfortable feelings of incongruity and incompletion, might upset the authenticity that tourists seek when they return to heritage sites. But her desire to do away with the specific past of slavery revealed not only a betrayal of national history but a broader refusal by the federal government to recognize slavery's reverberating effects on its black citizens specifically and all its citizens more generally.

While the Liberty Bell Center planned to acknowledge slavery—the cracks, as it were, of American history—its primary purpose was to celebrate the nation's founding freedom, with the narrative of slavery folded into the larger story of abolitionism. Fortunately, Lawler's article and the ensuing debate with INHP was quickly taken up by scholars such as Randall Miller and Gary B. Nash, author of the The Liberty Bell (2010), as well as political activists such as Michael Coard and his Avenging the Ancestors Coalition, an African American–based group that demands formal commemoration of the slave quarters adjacent to the city's icon of liberty. In an op-ed piece for the Philadelphia Inquirer in 2002, Miller and Nash argued against the racially homogenizing "civic myths" of the Liberty Bell Center, championing instead a celebration of the complex truths that inhabited the President's House. "Washington's slaves were living symbols of the most paradoxical part of the nation's birth," they wrote, "freedom and unfreedom side by side, with enslavement of some making possible the liberty of others. An exhibition of documents and artifacts should show slavery's and freedom's many meanings at the dawn of the new nation. Doing so will make the Liberty Bell's own story ring loud and true."[6] Rather than upholding the myth of American freedom by ignoring or covering up slavery, Miller and Nash believed that the parallel narratives of slavery and freedom could agitate an expansion of democracy that would help fulfill its original promise. "A free people," they concluded, "dare not bury evidence or silence long-forgotten African Americans, whose stories make the meaning of the Liberty Bell and the Revolution real and palpable, here and abroad."[7]

Miller's and Nash's demands to remember the enslaved African Americans at the President's House were echoed by the Avenging the Ancestors Coalition. Congress and the city of Philadelphia soon responded with funding for the project, with the city also establishing an oversight committee and soliciting redesigns of the house from architects. In 2007, an archaeological dig revealed the house's foundation and the remains of a tunnel once used by servants and slaves, providing visual proof of the house's history that further cemented its historical importance in the national consciousness and drawing more than 300,000 visitors.[8] While the initial response from the National Park Service was tepid and dismissive, the collaborative and interracial efforts of academics, activists, politicians, journalists, artists, and Philadelphia residents to preserve the site as a memorial to the President House's enslaved African Americans eventually prevailed. The remains of the kitchen and corridors where slaves once toiled were incorporated into the final design. The exhibition that began as a way of preserving the nation's first executive mansion transformed into a public conversation on how best to represent the United States' multiple and sometimes conflicting histories. In many ways, the process of making the exhibition, what Nash described as shifting "from controversy to cooperation," is a testament to the racial progress that occurred during the post–civil rights era. Moreover, by opening up the process of memorialization, including the discords and dissonances, to the public, the President's House produced a democratic aesthetic; it is the first and only federal site designed to acknowledge the founding contradiction of American freedom and slavery. Rather than suppressing the disruptive cacophony of voices that challenged the United States' most beloved civic myths of freedom and liberty, the voices of the National Park Service, Congress, the city of Philadelphia, and a multiracial citizenry entered into conversation and attempted to redefine the meaning of American freedom and democracy.

The physical design of the memorial reflects a desire for transparency, inclusion, and visibility and should be read as an extension of, rather than an exception to, the democratic aesthetic of post–civil rights African American artists and intellectuals. The city of Philadelphia committed two-thirds of the project's contracts to minority-owned businesses, and the minority-owned firm Kelly/Maiello Architects & Planners designed the exhibit. The result was an unfinished open-air brick house open 24/7 for all tourists. Inside the doorless frames to the exhibit are images and facts about its famous residents, video installations, and a granite wall plaque dedicated to nine of Washington's slaves— Austin, Christopher Sheels, Giles, Hercules, Joe Richardson, Moll, Oney "Ona" Judge, Paris, and Richmond. The smaller rooms are filled with illustrated histories that detail George and Martha Washington's personal investment in slavery, a short history of Philadelphia slavery, the political radicalism of the African American ministers Absalom Jones and Richard Allen and the African Methodist Church, and a timeline of early American policies (such as the Fugitive Slave Act of 1793 and Alien and Sedition Act of 1798) that determined who lawfully belongs to the nation. This timeline ends with the official first family photo of the Obamas, a gesture that seems to suggest that this road of civic and legal exclusion has ended at the doorsteps of our current White House.

It is the combination of video reenactments and the glass vitrine framing the original foundation of the house, however, that formalizes the democratic aesthetic for American tourists. Fireplaces interrupt walls, and videos are set above them featuring African American actors dressed in period costumes, literally embodying the nine enslaved African Americans to whom the memorial is dedicated. Written by Lorene Cary and directed by Louis Massiah, the visual display performs an act of surrogacy, with the actors filling in and reanimating the muted bodies and narratives that were once forgotten and silenced at Independence Hall. For Massiah, the exhibit both revealed and resisted black civic estrangement: "One of the things I learned from this process is that it is the silences of history that disempower us, that is, not knowing, not having evidence, history not being acknowledged is what makes us powerless."[9] In the dialectic of forgetting and remembering, the President's House publicly engaged in "the politics of recognition" and ultimately won the formal battle for equality that required a revision of symbols and images. Instead of suppressing the cacophony of voices that disrupt American civic myths, new voices and perspectives blare from the stereo floorboards that enclose the exhibit, inviting visitors further into the interior of the house. The glass vitrine that models the transparency and accessibility of these new histories also exposes the foundation of the house. Inside, carefully cropped, bleached-out bricks show the lived incongruity built into the structure of the President's House and, ultimately, into the nation. On one side, the base of the house's curved parlor window, the place where "Washington received official delegations and perhaps brooded over the fate of the new republic," is exposed. "Opposite that curve are the remains of the kitchen, where the enslaved Hercules prepared food for the first family and state event."[10] Standing in front of both the Liberty Bell and Independence Hall, the exhibition holds the promise that the twin narrative of American slavery and freedom could emerge as *the* American story.

The most riveting storylines, nonetheless, belong to Hercules and Oney Judge, former slaves who, with the help of black and white Philadelphia abolitionists, escaped Washington's home. Close to the glass vitrine (and likely where the original kitchen stood) is a video panel featuring Hercules, Washington's favorite cook, who took his freedom the night of Washington's birthday party in 1798. A video featuring an actress playing Oney Judge, Martha Washington's waiting maid, who escaped to freedom in 1796, is at the entrance of the exhibit. After Judge escaped to New Hampshire, Washington tried but failed to have her return to Philadelphia, first by persuasion and then by coercion. The story, which is also told in a children's book, *The Escape of Oney Judge*, and memorialized in Philadelphia's annual Oney Judge's Freedom Day, not only reveals Washington's personal investment in slavery, but also provides an alternative narrative of founding freedom.[11] According to Randall Miller, the excavation of Judge's story is "almost a gift from God," for "she does something for us, as well as does something for history. She speaks. You do not have black voices in the creation story of America. If you go to Independence Hall, they are not there; they are referenced as objects. Now, you have black people speaking by actions and actually speaking about what freedom meant."[12] Quoting Judge's actual interview in the *Granite Freeman* in 1845, the character in the video reenactment refuses to go back to Washington: "I am free now and choose to remain so."[13] Through her story, we find an answer to the provocative question asked by Saidiya Hartman quoted at the beginning of this book: "What happens if we assume that the female subject serves as a general case for explicating social death, property relations, and the pained and putative construction of Blackness? . . . What possibilities of resignification would then be possible?"[14] Judge's story not only disrupts masculinist narratives of black enslavement and rebellion, but also expands gendered and racialized discourses of American freedom. Juxtaposed with Washington's lucrative role as slave master and withholder of liberty, the black female subject emerges as a more appropriate symbol of freedom, the true patriot of American democracy.

But if there is anything we should learn from the emergence of contemporary African American narratives on slavery, it is that American citizenship is multivalent and elusive. Post–civil rights America has been defined by the paradox of African Americans possessing full legal citizenship (the right to vote) while being unable to access the more intangible components of citizenship, civic membership (the right to recognition), and economic equality (the right to earn). But the President's House suggests that the right to recognition is gaining substantial traction. This current moment, what Roy Brooks calls the "Age of Obama," has ushered in a new phase of racial politics and representations. Brooks describes this as a period in which "the problem of race . . . is not racism but racial inequality." Racial inequality manifests more as "a paucity of financial, human, and social capital than [as] white racism. It is, in other

words, the maldistribution of America's resources (resources disparities between blacks and whites) that defines the race problem insofar
as it relates to black Americans in the Obama phase of post–civil rights
America."[15] While earlier stages of the post–civil rights era witnessed
the emergence of narratives of slavery that grappled with the dyad of
slavery and freedom, Obama's presidency is historic because it means
that the ultimate national symbols, the head of state and the First Lady,
are inseparable from black corporeality. While the history of the White
House, as the story of Thomas Jefferson and Sally Hemings attests, has
always been intertwined with that of slavery, the White House is, for
the very first time, now inhabited by those who most directly bear that
history; according to Farah Griffin, Michelle Obama, as both the First
Lady and a descendant of slaves, gives "cause for an honest discussion
about our nation's painful past but inspiring history."[16]

Unfortunately, neither the residency of Michelle Obama in the
White House nor the recent unearthing of the foundation of the President's House have meant the ongoing practices of racial inequality
have dissipated.[17] Rhetorically, the rising popularity of white suprema-
cist historical revisionists, such as the New Confederates and members
of the Tea Party, are reminders that specific conservative groups are
reconstructing the founding pasts of slavery and freedom in order to
keep both past and contemporary African Americans invisible within
American civic culture. This is exactly the type of historical amnesia
that contemporary African American narratives on slavery have challenged. Against such an upsurge, the President's House alone cannot
change the ideology or the resulting inequality that continues to deny
African Americans full citizenship. The backlash against the exhibit
itself has already begun, with Edward Rothstein writing that the President's House "ends up distorting history by demanding the sacrifice of
other perspectives," most notably downplaying Washington and Adams
as statesmen.[18] This pushback against the museum and the rising trend
of Confederate nostalgia suggests that critical patriotism, the type es-
poused by Frederick Douglass's "The Meaning of July Fourth for the
Negro?" and embodied in the collective effort to preserve the President's House, must vigilantly serve as a corrective against the monolithic, cult-like narratives of an uncritical patriotism. The singularity
of the first African American president and the propagation of racial
inequality in the form of mass incarceration, disproportionately high

rates of unemployment, domestic and sexual violence, and homicide, unequal access to quality housing, health care, and education mark the paradoxical state of both the hyper-visibility and hyper-invisibility characteristic of African American life. And while complicated and honest representations of slavery in the civic sphere are paramount, the right to recognition is one part of the triad of full citizenship. As reparations advocates argue, mnemonic restitution or the forms of redress provided by memorials like the President's House cannot and should not compensate for the paucity of resources that African Americans inherited from slavery, a paucity that continues to overdetermine their life choices and limit their economic citizenship in the present. More than a plaque or a bench by the road, the President's House begins to tell the compelling story that is America, but until we restructure the foundation of racial inequality begat by slavery, the project of democracy is forever incomplete.

INTRODUCTION ⫴ PECULIAR CITIZENSHIPS

1 Charles Johnson, quoted in Kevin Nance, "The Spirit and the Strength," 51.

2 Charles Johnson, "The End of the Black American Narrative," www.theamericanscholar.org/the-end-of-the-black-american-narrative; the piece was published in the conservative journal *The American Scholar* in 2008. In many ways, Johnson's declaration about the "end" of the African American narrative anticipates Ken Warren's thesis in *What Was African American Literature?* (Cambridge: Harvard University Press, 2011), in which he argues "that with the legal demise of Jim Crow, the coherence of African American literature has been correspondingly, if sometimes imperceptibly, eroded as well" (2). Their differences are more nuanced than their similarities. While Warren and Johnson both question what it means to write, read, and teach African American literature after the end of Jim Crow, Warren is as interested in the origins of African American literature as he is with its end. Johnson, on the other hand, emphasizes a unique African American literary tradition even as he demands the "end" of the black narrative. For Johnson, black identity transformed with the end of legalized segregation, but this new identity might form the basis for "new and better stories, new concepts, and new vocabularies and grammar" for twenty-first-century African American literature.

3 "Toni Morrison Discusses *A Mercy*" with Lynn Neary, *National Public Radio*, New York. October 27, 2008.

4 Smith, *Civic Ideals*, 6.

5 Bennett, *Democratic Discourses*, 15. Bennett analyzes how Jacobs created a democratic aesthetic by supplanting the European con-

ception of the belles-lettres with realistic depictions of slavery and her use of a new, distinctively U.S. form of the slave narrative that incorporated the pre-existing genre of the sentimental novel, the captivity narrative, and the picturesque.

6 Tate, *Flyboy in the Buttermilk*, 200.

7 Bernard Bell originally used the term "neo-slave slave narrative" in his book *The Afro-American Novel and Its Tradition* (1987). In *Neo-Slave Narratives: Studies in the Social Logic of a Literary Form*, Ashraf Rushdy expands it to describe contemporary African American novels that "assume the form, adopt the conventions, and take on the first-person voice of the antebellum slave narrative" (3).

8 Nora, "Between Memory and History."

9 Morrison, "The Site of Memory," 110.

10 Ibid., 120.

11 In *Citizenship and Social Class and Other Essays*, T. H. Marshall analyzed the development of citizenship in a democratic society as the development of civil rights during the eighteenth century, political rights during the nineteenth, then social rights during the twentieth.

12 Myrdal, *An American Dilemma*, lxxii.

13 Lipset, *The First New Nation*, 103.

14 *Dred Scott v. John F. A. Sandford*, 60 U.S. 393 (1856).

15 See Blight, *Race and Reunion: The Civil War in American Memory*.

16 Du Bois, *Black Reconstruction in America*, 723.

17 Kammen, *Mystic Chords of Memory*, 121.

18 See Scruggs, *Whispered Consolations*.

19 Weiner, *Black Trials*, 8.

20 Dubey, *Signs and Cities*, 5.

21 Cheng, *The Melancholy of Race*, 10.

22 Ibid., 10.

23 Eng and Han, "A Dialogue on Racial Melancholia," 671.

24 In *Black Visions*, Michael Dawson defined as "disillusioned liberalism" among African Americans in which the majority of African Americans believe that they live in a "fundamentally racially unjust society." See Dawson, *Black Visions*, 280.

25 Munoz, *Disidentifications*, 74.

26 Taylor, "The Politics of Recognition."

27 In the "Notes" section of *Juneteenth*, Ralph Ellison restates the African American predicament: "This society is not likely to become free of racism, thus it is necessary for Negroes to free themselves by becoming their idea of what a free people should be" (356).

28 Smith, *Civic Ideals*, 504.

29 Ibid., 505.

30 Thomas, *Civic Myths*, 13.

31 Douglass, "The Meaning of July Fourth for the Negro," 192.

32 See Morgan, *American Slavery, American Freedom*.

33 Rogin, "The Two Declarations of American Independence," 75–76.

34 See Hartman, *Scenes of Subjection*.

35 For more on "antagonistic cooperation," see Ellison, *Collected Essays*, 188, 267, 500–504, 594–95.

36 Hutcheon, *A Poetics of Postmodernism*, 5.

37 See A. Timothy Spaulding, *Re-forming the Past: History, the Fantastic, and the Postmodern Slave Narrative* (Columbus: Ohio State University Press, 2005); Arlene Keizer, *Black Subjects: Identity Formation in the Contemporary Narrative of Slavery* (Ithaca, N.Y.: Cornell University Press, 2004); and Timothy Cox, *Postmodern Tales of Slavery in the Americas: From Alejo Carpentier to Charles Johnson* (New York: Garland, 2001).

38 hooks, *Yearning*, 125.

39 Riffing off Nelson George's *Buppies, B-boys, Baps & Bohos*, Greg Tate calls the Post-Soul "the African American equivalent of postmodernism" in *Everything but the Burden*. Another working definition of the Post-Soul aesthetic could include, but not be limited to, the following quotation from Thelma Golden, curator of the Studio Museum in Harlem (who prefers the term "post-black"): "For me, to approach a conversation about 'black art' ultimately meant embracing and rejecting the notion of such a thing at the very same time. . . . [The Post-Soul] was characterized by artists who were adamant about not being labeled as 'black' artists, though their work was steeped, in fact deeply interested, in redefining complex notions of blackness." See Thelma Golden, *Freestyle* [exhibition catalogue] (New York: Studio Museum in Harlem, 2001), 14. In many ways, the Post-Soul aesthetic is a prime example of what Charles Johnson meant when he called for a new grammar and vocabulary of blackness. However, unlike Johnson's charge, Post-Soul artists do not simply disengage from the past in order to reproduce multifaceted black narratives. They often return to the past of slavery and segregation, as well as the civil rights and Black Power movements, to redefine the very terms and tropes of blackness.

40 Neal, *Soul Babies*, 3.

41 Following his eloquent lament for the freedom he cannot have, represented by the ships sailing on Chesapeake Bay, Frederick Douglass wrote, "You have seen how a man was made a slave; you shall see how a slave was made a man" (*Narrative of the Life of Frederick Douglass: An American Slave*, 107).

42 Hartman, *Scenes of Subjection*, 100.

43 Spillers, "Interstices," 76.

44 See Carpio, *Laughing Fit to Kill*; Woolfork, *Embodying American Slavery in Contemporary Culture*; Spaulding, *Reforming the Past*; Keizer, *Black Subjects*; Dubey, *Signs and Cities*; and Rushdy, *Neo-Slave Narratives*.

45 Carpio, *Laughing Fit to Kill*, 28.

ONE ⚶ FREEDOM IN A BONDSMAID'S ARMS

1 These phrases appear in Thomas Paine's 1776 pamphlet *Common Sense*, in which he extols the virtues of creating a new republic and chides those "weak men" who remain loyal to England: "Interested men, who are not to be trusted, weak men who CANNOT see, prejudiced men who will not see, and a certain set of moderate men who think better of the European world than it deserves; and this last class, by an ill-judged deliberation, will be the cause of more calamities to this Continent than all the other three" (25). And "Should an independency be brought about by the first of those means, we have every opportunity and every encouragement before us, to form the noblest, purest constitution on the face of the earth. We have it in our power to begin the world over again. A situation, similar to the present, hath not happened since the days of Noah until now" (57).

2 The miniseries aired on February 13 and 16, 2000, more than twenty years after CBS executives were pressured by Jefferson historians to drop plans for a miniseries on Jefferson and Hemings based on Barbara Chase-Riboud's novel *Sally Hemings*.

3 Trescott, "The Hemings Affair," B1.

4 Hortense Spillers, "Toward an Ontology: Black Women and the Republic," address delivered at "The Black Women in the Ivory Tower: Research and Practice Conference," Rutgers University, March 5, 2009.

5 Andrews, *Sally Hemings*, 5.

6 Walker, "Denial Is Not River in Egypt," 192.

7 Foster et al., "Jefferson Fathered Slave's Last Child."

8 Farrison, "The Origins of Brown's *Clotel*," 350.

9 Sollors, "'Never Was Born,'" 306.

10 French and Ayers, "The Strange Career of Thomas Jefferson," 422.

11 Du Cille, "Where in the World Is William Wells Brown?" 447.

12 Foucault, *Language, Counter-Memory, Practice*, 139, 144, 150.

13 Lipsitz, *Time Passages*, 213.

14 Dawson, "Witnesses and Practitioners," 3.

15 Spillers, "Mama's Baby, Papa's Maybe," 73.

16 Peterson, *The Jefferson Image in the American Mind*, viii.

17 Rosen, *Terror in the Heart of Freedom*, 6.

18 Hill-Collins, *Black Feminist Thought*, 70.

19 Spillers, "Interstices," 76.

20 Adair, "The Jefferson Scandals," 163.

21 Quoted in Brodie, *Thomas Jefferson*, 465.

22 Rothman, "James Callender and Social Knowledge of Interracial Sex," 95.

23 Morgan, "Some Could Suckle over Their Shoulder."

24 Brodie, *Thomas Jefferson*, 473.

25 Adair, "The Jefferson Scandals," 163.

26 Carby, *Reconstructing Womanhood*, 32.

27 Spillers, "Mama's Baby, Papa's Maybe," 65.

28 In 1981, Virginius Dabney wrote *The Jefferson Scandals: A Rebuttal* to challenge the historical accuracy of Fawn Brodie's biography. The Jefferson historian "detoured and devoted an entire chapter to Chase-Riboud's book." Instead of evaluating the literary merits of her novel *Sally Hemings*, Dabney spent the bulk of his analysis questioning its historical accuracy. Dabney asserts that *Sally Hemings* is not a historical novel but rather "faction," fiction that masquerades itself as fact. He contends that Chase-Riboud's "serious inaccuracies" (72) create a design different from those described by most theories of the historical novel. For Dabney, *Sally Hemings* cannot be a historical novel because there is "the strong probability" that its plot of Thomas Jefferson falling in love with a slave woman is "spurious" (73).

29 Most of the leading Jefferson historians refuted the possibility of their relationship. Works that departed from this consensus view, however, were the literary critic W. Edward Farrison's "The Origins of Brown's *Clotel*" (1954), the historian Pearl Graham's "Thomas Jefferson and Sally Hemings" (1961), and Winthrop Jordan's *White over Black: American Attitudes toward the Negro 1550–1812* (1968).

30 Barbara Chase-Riboud as quoted in McHenry, "Sally Hemings," 37.

31 Ibid.

32 Camp, "Review-Essay," 275.

33 Chase-Riboud, *Sally Hemings*, 199. All subsequent references are to this edition and are given parenthetically in the text.

34 While Virginia laws prohibited interracial sex, white slave masters forcing enslaved women to have sex was both commonplace and privately accepted among many Virginians. See Jones, "Race, Sex, and Self-Evident Truths."

35 See Jefferson, *Notes on the State of Virginia*, 138.

36 Burstein, "Jefferson's Rationalizations," C21.

37 Brown, "Black Rapture," 45.

38 Russell, "A Believable Sally Hemings," C15.

39 Dawson, "Witnesses and Practitioners," 11.

40 Hartman, *Scenes of Subjection*, 81.

41 Christian, "'Somebody Forget to Tell Somebody Something," 332.

42 Rushdy, "'I Write in Tongues,'" 106.

43 hooks, *Talking Back*, 42.

44 Brooks, *Bodies in Dissent*, 175.

45 Rushdy, "'I Write in Tongues,'" 112.

46 In Barbara Christian's essay "Somebody Forget to Tell Somebody Something," she notes that in *Sally Hemings* Chase-Riboud is "faced with a dilemma: Hemings, the main character, is encased in myth; yet she lingers in the margins of historical records. Because Chase-Riboud must rescue her heroine from myth, she cannot completely free herself from the conventional trappings of the historical novel, trappings which constrain her imaginative use of historical data" (336).

47 Here, Gordon-Reed cites John Blassingame's *Slave Community* (1972) and Eugene Genovese's *Roll, Jordan, Roll* (1972) as texts that use "slave narratives to reconstruct the experiences of blacks during slavery." Additional texts that mark this historiographic shift are Herbert Gutman's *The Black Family in Slavery and Freedom* and White's *Aren't I a Woman*.

48 S. F. Wetmore, "Life among the Lowly, No. 1," *Pike County (Ohio) Republican*, March 13, 1873.

49 Malone and Hochman, "A Note on Evidence," 525.

50 Ibid., 524.

51 Le Goff, *Histoire et Mémoire*, 114.

52 Hodes, "Racism and the Craft of History," 513.

53 Gordon-Reed, *The Hemingses of Monticello*, 23. All subsequent references are to this edition and are given parenthetically in the text.

54 Gordon-Reed, "Engaging Jefferson," 179.

55 For alternative historical interpretations on enslaved women, consent, and rape, see Davis, "Reflections on the Black Woman's Role in the Slave Community"; White, *Aren't I a Woman*; Jones, *Labor of Love, Labor of Sorrow*; Painter, "Soul Murder and Slavery"; Morgan, *Laboring Women*; Warren, "The Cause of Her Grief"; Glymph, *Out of the House of Bondage*; and Feimster, *Southern Horrors*.

56 Raewyn Whyte describes McCauley's art as having "no beginning-middle-end, no narrative closure, no 'once upon a time' or happy endings, no stereotypes, familiar characters, no comforting moral messages." See Whyte, "Robbie McCauley," 291.

57 McCauley, *Sally's Rape*, 225. All subsequent references are to this edition and are given parenthetically in the text.

58 Nymann, "Sally's Rape," 581.

59 Whyte, "Robbie McCauley," 282.

60 Patraka, "Robbie McCauley," 30.

61 Ibid., 27.

62 Whyte, "Robbie McCauley," 285.

63 Mahone, "The Introduction," xxix.

64 Sonnega, "Beyond a Liberal Audience," 89.

65 Huggins, *Revelations*, 130.

66 Harris and Baum, "Jefferson's Legacies," 59.

67 Spencer, "Historical Memory," 508.

68 Hartman, *Scenes of Subjection*, 81.

TWO ⫸ MILDER, MORE AMUSING PHASES OF SLAVERY

1 Between 1852, when *Uncle Tom's Cabin* was published in book form, and 1855, when the novel's popularity began to taper, over two hundred articles appeared in black newspapers such as the *Herald of Freedom*, the *Voice of the Fugitive*, the *Provincial Freeman*, and *Frederick Douglass' Paper*. As a result of the instrumental role the black press played in recording nineteenth-century

African American political ideologies, the letters, poems, and opinion pieces about *Uncle Tom's Cabin* that appeared in these antebellum newspapers provide the most comprehensive record of African American responses toward the novel.

2 Baldwin, *Notes of A Native Son*, 13. All subsequent references are to this edition and are given parenthetically in the text.

3 See Levine, *Martin Delany, Frederick Douglass and the Politics of Representative Identity*.

4 Braithwaite, "The Negro in American Literature," 30–31.

5 Wright, *Uncle Tom's Children*.

6 Gossett, *Uncle Tom's Cabin and American Culture*, 110.

7 Moses, *Black Messiahs and Uncle Tom*, xii–xiii.

8 Yarborough, "Strategies of Black Characterization in *Uncle Tom's Cabin* and the Early Afro-American Novel," 47.

9 Eckman, *The Furious Passage of James Baldwin*, 41.

10 Baldwin, *The Devil Finds Work*, 19.

11 Fisher, *Hard Facts*, 100; Baldwin, *The Devil Finds Work*, 14.

12 Berlant, "Poor Eliza," 636.

13 Williams, "Uncle Tom's Women," 21.

14 Williams, *Playing the Race Card*, 79.

15 Turner, *Ceramic Uncles and Celluloid Mammies*, 76.

16 Lott, *Love and Theft*, 219.

17 See Brody, *Impossible Purities*.

18 Dorman, "The Strange Career of Jim Crow Rice," 118.

19 Roediger, *The Wages of Whiteness*, 115–32.

20 Yarborough, "Strategies of Black Characterization," 43.

21 Hartman, *Scenes of Subjection*, 29.

22 Whitman, Preface to *Twasinta's Seminoles; or, Rape of Florida*, 8.

23 While African Americans cannot lay a particular claim to satire, the genre has had a unique application within African American literature. Historically, black abolitionist writers, like William Wells Brown, used satire to critique the absurd logic of chattel slavery and racism itself. Countering the system of slavery, black satirists would use humor to both expose the contradictions between American democracy and racial slavery and prove their humanity in spite of the putative juridical and legislative inequality into which they were born. Moreover, for black writers seeking to upset Stowe's racial sentimentalism, satire would have been the perfect foil. The critic Ronald Paulson notes that both date back to the eighteenth century and that, from their inceptions, the sentimental novel and satire had an antagonistic relationship because they induce radically opposite emotional reactions from the reader or audience. (See Paulson, *Satire and the Novel in Eighteenth-Century England*, 238.) While the sentimental focused on pathos, suffering, and compassion to invoke sympathy from its audience, satire used irony, ridicule, and wit to produce humor. But instead of satirizing *Uncle Tom's Cabin*, most black abolitionists, like Frederick Douglass in the 1853 novella "The Heroic Slave," engaged Stowe's characters

by supplanting them with realistic yet noble portrayals of enslaved and newly freed African Americans.

24 Hutcheon, *A Poetics of Postmodernism*, 5.

25 Hernández, *Chicano Satire*, 5.

26 See Martin, *Ishmael Reed and the New Black Aesthetic Critics*, and Rushdy, *Neo-Slave Narratives*.

27 Ishmael Reed adopted the nineteenth-century term "HooDoo," referring to forms of West African religions practiced by blacks in the New World, to explore the idea of spiritual practice outside easily defined faiths or creeds and rituals in contemporary literature and art. "Neo-HooDoo," Reed writes in his collection of poetry *Conjure*, "believes that every man is an artist and every artist a priest." His seminal poems, "The Neo-HooDoo Manifesto" and "The Neo-HooDoo Aesthetic," delve even deeper into this artistic practice to demonstrate its vitality as a transnational, African diasporic—an individualized, improvisational aesthetic that embraces spiritual creativity and innovation. For Reed's "Neo-HooDoo Manifesto" see *Conjure*, 21–22.

28 Stepto, *From Behind the Veil*, 18.

29 Gates, Rev. of *Flight to Canada*, 121.

30 Dickson-Carr, *African American Satire*, 15.

31 Carpio, *Laughing Fit to Kill*, 4.

32 Reed, *Flight to Canada*, 7. All subsequent references are to this edition and will be given parenthetically in the text.

33 Rushdy, *Neo-Slave Narratives*, 125.

34 Alexander, "I Ain't Yo' Uncle," 25. All subsequent references are to this edition and are given parenthetically in the text.

35 Brantley, "Topsy Returns to Confront Another Century's Legacy," 13.

36 Elam and Alexander, *Colored Contradictions*, 3.

37 In 2001, Jack E. White criticized Supreme Court Justice Clarence Thomas's anti-affirmative decisions and dubious civil rights philosophies in "Uncle Tom Justice," *Time*, June 26, 1995.

38 Yarborough, "Strategies of Black Characterization," 58.

39 "Student Nonviolent Coordinating Committee Position Paper: The Basis of Black Power"; see www3.iath.virginia.edu.sixties/HTML_docs/Resources/Primary/Manifestos/SNCC_black_power.html.

40 Gates, *The Annotated Uncle Tom's Cabin*, xi.

41 Reed, "Music: Black, White, and Blue," 81.

42 Dickson-Carr, *African American Satire*, 123.

43 Spillers, "Changing the Letter," 48.

44 Reed, *Shrovetide in Old New Orleans*, 297–98.

45 Baker, "Scene Not Heard," 43.

46 In 1988, as Arnie Zane and Bill T. Jones brainstormed ideas for their next project, Arnie suggested the title *Last Supper at Uncle's Tom's Cabin/Featuring 52 Handsome Nudes*. Although Zane died later that year, Jones changed the title to *Last Supper at Uncle's Tom's Cabin/The Promised Land* and created and choreographed the piece as homage and a memorial to Zane.

47 Martin Luther King Jr.'s "I See the Promised Land" speech directly alludes to the biblical story of Exodus and Moses leading the Israelites out of bondage in Egypt to the "Promised Land"—the land of Canaan that God had given to Abraham, Isaac, and Jacob. For African Americans, Canaan has always held special significance as the symbol of legal and spiritual freedom from slavery and racial oppression. For more on the Promised Land within early African American spiritual practices, see Raboteau, *Slave Religion*.

48 I have never seen a performance of *Last Supper at Uncle Tom's Cabin/The Promised Land*, but I have relied on multiple viewings of a video of the November 9, 1990, Brooklyn Academy of Music performance. Additionally, I have chosen to minimally analyze the dancing and choreography of the work. I also refer to the film *Dancing to the Promised Land: The Making of the Last Supper at Uncle Tom's Cabin/The Promised Land* (dir. Bill T. Jones).

49 Jones, *Last Night on Earth*, 209.

50 Toll, *Blacking Up*, 97.

51 Lott, *Love and Theft*.

52 Jones, *Last Night on Earth*, 207.

53 Ibid.

54 Gottschild-Dixon, "Some Thoughts on Choreographing History," 172.

55 Moten, *In the Break*, 1.

56 Brown, *Babylon Girls*, 161.

57 Jones, *Last Night on Earth*, 222.

58 Gates, *Thirteen Ways of Looking at a Black Man*, 64.

59 Jameson, *Marxism and Form*, 111.

60 Bissel, "Bill T. Jones," 37.

61 Lyotard, *Lessons on the Analytic of the Sublime*.

62 Jones, *Last Night on Earth*, 223.

63 Hebdige, "The Impossible Object," 70.

64 Foster, "Choreographies of Gender," 17.

65 Derrida, *Negotiations: Interventions and Interviews*, 180; Jones, quoted in Shapiro, "Dancing in Death's House," 66.

66 Elias, *Sublime Desire*, xviii.

67 Jones, *Last Night on Earth*, 223.

68 Yarborough, "Strategies of Black Characterization," 48.

69 Birdoff, *The World's Greatest Hit*, 219.

70 In "'Acting the Nigger:' Topsy, Shirley Temple, and Toni Morrison's Pecola," Kimberley G. Hebert argues that Toni Morrison's *Bluest Eye* rewrites *Uncle Tom's Cabin* "to tell Topsy's story and describe the damage incurred by blacks from black performances" (194).

71 Hartman, *Scenes of Subjection*, 26.

72 Wallace, "*Uncle Tom*," 150.

73 Duckworth, "Stowe's Construction of an African Persona and the Creation of White Identity for a New World Order," 225.

74 Gregory, "The Drama of Negro Life," 155.

75 Brown, *Babylon Girls*, 91.

76 Walker, *The End of Uncle Tom and the Grand Allegorical Tableau of Eva in Heaven* (1995).

77 West, *Race Matters*, 1.

78 Baker, "Scene Not Heard," 45.

79 In the summer of 1997, Saar sent out over two hundred letters and packets to artists, academics, and activists imploring them to boycott the display and collection of Walker's art on the grounds that Walker's art foolishly perpetuates racist stereotypes of African Americans. Given Walker's unprecedented acclaim in the art world, Saar also felt that such images were more likely to be accepted by the white establishment in the art world because they reinforced rather than revised longstanding stereotypes and caricatures of enslaved African Americans. Furthermore, she submitted several of Walker's images in the packet, one of which was *The End of Uncle Tom and the Grand Allegorical Tableau of Eva in Heaven*.

80 Cameron, "Kara Walker," 11.

81 For a comprehensive analysis of the impact of the visual reproductions of Harriet Beecher Stowe's *Uncle Tom's Cabin* in American culture, see Jo-Ann Morgan's *Uncle Tom's Cabin as Visual Culture*.

82 For a wonderful discussion of the inequality of interracial friendships in *Uncle Tom's Cabin*, see P. Gabrielle Foreman's "This Promiscuous Housekeeping."

83 Edmunson, *Nightmare on Main Street*, 131.

84 See Lhamon, *Raising Cain*.

85 Lang, "Class and the Strategies of Sympathy," 138.

86 Dating back to the nineteenth century, silhouettes were domestic portraitures produced in Europe and the United States, and, like both sentimental novels and plantation romances, they were primarily produced and consumed by the middle class. While many silhouettes served as affordable family portraits, they were also used, especially by Johann Caspar Lavater, in the practice of physiognomy and to further perpetuate myths of white superiority.

87 Quoted in Saltz, "Kara Walker," 86.

88 "Extreme Times Call for Extreme Heroes," 12.

89 In *Ugly Feelings*, Sianne Ngai explores how affects of irritation, envy, and disgust, unlike the powerful and dynamic negative emotions like anger, are often considered non-cathartic and are associated with situations in which action is blocked or suspended. Ngai shows how these "ugly feelings" help us rethink the subtler forms of sociopolitical agency that may take place in late modernity.

90 Ignatieff, *The Warrior's Honor*, 188.

91 Nietzsche, *Thus Spoke Zarathustra*, 162.

92 See Jackson, *Racial Paranoia*.

93 Walker, *Kara Walker*, the Renaissance Society at the University of Chicago (January 12–February 23, 1997).

94 Sharpe, *Monstrous Intimacies*, 155.

95 Booth, "The Unforgotten," 787.

96 Wallace, "*Uncle Tom*," 139.

97 Henry Louis Gates Jr., quoted in "Extreme Times Call for Extreme Heroes," 5.

THREE ‖ A RACE OF ANGELS

1 Campbell, *Middle Passages*, xxiv.

2 Smith, *Civic Ideals*, 6.

3 Eng and Han, "A Dialogue on Racial Melancholia," 671.

4 Scott, "That Event, This Memory," 263.

5 Stephens, *Black Empire*, 14.

6 Gaines, *American Africans in Ghana*, 141.

7 Glissant, *Caribbean Discourse*, 26.

8 Hartman, *Lose Your Mother*, 42.

9 Lowenthal, *The Past Is a Foreign Country*, xv.

10 Timothy and Teye, "American Children of the African Diaspora," 114.

11 Anderson, "Exodus," 323–24.

12 Clifford, *Routes*, 250.

13 Stephens, *Black Empire*, 15.

14 See MacCannell, *The Tourist*.

15 See Holsey, *Routes of Remembrance*.

16 Curtin posted the following comments: "Goree was never important in the slave trade, which flourished in Senegambia only at the mouth of the Senegal to the north or the Gambia to the south. But Goree is an interesting nineteenth-century town that can be used to attract tourists, especially African Americans looking for their roots" on the newly founded listservs H-Africa and H-Slavery. This heated exchange can be found at http://www.h-net.org/~africa/threads/goree.html. De Roux's article in *Le Monde* appaeared on December 27, 1996.

17 Higgins, "Into Africa: The Search for Identity."

18 Higgins, *Feeling the Spirit*, 9.

19 Ibid., 37.

20 Quoted in Hughes, "Chester Higgins' *Feeling the Spirit*."

21 Higgins, *Feeling the Spirit*, 8.

22 Gilroy, *Black Atlantic*, 19.

23 "An Interview with Chester Higgins, Jr.," www.abesha.com/abesha10/higgins.htm.

24 Ibid.

25 Hall, "Cultural Identity and Diaspora," 224.

26 Ibid., 225.

27 Holsey, *Routes of Remembrance*, 189.

28 Higgins, *Feeling the Spirit*, 36.

29 Ibid., 36.

30 Flusser, *Towards a Philosophy of Photography*, 42.

31 Baer, *Spectral Evidence*, 152.

32 Patterson and Kelley, "Unfinished Migrations," 20.

33 Glissant, *Le Discours Antillais*, 150, 356.
34 Higgins, *Feeling the Spirit*, 42.
35 Roach, *Cities of the Dead*, 4.
36 Clifford, *Routes*, 264.
37 "An Interview with Chester Higgins Jr."
38 Hall, "Cultural Identity and Diaspora," 224.
39 Piche, "Reading Carrie Mae Weems," 17.
40 Ibid.
41 Piche, "Reading Carrie Mae Weems," 33.
42 Edwards, *The Practice of Diaspora*, 11.
43 Ibid., 15.
44 Lavie, *Displacement, Diaspora, and Geographies of Identity*, 15.
45 Turner, *The Ritual Process*, 94.
46 Hartman, "Time of Slavery," 763.
47 Richards, "What Is to Be Remembered," 636.
48 Finley, "Carrie Mae Weems," 26.
49 Clarke, *Odysseys Home*, 82.
50 Piche, "Reading Carrie Mae Weems," 17.
51 Ebron, "Tourists as Pilgrims," 920.
52 Sidhu, "Africa's Cinema: Setting the Record Straight."
53 Woolford, "Filming Slavery," 92.
54 Ibid., 102.
55 Ibid., 94.
56 *Sankofa*, dir. Haile Gerima, Mypheduh Films, 1993.
57 Mayer, *Artificial Africas*, 233.
58 Ibid., 223.
59 Keeling, *The Witch's Flight*, 47.
60 Dubey, *Black Women Novelists and the Nationalist Aesthetic*, 24–28.
61 Kandé, "Look Homeward, Angel," 132.
62 Howard, "A Cinema of Transformation," 29.
63 Woolford, "Filming Slavery," 91.
64 Ibid., 101.
65 Ibid., 102.
66 Ukpokodu, "African Heritage from the Lenses of African-American Theatre and Film," 71.
67 Holsey, *Routes of Remembrance*, 217.
68 Richards, "What Is to Be Remembered?," 620.
69 Douglass, "Confronting Slavery's Legacy," A21.
70 "President Bush Speaks at Gorée Island in Senegal" [transcript], georgew bushwhitehouse.archives.gov/news/releases/2003/07/20030708-1.html.
71 "President Obama Remarks at Cape Coast Castle" [transcript], www.america .gov/st/texttransenglish/2009/July/20090711135243abretnuho.7640955.html.
72 Gaines, *American Africans in Ghana*, 285.

FOUR ⚓ WHAT HAVE WE DONE TO WEIGH SO LITTLE

The chapter's title, "What Have We Done to Weigh So Little on Their Scale,"
is taken from Depestre, "Epiphanies of a Voodoo God," 162.

1 Remnick, *The Bridge*, 265.
2 Gates, "Ending the Slavery Blame-Game."
3 Aiyetoro and Davis, "Historic and Modern Social Movements for Reparations," 691.
4 See Dawson and Popoff, "Reparations: Justice and Greed in Black and White."
Other surveys found similar results; see, for example, *USA Today*, February 22,
2002.
5 Campbell, "Settling Accounts?," 972.
6 Foner, "Africa's Role in the Slave Trade."
7 Boyd, "Africa's Role in the Slave Trade."
8 Ransby, "Henry Louis Gates' Dangerously Wrong Slave History."
9 Verdun, "If the Shoe Fits, Wear It," 597.
10 See Booth, *Communities of Memory*.
11 Kelley, *Freedom Dreams*, 114.
12 See Douglass, "The Future of the Negro People in the Slave States." See also
Oubre, *Forty Acres and a Mule*, 76.
13 Shklar, *American Citizenship*, 15.
14 Kessler-Harris, *In Pursuit of Equity*, 12.
15 I would argue that it was the confluence of four distinct factors that marked
the beginnings of the modern-day reparations movement: first, the post–
Second World War reparations agreement between Germany and European
Jews who were victims of the Nazi Holocaust; second, Japanese American
reparations claims for having been interned by the federal government in
camps during the Second World War, as well as the passage of the Civil Liberties Act in 1989, which granted the former internees a national apology, an
educational fund, and $20,000 compensation for each survivor; third, Con-
gressman John Conyers's (D-Michigan) introduction in 1989 and continued
support for H.R. 40, which calls for the establishment of a commission that
examines the impact of slavery and segregation on the lives of contemporary African Americans; and fourth, the emergence of the grassroots National
Coalition of Blacks for Reparations in America (N'COBRA) in 1987, whose support from working-class African Americans is more responsible than that of
any other group for placing the issue of reparations on the national agenda.
16 Barkan, *The Guilt of Nations*, 348.
17 Soyinka, *The Burden of Memory*, 37.
18 Eng, *The Feeling of Kinship*, 188.
19 In his insightful essay "Racial Naturalization," Devon Carbado argues "that
American identity and American citizenship do not necessarily go hand in
hand," but "racial naturalization constitutes both, and that racial naturalization ought to be understood as a process or experience through which people

enter the imagined American community as cognizable racial subjects." In this sense, citizenship and belonging are not identical but rather symbiotic systems that are determined by racial privilege or disenfranchisement.

20 Verdun, "If the Shoe Fits, Wear It," 597.

21 *Johnson v. McAdoo*, 45 U.S. App. D.C. 440 (1916).

22 Sovereign immunity is the doctrine that the sovereign or government cannot commit a legal wrong and is immune from civil suit or criminal prosecution. In the United States, the federal government has sovereign immunity and may not be sued unless it has waived its immunity or consented to a suit.

23 *Cato v. United States*, 70 F. 3d 1103 (9th Cir. 1995).

24 Brooks, *Atonement and Forgiveness*, 123.

25 Aiyetoro and Davis, "Historic and Modern Social Movements for Reparations," 689.

26 Campbell, "Settling Accounts?," 967.

27 *Cato v. United States*, 70 F. 3d 1106 (9th Cir. 1995).

28 Nora, "Between Memory and History," 8.

29 *Cato v. United States*, 70 F. 3d 1106 (9th Cir. 1995).

30 Ibid.

31 Govier, *Forgiveness and Revenge*, 146.

32 Brooks, *Atonement and Forgiveness*, 148.

33 See Nobles, *The Politics of Official Apologies*.

34 Blustein, *The Moral Demands of Memory*, 143.

35 Minow, *Between Vengeance and Forgiveness*, 310–11.

36 Farmer-Paellman, "Excerpt from *Black Exodus*," 25.

37 Ibid.

38 The defendants included the following companies: FleetBoston Financial Corporation, csx Corporation, Aetna, Brown Brothers Harriman, New York Life, Norfolk Southern Corporation, Lehman Brothers, Lloyd's of London, Union Pacific Railroad, JP Morgan Chase Manhattan Bank, Westpoint Stevens, RJ Reynolds Tobacco Company, Brown and Williamson, Liggett Group, Loews Corporation, Canadian National Railway, Southern Mutual Insurance Company, and American International Group.

39 See *re African American Litigation*, 307 F. Supp. 2d 977 (N.D. Ill., 2004); see also Ogletree, "Repairing the Past," 295.

40 Brooks, *Atonement and Forgiveness*, 100.

41 See *Farmer-Paellmann v. FleetBoston Financial Corporation, Aetna, Inc., csx*, C.A. No 1:02–1862 (E.D.N.Y., 2002).

42 See *re African American Litigation*, 307 F. Supp. 2d 977 (N.D. Ill., 2004).

43 Ibid.

44 Hylton, "Slavery and Tort Law," 1251.

45 Dagan, "Restitution and Slavery," 1144.

46 Hylton, "Slavery and Tort Law," 1252.

47 Kirshenblatt-Gimblett, *Destination Culture*, 150.

48 Ogletree, "Litigating the Legacy of Slavery."

49 For more on this debate, see Torphy, *Making Whole What Has Been Smashed*, 123–27.

50 Le Goff, *Histoire et Mémoire*, 182.

51 Robinson, *The Debt: What America Owes to Blacks*, 204. All subsequent references are to this edition and are given parenthetically in the text.

52 McWhorter, "Against Reparations," 194.

53 Barkan, *Guilt of Nations*, xix.

54 Patterson, *Slavery and Social Death*.

55 Berry, "In Search of Callie House," 323.

56 Berry, "Reparations for Freedmen, 1890–1916," 219–30.

57 Ibid., 230.

58 Berry, "In Search of Callie House," 327.

59 Berry, *My Face Is Black Is True*, 62–63.

60 Shklar, *American Citizenship*, 3.

61 Regosin, *Freedom's Promise*, 185.

62 Blight, "If You Don't Tell It Like It Was," 19, 30.

63 Kelley, *Freedom Dreams*, 131–32.

64 One of the main arguments against reparations for slavery is that the perpetrators of slavery (slaveholders) and those shown to be the specific indirect beneficiaries of slavery (the descendants of slaveholders) would not bear the cost. Instead, the debt of reparations would simply be arbitrarily borne by present-day taxpayers. These opponents argue against the *descendibility* of the debt from slaveholders and the federal government to all living Americans, especially those whose ancestors immigrated to the United States after the Civil War. Another line of reasoning is that reparations for slavery cannot be justified on the basis that slave descendants are subjectively worse off because of slavery. In his treatise "Ten Reasons Why Reparations for Blacks Is a Bad Idea for Blacks—and Racist Too," white neo-conservative David Horowitz concludes that African Americans are better off than they would have been in Africa if the slave trade had never happened: "The claim for reparations is premised on the false assumption that only whites have benefited from slavery. If slave labor created wealth for Americans, then obviously it has created wealth for black Americans as well, including the descendants of slaves."

65 Fears, "Seeking More Than Apologies for Slavery."

66 John Lewis is quoted by Melanie Eversley, "Memorial Eyed for Slaves Who Helped Build Capitol," 4A.

67 "A Concurrent Resolution Apologizing for Enslavement and Racial Segregation of African Americans," H. Res. 194, 110th Cong., 1st sess. (2008).

68 Cheng, *The Melancholy of Race*, 174.

69 Ibid.

70 Hartman, *Lose Your Mother*, 133.

EPILOGUE ⚓ THE PRESIDENT'S HOUSE

1 Obama, "A More Perfect Union."

2 Lawler, "The President's House in Philadelphia."

3 Ogline, "Creating Dissonance for the Visitor," 52.

4 Nash, "For Whom Will The Liberty Bell Toll? From Controversy to Cooperation," 75.

5 Ogline, "Creating Dissonance for the Visitor," 55–56.

6 Nash and Miller, "Don't Bury the Past: Honor Liberty by Including the Stories of All."

7 Ibid.

8 Klein, "All the President's Men."

9 "President's House: Freedom and Slavery in Making a New Nation," *Radio Times with Marty Moss-Coane*, WHYY. Philadelphia. December 13, 2010. whyy.org/cms/radiotimes/2010/12/13/philadelphias-presidents-house-and-slave-memorial/.

10 Saffron, "Changing Skyline: Brick Pile's Colliding Tales,"

11 As the exhibition relates, Washington's will directed that his 123 slaves be freed after his wife's death. She liberated them herself in 1801. But Martha Washington did not emancipate her own 153 "dower" slaves, from the estate of her first husband; she left them instead to her grandchildren. Oney Judge, aware that she would willed to Martha's granddaughter, Elizabeth Parker Custis, escaped to New Hampshire in 1796. Unfortunately, Judge's younger sister, Delphy, was bequeathed to the bride and groom by Martha Washington; Delphy and her children were manumitted in 1807.

12 "President's House," *Radio Times with Marty Moss-Coane*.

13 Rev. T. H. Adams, "Washington's Runaway Slave, and How Portsmouth Freed Her." *The Granite Freeman*, Concord, New Hampshire (May 22, 1845); reprinted in *Frank W. Miller's Portsmouth New Hampshire Weekly*, June 2, 1877.

14 Hartman, *Scenes of Subjection*, 100.

15 Brooks, *Racial Justice in the Age of Obama*, 12.

16 Griffin, "At Last . . . ? Michelle Obama, Beyoncé, Race & History," 6.

17 For a more nuanced definition of the term "practices of racial inequality," see Imani Perry, *More Beautiful, More Terrible*, in which she writes that "racial inequality is a culture practice in the United States. This cultural practice creates a devastating accumulation of disadvantaging experiences. . . . Although it is based in individual action, these individual actions are all part of a consistent yet diversely expressed cultural logic" (9). Perry argues that it is through understanding racial inequality as a set of practices rather than an immovable and codified "stasis of structural racism" that a political revolution becomes more possible and, at the very least, "massive reform" (42) more probable.

18 Rothstein, "The President's House in Philadelphia."

BOOKS AND ARTICLES

Adair, Douglass. "The Jefferson Scandals." *Fame and the Founding Fathers*, ed. Trevor Colbourn, 160–91. New York: W. W. Norton, 1974.

Adeleke, Tunde. *Unafrican Americans: Nineteenth-Century Black Nationalists and the Civilizing Mission*. Lexington: University Press of Kentucky, 1998.

Aiyetoro, Adjoa A. "The National Coalition of Blacks for Reparations in America (N'COBRA), Its Creation and Contribution to the Reparations Movement." *Should America Pay? Slavery and the Raging Debate over Reparations*, ed. Raymond Winbush, 209–25. New York: Amistad, 2003.

Aiyetoro, Adjoa A., and Adrienne D. Davis. "Historic and Modern Social Movements for Reparations: The National Coalition of Blacks for Reparations in America and Its Antecedents." *Texas Wesleyan Law Review* 16 (2009–10), 687–766.

Albert, Octavia V. Rogers. *The House of Bondage, or Charlotte Brooks and Other Slaves*. New York: Hunt and Eaton, 1890.

Alexander, Robert. "I Ain't Yo' Uncle: The New Jack Revisionist Uncle Tom's Cabin." *Colored Contradictions: An Anthology of Contemporary African-American Plays*, ed. Harry J. Elam Jr. and Robert Alexander. New York: Plume, 1996.

Amamoo, Joseph G. *The Ghanaian Revolution*. London: Jafint, 1988.

Ammons, Elizabeth. *Critical Essays on Harriet Beecher Stowe*. Boston: G. K. Hall, 1980.

———. "Heroines in *Uncle Tom's Cabin*." *American Literature* 49, no. 2 (May 1977), 161–79.

Ammons, Elizabeth, and Susan Belasco, eds. *Approaches to Teach-*

ing Stowe's Uncle Tom's Cabin. New York: Modern Language Association of America, 2000.

Anderson, Benedict. "Exodus." *Critical Inquiry* 20 (winter 1994), 314–27.

———. *Imagined Communities: Reflections on the Origins and Spread of Nationalism.* London: Verso, 1991.

Andrews, Tina. *Sally Hemings: An American Scandal: The Struggle to Tell the Controversial True Story.* Malibu, Calif.: Malibu, 2002.

Angelou, Maya. *All God's Children Need Traveling Shoes.* New York: Random House, 1986.

Babb, Valerie. "The Color Purple: Writing to Undo What Writing Has Done." *Phylon* 47, no. 2 (summer 1986), 107–16.

Baer, Ulrich. *Spectral Evidence: The Photography of Trauma.* Cambridge: MIT Press, 2002.

Baker, Houston. "Scene Not Heard." *Reading Rodney King / Reading Urban Uprising,* ed. Robert Gooding Williams, 38–51. New York: Routledge, 1993.

Baldwin, James. *Notes of a Native Son.* Boston: Beacon, 1983. First published 1955.

Balfour, Lawrie. "Finding the Words: Baldwin, Race Consciousness, and Democratic Theory." *James Baldwin Now,* ed. Dwight A. McBride. New York: New York University Press, 1999.

Banks, Marva. "An Analysis of Nineteenth Century Black Responses to Uncle Tom's Cabin as Recorded in Selected Antebellum Newspapers: 1852–1855." Ph.D. diss., Rensselaer Polytechnic Institute, 1986.

Barkan, Elazar. *The Guilt of Nations: Restitution and Negotiating Historical Injustices.* New York: W. W. Norton, 2000.

Bennett, Michael. *Democratic Discourses: The Radical Abolitionist Movement and Antebellum American Literature.* New Brunswick, N.J.: Rutgers University Press, 2005.

Berlant, Lauren. "Poor Eliza." *American Literature* 70, no. 3 (September 1998), 635–68.

Berry, Mary Frances. "In Search of Callie House and the Origins of the Modern Reparations Movement." *Journal of African American History* 91, no. 3 (summer 2006), 323–27.

———. *My Face Is Black Is True: Callie House and the Struggle for Ex-Slave Reparations.* New York: Alfred A. Knopf, 2005.

———. "Reparations for Freedmen, 1890–1916: Fraudulent Practices or Justice Deferred." *Journal of Negro History* 57, no. 3 (July 1972), 219–30.

Birdoff, Harry. *The World's Greatest Hit: Uncle Tom's Cabin.* New York: S. F. Vanni, 1947.

Bissel, Bill. "Bill T. Jones." *High Performance* #55 14, no. 3 (1991), 37.

Bitker, Borris. *The Case for Black Reparations.* New York: Random House, 1973.

Blackett, Richard. "Martin Delany and Robert Campbell: Black Americans in Search of an African Colony." *Journal of Negro History* 62, no. 1 (January 1977), 1–25.

Blight, David W. "If You Don't Tell It like It Was, It Can Never Be as It Ought to

Be." *Slavery and Public History: The Tough Stuff of American Memory*, ed. James Oliver Horton and Lois E. Horton, 19–34. New York: New Press, 2006.

———. *Race and Reunion: The Civil War in American Memory*. Cambridge: Harvard University Press, 2001.

Blustein, Jeffrey. *The Moral Demands of Memory*. Cambridge: Cambridge University Press, 2008.

Booth, W. James. *Communities of Memory: On Witness, Identity, and Justice*. Ithaca: Cornell University Press, 2006.

———. "The Unforgotten: Memories of Justice." *American Political Science Review* 95, no. 4 (December 2001), 777–91.

Boyd, Herb. "Africa's Role in the Slave Trade" [letter to the editor]. *New York Times*, April 25, 2010, § A, 22.

Braithwaite, William Stanley. "The Negro in American Literature." 1925. *The New Negro*, ed. Alain Locke. New York: Atheneum, 1975.

Brantley, Ben. "Topsy Returns to Confront Another Century's Legacy." *New York Times*, November 25, 1995, 13.

Brodie, Fawn, *Thomas Jefferson: An Intimate History*. New York: W. W. Norton, 1974.

Brody, Jennifer D. V. *Impossible Purities: Blackness, Femininity, and Victorian Culture*. Durham: Duke University Press, 1998.

Brooks, Daphne. *Bodies in Dissent: Spectacular Performances of Race and Freedom, 1850–1910*. Durham: Duke University Press, 2006.

Brooks, Roy L. *Atonement and Forgiveness: A New Model for Black Reparations*. Berkeley: University of California Press, 2004.

———. *Racial Justice in the Age of Obama*. Princeton: Princeton University Press, 2009.

———. *When Sorry Isn't Enough: The Controversy over Apologies and Reparations for Human Injustice*. New York: New York University Press, 1999.

Brown, Jayna. *Babylon Girls: Black Women Performers and the Shaping of the Modern*. Durham: Duke University Press, 2008.

Brown, Kimberly Juanita. "Black Rapture: Sally Hemings, Chica da Silva, and the Slave Body of Sexual Supremacy." *Women's Studies Quarterly* 35, nos. 1–2 (2007), 45–66.

Brown, William Wells. *Clotel, or the President's Daughter*. 1853. New York: Arno, 1969.

Bruner, Edward. "Tourism in Ghana: The Representation of Slavery and the Return of the Black Diaspora." *American Anthropologist* 98, no. 2 (1996), 290–304.

Burstein, Andrew. "Jefferson's Rationalizations." *William and Mary Quarterly* 57, no. 1 (January 2000), 183–97.

———. *Jefferson's Secrets: Death and Desire at Monticello*. New York: Basic Books, 2005.

Cameron, Dan. "Kara Walker: Rubbing History the Wrong Way." *On Paper*, September–October 1997, 10–14.

Camp, Stephanie. "Review-Essay: Sally Hemings and Thomas Jefferson." *Mississippi Quarterly* 53, no. 2 (spring 2000), 275–83.

Campbell, James. *Middle Passages: African-American Journeys to Africa, 1787–2005.* New York: Penguin, 2006.

———. "Settling Accounts? An Americanist Perspective on Historical Reconciliation." *American Historical Review* 114, no. 4 (October 2009), 963–77.

Campbell, Robert. "A Pilgrimage to My Motherland: An Account of a Journey among the Egbas and Yorubas of Central Africa in 1859–1860" (1861). *Search for a Place: Black Separatism and Africa, 1860*, ed. Howard H. Bell. Ann Arbor: University of Michigan Press, 1969.

Cancel, Robert. "Whose Africa Is It, Anyway? Or, What Exactly Is Skip Gates Signifyin'?" *African Arts* 33, no. 2 (summer 2000), 1–9, 86–88.

Carbado, Devon. "Racial Naturalization." *American Quarterly* 57, no. 3 (2005), 633–58.

Carby, Hazel. *Reconstructing Womanhood: The Emergence of the Afro-American Novelists.* New York: Oxford University Press, 1987.

Carpio, Glenda. *Laughing Fit to Kill: Black Humor in the Fictions of Slavery.* New York: Oxford University Press, 2008.

Cassells, Cyrus. "Sally Hemings to Thomas Jefferson." *Callaloo* 18 (spring–summer 1983), 1–4.

Chase-Riboud, Barbara. *The President's Daughter.* New York: Ballantine, 1994.

———. *Sally Hemings.* New York: St. Martin's/Griffin, 1979.

Cheng, Anne Anlin. *The Melancholy of Race: Psychoanalysis, Assimilation, and Hidden Grief.* New York: Oxford University Press, 2001.

Christian, Barbara. *Black Feminist Criticism: Perspectives on Black Women Writers.* New York: Pergamon, 1985.

———. *Black Women Novelists: The Development of a Tradition, 1892–1976.* Westport, Conn.: Greenwood, 1980.

———. "'Somebody Forget to Tell Somebody Something': African-American Women's Historical Novels." *Wild Women in the Whirlwind: Afro-American Culture and the Contemporary Literary Renaissance*, ed. Joanne M. Braxton and Andree Nicola McLaughlin, 326–41. New Brunswick, N.J.: Rutgers University Press, 1990.

Citron, Paul. "Uncle Tom's Shock-Filled Road to Salvation." *Toronto Star*, April 19, 1999, § D, 3.

Clarke, George E. *Odysseys Home: Mapping African-Canadian Literature.* Toronto: University of Toronto Press, 2002.

Clifford, James. *Routes: Travel and Translation in the Late Twentieth Century.* Cambridge: Harvard University Press, 1997.

Connerton, Paul. *How Societies Remember.* Cambridge: Cambridge University Press, 1989.

Contave, Sophia. "Who Gets to Create the Lasting Images? The Problem of Black Representation in *Uncle Tom's Cabin*." *Approaches to Teaching Stowe's Uncle Tom's Cabin*, ed. Elizabeth Ammons and Susan Belasco. New York: Modern Language Association, 2000.

Cose, Ellis. *Bone to Pick: Of Forgiveness, Reconciliation, Reparation, and Revenge.* New York: Atria, 2004.

Cox, James. "Reparations Activist: 'We're Still Living with the Vestiges of Slavery.'" *USA Today,* February 21, 2002, 8A.

Cullen, Countee. *On These I Stand.* New York: Harper and Row, 1927.

Dabney, Virginius. *The Jefferson Scandals: A Rebuttal.* New York: Dodd, Mead, 1981.

Dagan, Hanoch. "Restitution and Slavery: On Incomplete Commodification, Intergenerational Justice, and Legal Transitions." *Boston University Law Review* 84 (December 2004), 1139–76.

Davis, Angela. "Reflections on the Black Woman's Role in the Slave Community." *Massachusetts Review* 13, nos. 1–2 (winter 1972), 81–100.

Davis, Charles T., and Henry Louis Gates Jr., eds. *The Slave's Narrative.* New York: Oxford University Press, 1985.

Dawson, Emma Waters. "Witnesses and Practitioners: Attitudes toward Miscegenation in Barbara Chase-Riboud's *Sally Hemings.*" *Recovered Writers/Recovered Texts,* ed. Dolan Hubbard, 1–14. Knoxville: University of Tennessee Press, 1997.

Dawson, Michael C. *Black Visions: The Roots of Contemporary African-American Political Ideologies.* Chicago: University of Chicago Press, 2001.

Dawson, Michael, and Rovana Popoff. "Reparations: Justice and Greed in Black and White." *Du Bois Review* 1, no. 1 (2004), 47–91.

Delany, Martin. *The Condition, Elevation, Emigration, and Destiny of the Colored People of the United States, Politically Considered.* New York: Arno, 1968. First published 1852.

———. "Official Report of the Niger Valley Exploring Party" (1861). *Search for a Place: Black Separatism and Africa, 1860,* ed. Howard H. Bell. Ann Arbor: University of Michigan Press, 1969.

Depestre, Rene. *A Rainbow for the Christian West,* trans. Joan Dayan. Amherst: University of Massachusetts Press, 1977.

Derricotte, Toi. "Exits from Elmina Castle: Cape Coast, Ghana." *Callaloo* 19, no. 1 (winter 1996), 107–10.

Derrida, Jacques. *Negotiations: Interventions and Interviews, 1971–2001,* ed. Elizabeth Rottenberg, 147–98. Stanford: Stanford University Press, 2002.

Dickson-Carr, Darryl. *African American Satire: The Sacredly Profane Novel.* Columbia: University of Missouri Press, 2001.

Dorman, James. "The Strange Career of Jim Crow Rice." *Journal of Social History* 3, no. 2 (1969–70), 109–22.

Douglass, Frederick. "The Future of the Negro People in the Slave States." *Douglass's Monthly,* March 1862.

———. "The Heroic Slave." 1852. *Three Classic African-American Novels,* ed. William Andrews. New York: Signet, 1990.

———. "The Meaning of July Fourth for the Negro." *Frederick Douglass: Selected Speeches and Writings,* ed. Eric Foner. Chicago: Lawrence Hill, 1999.

————. *Narrative of Frederick Douglass: An American Slave, Written by Himself.* New York: Penguin, 1986. First published 1845.

Douglass, William. "Confronting Slavery's Legacy: Clinton's Island Visit a Test of. Sensitivity." *Newsday*, April 2, 1998, § A, 21.

Dubey, Madhu. *Black Women Novelists and the Nationalist Aesthetic.* Bloomington: Indiana University Press, 1994.

————. *Signs and Cities: Black Literary Postmodernism.* Chicago: University of Chicago Press, 2003.

Du Bois, W. E. B. *Black Reconstruction in America: 1860–1880.* New York: Free Press, 1992. First published 1935.

Du Cille, Ann. "Where in the World Is William Wells Brown? Thomas Jefferson, Sally Hemings, and the DNA of African-American Literary History." *American Literary History* 12, no. 3 (2000), 443–62.

Duckworth, Sarah. "Stowe's Construction of an African Persona and the Creation of White Identity for a New World Order." *The Stowe Debate: Rhetorical Strategies in Uncle Tom's Cabin*, ed. Ellen E. Westbrook et al. Amherst: University of Massachusetts Press, 1994.

Dunbar, Paul Laurence. *Lyrics of the Hearthside.* New York: Dodd, Mead, 1899.

Ebron, Paulla A. "Tourists as Pilgrims: Commercial Fashioning of Transatlantic Politics." *American Ethnologist* 26, no. 4 (November 1999), 910–32.

Eckman, Fern M. *The Furious Passage of James Baldwin.* London: Michael Joseph, 1968.

Edmunson, Mark. *Nightmare on Main Street: Angels, Sadomasochism, and the Culture of the Gothic.* Cambridge: Harvard University Press, 1997.

Edwards, Brent H. *The Practice of Diaspora: Literature, Translation, and the Rise of Black Internationalism.* Cambridge: Harvard University Press, 2003.

————. "The Uses of Diaspora." *Social Text* 19, no. 1 (spring 2001), 45–73.

Eichstedt, Jennifer L., and Stephen Small. *Representations of Slavery: Race and Ideology in Southern Plantation Museums.* Washington: Smithsonian Institution Press, 2002.

Elam, Harry J., and Robert Alexander. *Colored Contradictions: An Anthology of Contemporary African-American Plays.* New York: Plume, 1996.

Elam, Harry J., and David Krasner. *African American Performance and Theatre History: A Critical Reader.* New York: Oxford University Press, 2000.

Elias, Amy J. *Sublime Desire: History and Post-1960s Fiction.* Baltimore: Johns Hopkins University Press, 2001.

Ellis, Joseph. "Jefferson: Post-DNA." *William and Mary Quarterly* 57, no. 1 (January 2000), 125–38.

Ellison, Ralph. *The Collected Essays of Ralph Ellison*, ed. John F. Callahan. New York: Modern Library, 1995.

————. *Juneteenth*, ed. John F. Callahan. New York: Random House, 1999.

Eng, David L. *The Feeling of Kinship: Queer Liberalism and the Racialization of Intimacy.* Durham: Duke University Press, 2010.

Eng, David, and Shinhee Han. "A Dialogue on Racial Melancholia." *Psychoanalytic Dialogues* 10, no. 1 (2000), 671.

Eversley, Melanie. "Memorial Eyed for Slaves Who Helped Build Capitol." *USA Today*, February 28, 2006, 4A.

"Extreme Times Call for Extreme Heroes." *International Review of African American Review* 14, no. 3 (1997), 2–15.

Eyerman, Ron. *Cultural Trauma: Slavery and the Formation of African American Identity*. Cambridge: Cambridge University Press, 2001.

Fabre, Geneviève, and Robert O'Meally. *History and Memory in African-American Culture*. New York: Oxford University Press, 1994.

Farmer-Paellman, Deadria C. "Excerpt from *Black Exodus: The Ex-slave Pension Movement Reader*." *Should America Pay? Slavery and the Raging Debate over Reparations*, ed. Raymond Winbush, 22–32. New York: Amistad, 2003.

Farrison, Edward W. "The Origins of Brown's *Clotel*." *Phylon* 15, no. 4 (1954), 347–54.

Feagin, Joe R. *Racist America: Roots, Current Realities, and Future Reparations*. New York: Routledge, 2000.

Fears, Darryl. "Seeking More Than Apologies for Slavery: Activists Hope Firms' Disclosure of Ties Will Lead to Reparations." *Washington Post*, June 20, 2005, § A, 1.

Feimster, Crystal N. *Southern Horrors: Women and the Politics of Rape and Lynching*. Cambridge: Harvard University Press, 2009.

Fiedler, Leslie. *The Inadvertent Epic: From "Uncle Tom's Cabin" to "Roots."* New York: Simon and Schuster, 1979.

Finley, Cheryl. "Carrie Mae Weems: Grabbing, Snatching, Blink and You Be Gone, 1993." *Imagining African Art: Documentation and Transformation*. New Haven: Yale Art Gallery, 2000.

Fisher, Philip. *Hard Facts: Setting and Form in the American Novel*. New York: Oxford University Press, 1985.

Fleming, Walter. "Ex-Slaves Pension Frauds." *South Atlantic Quarterly* 9 (April 11, 1910), 123–35.

Flusser, Vilém. *Towards a Philosophy of Photography*. London: Reaktion, 2000.

Foner, Eric. "Africa's Role in the Slave Trade" [letter to the editor]. *New York Times*, April 25, 2010, § A, 22.

———. *A Short History of Reconstruction, 1863–1877*. New York: Harper and Row, 1990.

Forbath, William E. "Caste, Class, and Equal Citizenship." *Michigan Law Review* 98, no. 1 (October 1999), 1–91.

Foreman, P. Gabrielle. "'This Promiscuous Housekeeping': Death, Transgression, and Homoeroticism in *Uncle Tom's Cabin*" *Representations* 43 (1993), 51–72.

Foster, Eugene A., et al. "Jefferson Fathered Slave's Last Child." *Nature* 396 (November 1998), 27–28.

Foster, Susan. "Choreographies of Gender." *Signs* 24, no. 1 (autumn 1998), 1–33.

Foucault, Michel. *Language, Counter-Memory, Practice: Selected Essays and Interview*. Trans. Donald Bouchard. Ithaca: Cornell University Press, 1980.

Frederickson, George M. *The Black Image in the White Mind: The Debate on Afro-American Character and Destiny, 1817–1914*. New York: Harper and Row, 1971.

French, Scot A., and Edward L. Ayers. "The Strange Career of Thomas Jefferson: Race and Slavery in American Memory, 1943–1993." *Jeffersonian Legacies*, ed. Peter S. Onuf, 418–56. Charlottesville: University of Virginia Press, 1993.

Furnas, J. C. *Goodbye to Uncle Tom*. New York: William Sloane, 1956.

Gaines, Kevin. *American Africans in Ghana: Black Expatriates and the Civil Rights Era*. Chapel Hill: University of North Carolina Press, 2006.

———. *Uplifting the Race: Black Leadership, Politics, and Culture in the Twentieth Century*. Chapel Hill: University of North Carolina Press, 1996.

Gates, Henry L., Jr. "Ending the Slavery Blame-Game." *New York Times*, April 23, 2010, § A, 27.

———. Introduction. *The Annotated Uncle Tom's Cabin*. By Henry L. Gates, Hollis Robbins, and Harriet B. Stowe. New York: W. W., 2007.

———. Review of *Flight to Canada by Ishmael Reed*. 1976. *The Critical Response to Ishmael Reed*, ed. Dick Bruce and Pavel Zemliansky. Westport, Conn: Greenwood, 1999.

———. *Thirteen Ways of Looking at a Black Man*. New York: Vintage, 1998.

———. "The Trope of the New Negro and the Reconstruction of the Image of the Black." *Representations* (fall 1988), 129–55.

Gates, Henry L., Hollis Robbins, and Harriet B. Stowe. *The Annotated Uncle Tom's Cabin*. New York: W. W. Norton, 2007.

Gilroy, Paul. *Black Atlantic: Modernity and Double Consciousness*. Cambridge: Harvard University Press, 1993.

———. *"There Ain't No Black in the Union Jack": The Cultural Politics of Race and Nation*. London: Hutchinson, 1987.

Giovanni, Nikki. Preface. *Abandoned Baobab* by Ken Bugal. Chicago: Lawrence Hill, 1991.

Glissant, Édouard. *Le discours antillais*. Paris: Le Seuil, 1981.

———. *Caribbean Discourse: Selected Essays*. Charlottesville: University Press of Virginia, 1989.

Glymph, Thavolia. *Out of the House of Bondage: The Transformation of the Plantation Household*. Cambridge: Cambridge University Press, 2008.

Goldberg, Cary. "DNA Offers Link to Black History." *New York Times*, August 28, 2000 § A, 10.

Gordon-Reed, Annette. "Engaging Jefferson: Blacks and the Founding Father." *William and Mary Quarterly* 57, no. 1 (January 2000), 171–82.

———. *The Hemingses of Monticello: An American Family*. New York: W. W. Norton, 2008.

———. *Thomas Jefferson and Sally Hemings: An American Controversy*. Charlottesville: University Press of Virginia, 1997.

Gossett, Thomas. *Uncle Tom's Cabin and American Culture*. Dallas: Southern Methodist University Press, 1985.

Gottschild-Dixon, Brenda. "Some Thoughts on Choreographing History." *Mean-*

ing in Motion: New Cultural Studies of Dance, ed. Jane C. Desmond. Durham: Duke University Press, 1997.

Govier, Trudy. *Forgiveness and Revenge*. London: Routledge, 2002.

Gregory, Montgomery. "The Drama of Negro Life." *The New Negro: Voices of the Harlem Renaissance*, ed. Alain Locke. 1925. New York: Simon and Schuster, 1997.

Griffin, Farah Jasmine. "At Last . . . ? Michelle Obama, Beyoncé, Race & History." *Daedalus* 140, no. 1 (winter 2011), 131–41.

———. *Who Set You Flowin'? The African-American Migration Narrative*. New York: Oxford University Press, 1995.

Guerrero, Ed. *Framing Blackness: The African American Image in Film*. Philadelphia: Temple University Press, 1993.

Gutman, Herbert G. *The Black Family in Slavery and Freedom, 1750–1925*. New York: Pantheon, 1976.

Halbwachs, Maurice. *On Collective Memory*, trans. Lewis A. Coser. Chicago: University of Chicago Press, 1992. First published 1952.

Haley, Alex. "My Furthest-Back-Person — The African." *New York Times Magazine*, July 16, 1972, 13.

———. *Roots: The Saga of an American Family*. Garden City, N.Y.: Doubleday, 1976.

Hall, Stuart. "Cultural Identity and Diaspora." *Identity: Community, Culture, and Difference*, ed. Jonathan Rutherford, 222–37. London: Lawrence and Wishart, 1990.

Hamilton, Anita. "A Family Divided: Sex, Race, and the Jefferson Feud." *Time*, July 5, 2004, 65–69.

Harris, Duchess, and Bruce Baum. "Jefferson's Legacies: Racial Intimacies and American Identity." *Racially Writing the Republic: Racists, Race Rebels, and Transformations of American Identity*, ed. Bruce Baum and Duchess Harris, 44–63. Durham: Duke University Press, 2009.

Harris, Trudier. *Exorcising Blackness: Historical and Literary Lynching and Burning Rituals*. Bloomington: Indiana University Press, 1984.

Hartigan, Patti. "Setting the Table for the 'Last Supper.'" *Boston Globe*, April 15, 1991, 32.

Hartman, Saidiya V. *Lose Your Mother: A Journey along the Atlantic Slave Route*. New York: Farrar, Straus and Giroux, 2007.

———. *Scenes of Subjection: Terror, Slavery, and Self-Making in Nineteenth-Century America*. New York: Oxford University Press, 1997.

———. "Time of Slavery." *South Atlantic Quarterly* 101, no. 4 (fall 2002), 774.

Hayes, Bernetta. "Claiming Our Heritage Is a Booming Industry." *American Visions*, 12 no. 5 (1997), 44.

Hebdige, Dick. "The Impossible Object: Toward a Sociology of the Sublime." *Cultural Studies and Communications*, ed. James Curran et al. London: Arnold, 1996.

Hebert, Kimberley G. "'Acting the Nigger:' Topsy, Shirley Temple, and Toni

Morrison's Pecola." *Approaches to Teaching Stowe's Uncle Tom's Cabin*, ed. Elizabeth Ammons and Susan Belasco. New York: Modern Language Association, 2000.

Henderson, Mary C. *Theater in America: 200 Years of Plays, Players, and Productions.* New York: Harry N. Abrams, 1996.

Henson, Josiah. *The Life of Josiah Henson, Formerly a Slave, Now an Inhabitant of Canada, as Narrated by Himself.* Boston: Arthur D. Phelps, 1849.

Hernández, Guillermo. *Chicano Satire: A Study in Literary Culture.* Austin: University of Texas Press, 1991.

Higgins, Chester. *Feeling the Spirit: Searching the World for the People of Africa.* New York: Bantam, 1994.

———. "Into Africa: The Search for Identity." *American Legacy Magazine,* winter 2001.

Hill-Collins, Patricia. *Black Feminist Thought: Knowledge, Consciousness, and the Politics of Empowerment.* New York: Routledge, 2000.

Hobsbawm, Eric J., and Terence Ranger. *The Invention of Tradition.* Cambridge: Cambridge University Press, 1983.

Hochschild, Jennifer. *Facing Up to the American Dream: Race, Class and the Soul of the Nation.* Princeton: Princeton University Press, 1995.

Hodes, Martha. "Racism and the Craft of History." *American History* 26, no. 3 (1998), 510–15 [review of *Thomas Jefferson and Sally Hemings: An American Controversy*, by Annette Gordon-Reed].

Holsey, Bayo. *Routes of Remembrance: Refashioning the Slave Trade in Ghana.* Chicago: University of Chicago Press, 2007.

hooks, bell. *Talking Back: Thinking Feminist, Thinking Black.* Boston: South End, 1989.

———. *Yearning: Race, Gender, and Cultural Politics.* Boston: South End, 1998.

Horne, Gerald. *Black and Red.* Albany: State University of New York Press, 1986.

Horowitz, David. *Uncivil Wars: The Controversy over Reparations for Slavery.* San Francisco: Encounter, 2003.

Howard, Steve. "A Cinema of Transformation: The Films of Haile Gerima." *Cineaste* 14, no. 1 (1985), 28–29, 39.

Huggins, Nathan. *Revelations: American History, American Myths.* New York: Oxford University Press, 1995.

Hughes, Holly Stuart. "Chester Higgins' *Feeling the Spirit.*" *Photo District News.* February 2005.

Huntington, Samuel P. *Who Are We? The Challenges to America's Identity.* New York: Simon and Schuster, 2004.

Hurston, Zora Neale. "How It Feels to Be Colored Me" (1928). *I Love Myself When I Am Laughing and Then Again When I Am Looking Mean and Impressive,* ed. Alice Walker. Old Westbury, N.Y.: Feminist Press, 1979.

Hutcheon, Linda. *A Poetics of Postmodernism: History, Theory, Fiction.* London: Routledge, 1988.

Hylton, Keith. "Slavery and Tort Law." *Boston University Law Review* 84 (December 2004), 46–51.

Ignatieff, Michael. "Articles of Faith." *Index on Censorship* 5 (1996), 110–22.

———. *The Warrior's Honor: Ethnic War and the Modern Conscience*. London: Chatto and Windus, 1998.

Jackson, John L. *Racial Paranoia: The Unintended Consequences of Political Correctness: The New Reality of Race in America*. New York: Basic Civitas, 2008.

Jacobs, Harriet. *Incidents in the Life of a Slave Girl: Written by Herself*. 1861. Cambridge: Harvard University Press, 1987.

Jacobs, Mary Jane. Introduction, *Carrie Mae Weems: The Fabric Workshop/Museum*. Philadelphia: Fabric Workshop, 1994.

James, Henry. *A Small Boy and Others*. New York: C. Scribner's Sons, 1913.

Jameson, Fredric. *Marxism and Form: Twentieth-Century Dialectical Theories of Literature*. Princeton: Princeton University Press, 1972.

Jefferson, Thomas. *Notes on the State of Virginia*. Chapel Hill: University of North Carolina Press, 1954. First published 1781.

Johnson, Charles R. "The End of the Black American Narrative." 2008. Available at www.theamericanscholar.org/the-end-of-the-black-american-narrative.

Johnson, Charles S. "The New Frontage on American Life." *The New Negro*, ed. Alain Locke. New York: Atheneum, 1977. First published 1925.

Jones, Bill T. *Last Night on Earth*. New York: Pantheon, 1997.

Jones, Jacqueline. *Labor of Love, Labor of Sorrow: Black Women, Work, and the Family from Slavery to the Present*. New York: Basic Books, 1985.

———. "Race, Sex, and Self-Evident Truths: The Status of Slave Women during the Era of the American Revolution." *Half Sisters of History: Southern Women and the American Past*, ed. Catherine Clinton. Durham: Duke University Press, 1994.

Jordan, Winthrop. "Hemings and Jefferson: Redux." *Sally Hemings and Thomas Jefferson: History, Memory, and Civic Culture*, ed. Jan Ellen Lewis and Peter S. Onuf, 35–51. Charlottesville: University Press of Virginia, 1999.

———. *White over Black: American Attitudes toward the Negro 1550–1812*. New York: W. W. Norton, 1968.

Kammen, Michael. *Mystic Chords of Memory: The Transformation of Tradition in American Culture*. New York: Alfred A. Knopf, 1991.

Kandé, Sylvie. "Look Homeward, Angel: Maroons and Mulattos in Haile Gerima's Sankofa." *Research in African Literatures* 29 (summer 1998), 128–46.

Keeling, Kara. *The Witch's Flight: The Cinematic, the Black Femme, and the Image of Common Sense*. Durham: Duke University Press, 2007.

Kelley, Robin D. G. *Freedom Dreams: The Black Radical Imagination*. Boston: Beacon, 2002.

Kerber, Linda K. *Women of the Republic: Intellect and Ideology in Revolutionary America*. Chapel Hill: University of North Carolina Press, 1980.

Kessler-Harris, Alice. *In Pursuit of Equity: Women, Men, and the Quest for Economic Citizenship in Twentieth Century America*. Oxford: Oxford University Press, 2001.

Kim, Kichung. "Wright, the Protest Novel, and Baldwin's Faith." *College Language Association Journal* 17 (1974), 387–96.

King, Martin Luther, Jr. "I Have a Dream." *I Have a Dream: Writings and Speeches That Changed the World*, ed. James Melvin Washington, 101–6. San Francisco: Harper Collins, 1992.

Kirshenblatt-Gimblett, Barbara. *Destination Culture: Tourism, Museums, and Heritage*. Berkeley: University of California Press, 1998.

Klein, Julia A. "All the President's Men." *Wall Street Journal*. January 4, 2011, § D, 5.

Kook, Rebecca. "The Shifting States of African-Americans in the American Collective Identity." *Journal of Black Studies* 29, no. 2 (November 1998), 154–78.

Kreamer, Christine Mullen. "Cultural Negotiation and Ghana's Cape Coast Castle Exhibition: 'Crossroads of a People, Crossroads of Trade.'" *The Slave Trade in African and African-American Memory*, ed. R. Austen and K. Warren. Unpublished manuscript.

Kriegsman, Alan M. "By Dance Possessed: The Kinetic Energy of Bill T. Jones." *Washington Post*, March 17, 1991, § G, 1.

Lacy, Leslie. *The Rise and Fall of a Proper Negro: An Autobiography*. New York: Macmillan, 1970.

Lang, Amy. "Class and the Strategies of Sympathy." *The Culture of Sentiment: Race, Gender, and Sentimentality in Nineteenth-Century America*, ed. Shirley C. Samuels, 128–42. New York: Oxford University Press, 1992.

Lavie, Smadar. *Displacement, Diaspora, and Geographies of Identity*. Durham: Duke University Press, 1996.

Lawler, Edward. "The President's House in Philadelphia: The Rediscovery of a Lost Landmark." *Pennsylvania Magazine of History and Biography* 26, no. 1 (January 2002), 5–95.

Le Goff, Jacques. *Histoire et Mémoire*. Paris: Gallimard, 1988.

Levine, Robert S. *Martin Delany, Frederick Douglass, and the Politics of Representative Identity*. Chapel Hill: University of North Carolina Press, 1997.

Lewis, Jan, and Peter Onuf. "American Synecdoche: Thomas Jefferson as Image, Icon, Character, and Self." *American History*, February 1998, 125–36.

————. *Sally Hemings and Thomas Jefferson: History, Memory, and Civic Culture*. Charlottesville: University Press of Virginia, 1999.

Lhamon, W. T. *Raising Cain: Blackface Performance from Jim Crow to Hip Hop*. Cambridge: Harvard University Press, 1998.

Lipset, Seymour Martin. *The First New Nation: The United States in Historical and Comparative Perspectives*. New York: W. W. Norton, 1973.

Lipsitz, George. *Time Passages: Collective Memory and American Popular Culture*. Minneapolis: University of Minnesota Press, 1990.

Litwack, Leon F. *Been in the Storm So Long: The Aftermath of Slavery*. New York: Vintage, 1980.

Lott, Eric. *Love and Theft: Blackface Minstrelsy and the American Working Class*. New York: Oxford University Press, 1995.

Lowenthal, David. *The Past Is a Foreign Country*. Cambridge: Cambridge University Press, 1985.

Lutz, Catherine A., and Jane L. Collins. *Reading National Geographic*. Chicago: University of Chicago Press, 1993.

Lyons, David. "Corrective Justice, Equal Opportunity, and the Legacy of Slavery and Jim Crow." *Boston University Law Review* 84 (December 2004), 1375–1404.

Lyotard, Jean-François. *Lessons on the Analytic of the Sublime: Kant's Critique of Judgment, [sections] 23–29*. Stanford: Stanford University Press, 1994.

MacCannell, Dean. *The Tourist: A New Theory of the Leisure Class*. New York: Schocken, 1976.

Magdol, Edward. *A Right to the Land: Essays on the Freedmen's Community*. Westport, Conn.: Greenwood, 1977.

Mahone, Sydne. "The Introduction." *Moon Marked and Touched by the Sun: Plays by African-American Women*, xiii–xxxiii. New York: Theater Communications Group, 1994.

Malone, Dumas. *Jefferson the President: The First Term, 1891–1805*. Boston: Little, Brown, 1970.

Malone, Dumas, and Stephen H. Hochman. "A Note on Evidence: The Personal History of Madison Hemings." *Journal of Southern History* 41 (1975), 523–28.

Marshall, T. H. *Citizenship and Social Class and Other Essays*. Cambridge: Cambridge University Press, 1950.

Martin, Randy. *Critical Moves: Dance Studies in Theory and Politics*. Durham: Duke University Press, 1998.

Martin, Reginald. *Ishmael Reed and the New Black Aesthetic Critics*. New York: St. Martin's, 1988.

Mayer, Ruth. *Artificial Africas: Colonial Images in the Times of Globalization*. Hanover, N.H.: University Press of New England, 2002.

Mbabuike, Michael C. "Wonders Shall Never Cease: Decoding Henry Louis Gates's Ambiguous Adventure." *Journal of Black Studies* 31, no. 2 (November 2000), 232–46.

McCarthy, Michael. *Dark Continent: Africa as Seen by Americans*. Westport, Conn.: Greenwood, 1983.

McCauley, Robbie. "Sally's Rape." *Moon Marked and Touched by Sun: Plays by African American Women*, ed. Sydné Mahone, 211–38. New York: Theatre Communications Group, 1994.

McHenry, Susan. "'Sally Hemings': A Key to a National Identity." *Ms.*, October 1980, 37–40.

McMurry, Rebecca L., and James F. McMurry Jr. *Anatomy of a Scandal: Thomas Jefferson and the Sally Story*. Shippensburg, Pa.: White Mane, 2002.

McWhorter, John. "Against Reparations." *Should America Pay? Slavery and the Raging Debate over Reparations*, ed. Raymond Winbush, 180–97. New York: Amistad, 2003.

Meriwether, James H. *Proudly We Can Be Africans: Black Americans and Africa, 1935–1961*. Chapel Hill: University of North Carolina Press, 2001.

Mitchell, W. J. T. *Picture Theory: Essays on Verbal and Visual Representation*. Chicago: University of Chicago Press, 1994.

Minow, Martha. *Between Vengeance and Forgiveness: Facing History after Genocide and Mass Violence*. Boston: Beacon, 1998.

Moore, Audley (Queen Mother). Interview with Cheryl Townsend-Gilkes, June 6 and 8, 1978. *The Black Women Oral History Project: 8*, ed. Ruth Edmonds Hill. Westport, Conn.: Meckler, 1991.

Moore, Thomas. "Epistle VII. To Thomas Hume ESQ., M.D. From the City of Washington." *Epistles, Odes, and Other Poems*. Philadelphia: John Watts, 1806.

Morgan, Edmund S. *American Slavery, American Freedom: The Ordeal of Colonial Virginia*. New York: W. W. Norton, 1975.

Morgan, Jennifer L. *Laboring Women: Reproduction and Gender in New World Slavery*. Philadelphia: University of Pennsylvania Press, 2004.

———. "'Some Could Suckle over Their Shoulder': Male Travelers, Female Bodies, and the Gendering of Racial Ideology, 1550–1770." *William and Mary Quarterly* 54, no. 1 (January 1997), 167–92.

Morgan, Jo-Ann. *Uncle Tom's Cabin as Visual Culture*. Columbia: University of Missouri Press, 2007.

Morrison, Toni. *Beloved*. New York: Penguin, 1987.

———. "The Site of Memory." *Inventing the Truth: The Art and Craft of Memoir*, ed. William Zinsser. Boston: Houghton Mifflin, 1995.

Morrison, Toni, and Robert Richardson. "A Bench by the Road: *Beloved*." *World* 3 (January–February 1989), 4, 5, 37–41.

Moses, Wilson J. *Black Messiahs and Uncle Toms*. University Park: Pennsylvania State University Press, 1981.

Moten, Fred. *In the Break: The Aesthetics of the Black Radical Tradition*. Minneapolis: University of Minnesota Press, 2003.

Murphy, Jacqueline Shea. "Unrest and Uncle Tom: Bill T. Jones/Arne Zane Dance Company's Last Supper at Uncle Tom's Cabin/The Promised Land." *Bodies of the Text: Dance as Theory, Literature as Dance*, ed. Ellen W. Goellner and Jacqueline Shea Murphy. New Brunswick, N.J.: Rutgers University Press, 1995.

Munoz, Jose Esteban. *Disidentifications: Queers of Color and the Performance of Politics*. Minneapolis: University of Minnesota Press, 1999.

Myrdal, Gunnar. *An American Dilemma: The Negro Problem and Modern Democracy*. New York: Harper Collins, 1944.

Nance, Kevin. "The Spirit and the Strength: A Profile of Toni Morrison." *Poets and Writers* (November–December 2008), 47–83.

Nash, Gary B. "For Whom Will the Liberty Bell Toll? From Controversy to Cooperation." *Slavery and Public History: The Tough Stuff of American Memory*, ed. James Oliver Horton and Lois E. Horton, 75–102. New York: New Press, 2006.

Nash, Gary B. and Miller, Randall M. "Don't Bury the Past: Honor Liberty by Including the Stories of All." *Philadelphia Inquirer*. March 31, 2002. http://articles.philly.com/2002-03-31/news/25341894_1_slave-quarters-liberty-bell-new-pavilion.

Neal, Mark Anthony. *Soul Babies: Black Popular Culture and the Post-Soul Aesthetic*. New York: Routledge, 2002.

Ngai, Sianne. *Ugly Feelings*. Cambridge: Harvard University Press, 2004.

Nietzsche, Friedrich. *Thus Spoke Zarathustra: A Book for All and None* (1883–1885), trans. R. J. Hollingdale. London: Penguin, 1969.

Nobles, Melissa. *The Politics of Official Apologies*. New York: Cambridge University Press, 2008.

Nora, Pierre. "Between Memory and History: Les Lieux de Mémoire." *Representations* 26 (spring 1989), 7–25.

Nuernberg, Susan. "The Rhetoric of Race." *The Stowe Debate: Rhetorical Strategies in* Uncle Tom's Cabin, ed. Mason Lowance et al. Amherst: University of Massachusetts Press, 1994.

Nymann, Ann E. "Sally's Rape: Robbie McCauley's Survival Art." *African-American Review* 33, no. 4 (winter 1999), 577–87.

Obama, Barack. "A More Perfect Union." Speech at Constitution Center, Philadelphia, March 18, 2008. www.barackobama.com/2008/03/18/remarks_of_senator _barack _obam_53.php.

Ogletree, Charles. "Litigating the Legacy of Slavery." *New York Times* April 4, 2002, § A, 22.

———. "Repairing the Past: New Efforts in the Reparations Debate in America." *Harvard Civil Rights–Civil Liberties Law Review* 38, no. 2 (2003), 279–320.

Ogline, Jill. "'Creating Dissonance for the Visitor': The Heart of the Liberty Bell Controversy." *Public Historian* 26 (2004), 49–57.

Ong, Aihwa. *Flexible Citizenship: The Cultural Logics of Transnationality*. Durham: Duke University Press, 1999.

Opoku-Agyemang, Kwadwo. "Dancing with Mr. Dizzy (or Manteca, by Mr. Birks)." *African American Review* 29, no. 2 (summer 1995), 257–58.

———. "In the Shadow of the Castle." *Cape Coast Castle*. Accra, Ghana: Afram, 1996.

Oubre, Claude F. *Forty Acres and a Mule: The Freedmen's Bureau and Black Land Ownership*. Baton Rouge: Louisiana State University Press, 1978.

Paine, Thomas. *Common Sense: Addressed to the Inhabitants of America, on the Following Interesting Subjects*. New York: Peter Eckler, 1918. First published 1776.

Painter, Nell Irvin. *Soul Murder and Slavery*. Waco: Baylor University Press, 1995.

Patraka, Vicki. "Robbie McCauley: Obsessing in Public." *Drama Review* 37, no. 2 (summer 1993), 25–55.

Patrick, Rembert W. *The Fall of Richmond*. Baton Rouge: Louisiana State University Press, 1960.

Patterson, Orlando. *Slavery and Social Death: A Comparative Study*. Cambridge: Harvard University Press, 1982.

Patterson, Tiffany Ruby, and Robin D. G. Kelley. "Unfinished Migrations: Reflections on the African Diaspora and the Making of the Modern World." *Africa Studies Review* 43, no. 1 (April 2000), 11–45.

Patton, Venetria K. *Women in Chains: The Legacy of Slavery in a Black Women's Fiction*. Albany: State University of New York Press, 1999.

Paulson, Ronald. *Satire and the Novel in Eighteenth-Century England*. New Haven: Yale University Press, 1967.

Perry, Imani. *More Beautiful and More Terrible: The Embrace and Transcendence of Racial Inequality in the United States*. New York: New York University Press, 2011.

Peterson, Merrill. *The Jefferson Image in the American Mind*. Charlottesville: University Press of Virginia, 1960.

Piche, Thomas. "Reading Carrie Mae Weems." *Carrie Mae Weems, Recent Work, 1992–1998*, ed. Thelma Golden and Thomas Piche. New York: W. W. Norton, 1999.

Raboteau, Albert J. *Slave Religion: The "Invisible Institution" in the Antebellum South*. New York: Oxford University Press, 1978.

Ransby, Barbara. "Henry Louis Gates' Dangerously Wrong Slave History." *Colorlines* (May 2010). http://colorlines.com/archives/2010/05/henry_louis_gates_dangerously_wrong_slave_history.html.

Reckley, Ralph, Sr. "The Love-Hate Syndrome of Master-Slave Relationships: Sally Hemings." *20th Century Black American Women in Print: Essays*, ed. Ralph Reckley and Lola E. Jones. Acton, Mass: Copley, 1991.

Reed, Ishmael. *Conjure; Selected Poems, 1963–1970*. Amherst: University of Massachusetts Press, 1972.

———. *Flight to Canada*. New York: Atheneum, 1979.

———. "Music: Black, White, and Blue." *Black World / Negro Digest*, April 1973, 79–81, 97.

———. *Shrovetide in Old New Orleans*. Garden City, N.Y: Doubleday, 1978.

Regosin, Elizabeth. *Freedom's Promise: Ex-slave Families and Citizenship in the Age of Emancipation*. Charlottesville: University Press of Virginia, 2002.

Remnick, David. *The Bridge: The Life and Rise of Barack Obama*. New York: Alfred A. Knopf, 2010.

Richards, Sandra. "What Is to Be Remembered? Tourism to Ghana's Slave Castle—Dungeons." *Theatre Journal* 57, no. 4 (December 2005), 617–37.

Roach, Joseph R. *Cities of the Dead: Circum-atlantic Performance*. New York: Columbia University Press, 1996.

Robinson, Randall. *The Debt: What America Owes to Blacks*. New York: Dutton, 2000.

Roediger, David R. *The Wages of Whiteness: Race and the Making of the American Working Class*. New York: Verso, 1991.

Rogin, Michael. "The Two Declarations of American Independence." *Representations* 55 (summer 1996), 13–30.

Root, Maria P. P. "Five Mixed-Race Identities: From Relic to Revolution." *New Faces in a Changing America: Multiracial Identity in the 21st Century*, ed. Loretta I. Winters and Herman L. DeBose. Thousand Oaks, Calif.: Sage, 2003.

Rosen, Hannah. *Terror in the Heart of Freedom: Citizenship, Sexual Violence, and the Meaning of Race in Postemancipation South*. Chapel Hill: University of North Carolina Press, 2009.

Rothman, Joshua D. "James Callender and Social Knowledge of Interracial Sex and Antebellum Virginia." *Sally Hemings and Thomas Jefferson: History, Memory, and Civic Culture*, ed. Jan Ellen Lewis and Peter S. Onuf, 87–113. Charlottesville: University Press of Virginia, 1999.

Rothstein, Edward. "Museum Review: Reopening a House That's Still Divided." *New York Times*, December 14, 2010, § C, 1.

Rushdy, Ashraf. "'I Write in Tongues': The Supplement of Voice in Barbara Chase-Riboud's *Sally Hemings*." *Contemporary Literature* 35, no. 1 (1994), 100–135.

———. *Neo-Slave Narratives: Studies in the Social Logic of a Literary Form*. New York: Oxford University Press, 1999.

Russell, John. "A Believable Sally Hemings." Rev. of *Sally Hemings*, by Barbara Chase-Riboud. *New York Times*, September 5, 1979, § C, 21.

Saffron, Inga. "Changing Skyline: Brick Pile's Colliding Tales," *Philadelphia Inquirer*, December 17, 2010, § F, 1.

Saltz, Jerry. "Kara Walker: Ill-Will and Desire." *Flash Art* 29, no. 191 (1996), 83–86.

Savage, Kirk. *Standing Soldiers, Kneeling Slaves: Race, War, and Monument in Nineteenth-Century*. Princeton: Princeton University Press, 1997.

Schudson, Michael. *Watergate in American Memory: How We Remember, Forget, and Reconstruct the Past*. New York: Harper Collins, 1992.

Schulman, Norma. "Laughing across the Color Barriers: *In Living Color*." *Gender, Race, and Class in Media: A Text-Reader*, ed. Gail Dines and Jean M. Humez. Thousand Oaks, Calif.: Sage, 1995.

Schwartz, Barry. "The Reconstruction of Abraham Lincoln." *Collective Remembering*, ed. David Middleton and Derek Edwards. London: Sage, 1990.

Scott, David. "That Event, This Memory: Notes on the Anthropology of African Diasporas in the New World." *Diaspora* 1, no. 3 (1991), 261–84.

Scruggs, Jon Christian. *Whispered Consolations: Law and Narrative in African American Life*. Ann Arbor: University of Michigan Press, 2000.

Shapiro, Laura. "Dancing in Death's House." *Newsweek*, November 7, 1994. 66.

Sharpe, Christina E. *Monstrous Intimacies: Making Post-Slavery Subjects*. Durham: Duke University Press, 2010.

Shaw, Gwendolyn D. B. *Seeing the Unspeakable: The Art of Kara Walker*. Durham: Duke University Press, 2004.

Shklar, Judith N. *American Citizenship: The Quest for Inclusion*. Cambridge: Harvard University Press, 1991.

Sidhu, Jatinder. "Africa's Cinema: Setting the Record Straight." *BBC News*, December 7, 1999.

Smith, Rogers M. *Civic Ideals: Conflicting Visions of Citizenship in U.S. History*. New Haven: Yale University Press, 1997.

Smith, William Gardner. *Return to Black America*. Englewood Cliffs, N.J.: Prentice-Hall, 1970.

Snead, James A. "Images of Blacks in Black Independent Films: A Brief Survey." *Cinemas of the Black Diaspora: Diversity, Dependence, and Oppositionality*, ed. Michael Martin. Detroit: Wayne State University Press, 1995.

Sollors, Werner. "National Identity and Ethnic Diversity: 'Of Plymouth Rock and Jamestown and Ellis Island': or, Ethnic Literature and Some Redefinitions of 'America.'" *History and Memory in African-American Culture*, ed. Genevieve Fabre and Robert O'Meally. New York: Oxford University Press, 1994.

———. "'Never Was Born': The Mulatto, an American Tragedy." *Massachusetts Review* 27, no. 2 (1986), 293–316.

———. "Presidents, Race, and Sex." *Sally Hemings and Thomas Jefferson: History, Memory, and Civic Culture*, ed. Jan Ellen Lewis and Peter S. Onuf, 109–209. Charlottesville: University Press of Virginia, 1999.

Sonnega, William. "Beyond a Liberal Audience." *African American Performance and Theatre History: A Critical Reader*, ed. Harry J. Elam and David Krasner, 81–98. New York: Oxford University Press, 2000.

Sontag, Susan. *Regarding the Pain of Others*. New York: Farrar, Straus and Giroux, 2003.

Soyinka, Wole. *The Burden of Memory, the Muse of Forgiveness*. New York: Oxford University Press, 1999.

Spencer, Suzette. "Historical Memory, Romantic Narrative, and Sally Hemings." *African American Review* 40, no. 3 (fall 2006), 507–31.

Spillers, Hortense. "Changing the Letter: The Yokes, the Jokes of Discourse, or, Mrs. Stowe, Mr. Reed." *Slavery and the Literary Imagination*, ed. Deborah E. McDowell and Arnold Rampersad, 25–61. Baltimore: Johns Hopkins University Press, 1989.

———. "Interstices: A Small Drama of Words." *Pleasure and Danger: Exploring Female Sexuality*, ed. Carole S. Vance, 267–319. Boston: Routledge, 1996.

———. "Mama's Baby, Papa's Maybe: An American Grammar Book." *Diacritics* 17, no. 2 (1987), 64–81.

Spruill-Redford, Dorothy. *Somerset Homecoming: Recovering a Lost Heritage*. New York: Doubleday, 1988.

Steele, Shelby. ". . . Or a Childish Illusion of Justice? Reparations Enshrine Victimhood, Dishonoring Our Ancestors." *Should America Pay? Slavery and the Raging Debate over Reparations*, ed. Raymond Winbush. New York: Amistad, 2003.

Stephens, Michelle A. *Black Empire: The Masculine Global Imaginary of Caribbean Intellectuals in the United States, 1914–1962*. Durham: Duke University Press, 2005.

Stepto, Robert. *From behind the Veil: A Study of Afro-American Narratives*. Urbana: University of Illinois Press, 1979.

———. "Sharing the Thunder: The Literary Exchanges of Harriet Beecher Stowe, Henry Bibb, and Frederick Douglass." *New Essays on Uncle Tom's Cabin*, ed. Eric Sundquist Jr. New York: Cambridge University Press, 1986.

Stowe, Harriet Beecher. *Men of Our Times or Leading Patriots of the Day*. Hartford: Hartford Publishing, 1868.

———. *Uncle Tom's Cabin*. New York: W. W. Norton, 1994. First published 1854.

Sturken, Marita. *Tangled Memories: The Vietnam War, the Aids Epidemic, and the Politics of Remembering*. Berkeley: University of California Press, 1997.

Sundquist, Eric, Jr., ed. *New Essays on Uncle Tom's Cabin*. New York: Cambridge University Press, 1986.

Tai, Hue-Tam Ho. *The Country of Memory: Remaking the Past in Late Socialist Vietnam*. Berkeley: University of California Press, 2001.

Tate, Greg. *Everything but the Burden: What White People Are Taking from Black Culture*. New York: Broadway, 2003.

———. *Flyboy in the Buttermilk: Essays on Contemporary America*. New York: Fireside, 1992.

Taylor, Charles. "The Politics of Recognition." *Multiculturalism: Examining the Politics of Recognition*, ed. Amy Gutmann, 25–74. Princeton: Princeton University Press, 1994.

Thomas, Brook. *Civic Myths: A Law-and-Literature Approach to Citizenship*. Chapel Hill: University of North Carolina Press, 2007.

Thompson, Janna. *Taking Responsibility for the Past: Reparation and Historical Injustice*. Cambridge, England: Polity, 2002.

Timothy, Dallen J., and Victor B. Teye. "American Children of the African Diaspora: Journeys to the Motherland." *Tourism, Diasporas and Space*, ed. Tim Coles and Dallen J. Timothy, 111–23. London: Routledge, 2004.

Toll, Robert C. *Blacking Up: The Minstrel Show in Nineteenth Century America*. New York: Oxford University Press, 1974.

Tompkins, Jane P. "Sentimental Power: *Uncle Tom's Cabin* and the Politics of Literary History." *The New Feminist Criticism: Essays on Women, Literature, and Theory*, ed. Elaine Showalter. New York: Pantheon, 1985.

Torphy, John. *Making Whole What Has Been Smashed: On Reparations Politics*. Cambridge: Harvard University Press, 2006.

Trescott, Jacqueline. "The Hemings Affair." *Washington Post*, June 15, 1979, § B, 1.

Turner, Patricia. *Ceramic Uncles and Celluloid Mammies: Black Images and Their Influence on Culture*. Charlottesville: University Press of Virginia, 2002.

Turner, Victor. *The Ritual Process: Structure and Anti-structure*. Ithaca: Cornell University Press, 1977.

Tyler-McGraw, Marie. "Southern Comfort Levels." *Slavery and Public History: The Tough Stuff of American Memory*, ed. James Oliver Horton and Lois E. Horton. New York: New Press, 2006.

Ukpokodu, Peter I. "African Heritage from the Lenses of African-American Theatre and Film." *Journal of Dramatic Theory and Criticism* 16, no. 2 (spring 2002), 69–93.

Van DeBurg, William. *New Day in Babylon: The Black Power Movement and American Culture, 1965–1975*. Chicago: University of Chicago Press, 1992.

———. *Slavery and Race in American Popular Culture*. Madison: University of Wisconsin Press, 1984.

Verdun, Vincene. "If the Shoe Fits, Wear It: An Analysis of Reparations to African-Americans." *Tulane Law Review* 67 (1993), 619–44.

Walker, Clarence. "Denial Is Not River in Eygpt." *Sally Hemings and Thomas Jefferson: History, Memory, and Civic Culture*, ed. Jan Ellen Lewis and Peter S. Onuf. Charlottesville: University of Virginia Press, 1999.

Walker, Kamza. "Nigger Lover or Will There Be Any Black People in Utopia." *Parkett* 59 (2000), 152–65.

Walker, Kara E. *Kara Walker: The Renaissance Society at the University of Chicago. January 12–February 23, 1997.* Chicago: Renaissance Society at the University of Chicago, 1997.

Wallace, Michelle. "*Uncle Tom*: Before and after the Jim Crow." *Drama Review* 44, no. 1 (spring 2000), 137–56.

Walsh, Richard. "'A Man's Story Is His Gris-Gris': Cultural Slavery, Literary Emancipation, and Ishmael Reed's *Flight to Canada*." *Journal of American Studies* 27, no. 1 (April 1993), 55–71.

Warren, Wendy Anne. "'The Cause of Her Grief': The Rape of a Slave in Early New England." *Journal of American History* 93, no. 4 (2007), 1031–49.

Weeks, Edward C. "The Practice of Deliberative Democracy: Results from Four Large-Scale Trials." *Public Administration Review* 60, no. 4 (July–August 2000), 360–72.

Weiner, Mark S. *Black Trials: Citizenship from the Beginnings of Slavery to the End of Caste.* New York: Alfred A. Knopf, 2004.

Weisbord, Robert G. *Ebony Kinship: Africa, Africans, and the Afro-American.* Westport, Conn.: Greenwood, 1973.

Welter, Barbara. *Dimity Convictions: The American Woman in Nineteenth Century.* Athens: Ohio University Press, 1976.

West, Cornel. *Race Matters.* Boston: Beacon, 1993.

Westbrook, Ellen E., et al. *The Stowe Debate: Rhetorical Strategies in Uncle Tom's Cabin.* Amherst: University of Massachusetts Press, 1994.

Whetmore, S. F. "Life among the Lowly, No. 1." *Pike County (Ohio) Republican.* March 13, 1873.

White, Deborah Gray. *Ar'n't I a Woman? Female Slaves in the Plantation South.* New York: W. W. Norton, 1999.

Whitman, Albery A. Preface to *Twasinta's Seminoles; or, Rape of Florida.* Upper Saddle River, N.J.: Greg, 1970. First published 1885.

Whyte, Raewyn. "Robbie McCauley: Speaking History Other-wise." *Acting Out: Feminist Performances*, ed. Lynda Hart and Peggy Phelan, 277–94. Ann Arbor: University of Michigan Press, 1993.

Williams, Armstrong. "Presumed Victims." *Should America Pay? Slavery and the Raging Debate over Reparations*, ed. Raymond Winbush. New York: Amistad, 2003.

Williams, Judith. "Uncle Tom's Women." *African American Performance and Theatre History: A Critical Reader*, ed. Harry J. Elam and David Krasner. New York: Oxford University Press, 2000.

Williams, Linda. *Playing the Race Card: Melodramas of Black and White from Uncle Tom to O. J. Simpson.* Princeton: Princeton University Press, 2001.

Winbush, Raymond, ed. *Should America Pay? Slavery and the Raging Debate over Reparations.* New York: Amistad, 2003.

Winks, Robin. "The Making of Fugitive Slave Narrative: Josiah Henson and

Uncle Tom—Case Study." *The Slave's Narrative*, ed. Charles T. Davis and Henry Louis Gates Jr. New York: Oxford University Press, 1985.

Woolford, Pamela. "Filming Slavery: Interview with Haile Gerima." *Transitions* 64 (1994), 90–104.

Woolfork, Lisa. *Embodying American Slavery in Contemporary Culture*. Urbana: University of Illinois Press, 2008.

Wright, Richard. *Twelve Million Black Voices: A Folk History of the Negro in the United States*. London: L. Drummond, 1947.

———. *Uncle Tom's Children*. New York: Harper and Row, 1940.

———. *White Man Listen!* New York: Anchor, 1957.

Yarborough, Richard. "Race, Violence, and Manhood: The Masculine Ideal in Frederick Douglass's 'Heroic Slave.'" *Haunted Bodies: Gender and Southern Texts*, ed. Anne Goodwyn Jones and Susan V. Donaldson. Charlottesville: University of Virginia Press, 1997.

———. "Strategies of Black Characterization in *Uncle Tom's Cabin* and the Early Afro-American Novel." *New Essays on Uncle Tom's Cabin*, ed. Eric Sundquist Jr. New York: Cambridge University Press, 1986.

Yellin, Jean Fagan. *The Intricate Knot: Black Figures in American Literature, 1776–1863*. New York: New York University Press, 1972.

Zaeske, Susan. *Signatures of Citizenship: Petitioning, Antislavery, and Women's Political Identity*. Chapel Hill: University of North Carolina Press, 2003.

CASES AND EXECUTIVE ORDERS

African-American Litigation, 307 F. Supp. 2d 977 (N.D. Ill. 2004).

Berry v. United States, 1994 WL 374537 (N.D. Cal.).

Cato v. United States, 70 F. 3d 1103 (9th Cir. 1995).

"Commission to Study Reparations Proposals." House Res. 40. 101st Congress, 1st Session. *Congressional Record* 135, E 4007. November 21, 1989.

Dred Scott v. John F. A. Sandford, 60 U.S. 393 (1856).

Farmer-Paellmann v. FleetBoston Financial Corporation, Aetna, Inc., CSX, C.A. No 1:02-1862 (E.D.N.Y. 2002).

Johnson v. McAdoo, 45 U.S. App. D.C. 440 (1917).

Pigford v. Glickman, 182 F.R.D. 341 (D.D.C. 1998), consent decree approved and entered, 185 F.R.D. 82 (1999), reversing district court's order, inter alia, extending filing deadlines under consent decree, 292 F. 3rd 918 (D.C. Cir. 2002).

Presidential Proclamation, Executive Order No. 9066, *Federal Registry* 7 no. 1407 (February 25, 1942).

FILMS AND VISUAL ART

Andrews, Tina. *Sally Hemings and Thomas Jefferson: An American Scandal* [teleplay]. Dir. Charles Haid. Artisan Home Entertainment, 2000. Videocassette.

Gates, Henry Louis, Jr. *African-American Live: Beyond the Middle Passage*. Dir. Graham Judd. Kunhart Productions and Thirteen/WNET New York, 2006.

————. *Wonders of the African World: The Slave Kingdoms*. Dir. Nicola Colton. Kunhart Productions and Thirteen/WNET. New York, 2000.

Gerima, Haile, dir. *Sankofa*. Mypheduh Films. Washington, 1993.

Higgins, Chester, Jr. *Dakar, Senegal, 1972. The Door of No Return in the House of Slaves*. 1972. 1 silver print. Reproduced in Chester Higgins, *Feeling the Spirit: Searching the World for the People of Africa*. New York: Bantam, 1994.

Jones, Bill T., dir. *Dancing to the Promised Land: The Making of the Last Supper at Uncle Tom's Cabin/The Promised Land*. V.I.E.W., 1994.

Spielberg, Steven, dir. *Amistad*. DreamWorks, 1997.

Walker, Kara. *The End of Uncle Tom and the Grand Allegorical Tableau of Eva in Heaven*. 1995. Cut paper and adhesive paper on wall, 15 × 35′. Private Collection, Brent Sikkema Galley, New York City.

Weems, Carrie Mae. *Elmina Cape Coast Ile de Goree: The Slave Coast Series*. 1994. 3 silver prints, Fabric Museum and Workshop, Philadelphia.

MUSIC AND PERFORMANCE ART

Brown, Oscar. "Forty Acres and a Mule." *Mr. Oscar Brown Jr. Goes to Washington*. Compact disc. Verve Records, 1998.

Jones, Bill T., choreographer. *Last Supper at Uncle Tom's Cabin/The Promised Land*. Brooklyn Academy of Music, New York, November 9, 1990.

SALAMISHAH TILLET is an assistant professor of English and
Africana studies at the University of Pennsylvania.

Library of Congress Cataloging-in-Publication Data

Tillet, Salamishah.
Sites of slavery : citizenship and racial democracy in the
post-civil rights imagination / Salamishah Tillet.
p. cm.
Includes bibliographical references and index.
ISBN 978-0-8223-5242-6 (cloth : alk. paper)
ISBN 978-0-8223-5261-7 (pbk. : alk. paper)
1. African Americans—Political activity.
2. United States—Race relations—History—20th century.
3. United States—Race relations—History—21st century.
4. Slavery—United States—History.
5. Memory—Social aspects—United States.
I. Title.
E185.615.T575 2012
326.0973—dc23   2011053371